Population in an Interacting World

POPULATION
IN AN INTERACTING WORLD

Edited by William Alonso

HARVARD UNIVERSITY PRESS
Cambridge, Massachusetts, and London, England   1987

Library of Congress Cataloging-in-Publication Data

Population in an interacting world.

   Bibliography: p.
   Includes index.
   1. Population—Congresses. 2. Emigration and
immigration—Congresses. I. Alonso, William.
HB849.P682 1987   304.6   86-20133
ISBN 0-674-69008-7 (alk. paper)

Acknowledgments

THE ESSAYS in this volume are the work of individual authors, but the sum total is the product of extensive collaboration. The project was conceived by a group at the Harvard Center for Population Studies and was supported by a grant from the Dräger Foundation of the German Federal Republic. A prospective essay on the themes of the conference was circulated to the invited authors, and the early drafts of their papers were discussed around the table at an Authors' Conference on Population Interactions between Poor and Rich Countries that was held at Harvard University in October 1983. The various essays were then revised in view of what was said there and the comments of several outside readers. Needless to say, not all advice and criticism were heeded, and the reader will find a lively variety of perspectives in the various essays.

Deeply felt thanks are due to Dr. Heinrich Dräger, president, Dr. Dieter Feddersen, vice-president, and Hildegard Bartschat, scientific manager, of the Dräger Foundation and to David Bell, director of the Harvard Center for Population Studies, for their early and late support of this enterprise. Francis X. Sutton contributed greatly to the organization and conceptualization. Ellen Hopkins, of the Center, gave essential help to the administration of the enterprise. Deborah Ridings showed her intelligence and resourcefulness in the final preparation of the manuscript. The authors have my special gratitude for the diligence and good grace with which they responded to my many requests.

W.A.

Contents

Population in an Interacting World

Population North and South

William Alonso

THE RAPID GROWTH of the world's population is one of mankind's more serious problems, but the aggregate figures for the world obscure a fundamental fact: in the last two decades the demographic trajectories of the poor and the rich countries have bifurcated. Although fertility is starting to decline, in the poor countries it is still at a level which more than doubles the population for each succeeding generation. Even if by some miracle their fertility were to fall today to mere replacement, their overall population would still double in the next few decades before stabilizing because, with about half their population fifteen years old or under, their demographic momentum ensures billions of additional births as these young people reach reproductive age in the coming years.

The situation is quite different in the rich countries. For many years their fertility has been below generational replacement and shows no sign of rising significantly. Thus their intrinsic rate of population growth is negative, and only the demographic momentum of their baby booms of the 1950s and 1960s masks this fact. Overall, the fertility of the nineteen countries which the World Bank designates as "industrial market economies" was one-fifth below the generational replacement rate in 1982. Only the poorest of these countries, Ireland and Spain, had rates above replacement (and Spain just barely); the German Federal Republic had the lowest rate, fully one-third below replacement. Three of these countries (Italy, Belgium, and Sweden) already had as many deaths as births, while two (Germany and Denmark) had more deaths than births (World Bank, 1984).

This volume is concerned with these diverging demographic trajectories. But the populations of rich and poor countries are not ballistic missiles traveling on independent courses, as they may appear in neat statistical tables presenting data and projections for one and the other group. The population processes in both rich and poor nations are determined, of course, largely by their own internal dynamics, but they are not truly independent. The basic elements of their demographic processes — births, deaths, and migration — are often linked and modified through social, economic, cultural, political, military, and biological interactions. This interdependence, transacted through the full historical complexity of human and biological processes, is the theme of this volume.

Once one starts looking for them, the interactions seem to be everywhere, some quite obvious and some more subtle. Perhaps the most obvious interaction is migration, whether caused by economics or by politics. For instance, millions of workers from the third world have come to the industrialized nations since World War II because of disparities in income; in this same period, largely as the result of the geopolitics of world powers, tens of millions of refugees have fled across national boundaries, some to the industrialized countries but most within the third world.

Less visible, because they are not reflected in censuses, are other forms of migration — usually from rich to poor countries — which sometimes have strong demographic effects. A vacation in a less developed country may be a fleeting experience to a citizen from a rich country, but the stream of transient vacationers may represent a steady third of the population in some of the smaller receiving countries, and this collective permanency will reshape the material and cultural bases of the local society, and thus its demographic performance. Or alternatively, small foreign groups — missionaries, scientists, merchants, ideologues, and military and economic experts — may have effects disproportionate to their numbers in the social transformation of a society.

The interaction of populations is not limited to migration, however; it extends, at least as importantly, to the other basic components of the demographic process: births and deaths. Today's image of a juggernaut population growth in the third world is so prevalent that it is hard to remember that this is a relatively new development. As recently as the 1910s, countries such as Mexico and India actually lost population to disease and famine, and sustained growth of population in the poorer regions of the world could not be taken for granted. Indeed, through much of history, when powerful societies came in contact with peripheral populations in search of commerce or conquest, they brought with them diseases to which their inhabitants had become immune but which were new and devastating to the more isolated populations. To cite one instance, when the Spaniards came to the Americas they carried in their veins microorganisms so deadly to the unprotected Amerindians that the native population of what today is Mexico was reduced by some nine-tenths (McNeill, 1976); it did not return to the pre-Columbian level until the middle of this century.

In the last half-century, however, the rise of third world population has been vertiginous and will continue, albeit at slower rates in most places, into the indefinite future. The cause for this population explosion has not been a rise in fertility but a reduction of mortality, a dramatic extension in the expectation of life at birth. Increased longevity acts on population growth as the lingering of onlookers determines the size of a crowd looking at an accident. If each passerby stops for a minute and then moves on, the crowd will reach a certain size; but let the average gazer stay for two minutes, and the size of the crowd will double. Thus one of the world's most difficult problems stems from what is undoubtedly a great improvement in mankind's condition.

The precise balance of causes for the fall of the third world's death rate cannot be fixed, but it is clear that scientific advances originating in the industrialized countries have played a central role, beginning at the turn of the century and accelerating after World War II. In the area of health these advances include better strategies for combating infectious diseases, antibiotics, insecticides to control the vectors of parasitic diseases, vaccination, public health measures, and improvements in maternal and child care. The area of food produced improvements in plant genetics and agricultural methods and in the preservation and distribution of food.

Although the rich countries' contribution to the population explosion in the poor countries was in a sense fortuitous, when the reality of this phenomenon became apparent in the decades after World War II, the rich countries led an international effort for family planning and lowered birth rates (Gille, 1982). The beginnings were timid. In the early 1950s the United Nations began to aid and encourage developing countries in census-taking and demographic studies, and four nongovernmental organizations (the International Planned Parenthood Federation, the Population Council, and the Ford and Rockefeller Foundations) initiated and carried out the bulk of population program assistance to developing countries until large-scale govern-

ment assistance became available in the late 1960s. Sweden's government was the first to enter the field with a program in Sri Lanka,
and the United Kingdom and the United States joined in the mid-
1960s. By the early 1970s the governments of Canada, Denmark,
West Germany, Japan, the Netherlands, and Norway had also developed programs. In the United Nations, the Fund for Population
Activities (UNFPA) and other UN agencies became active in the late
1960s, and the World Bank issued its first loan in this area in 1970.
By 1981 total international contributions had amounted to $7 billion
and stood at just under $500 million that year (World Bank, 1984; all
figures in 1982 dollars).

And so within the span of a human lifetime (under present life
expectancies) the developed countries have first helped to trigger
population growth in the poor countries and then tried to curb it.
Within this same period the fertility of the industrialized countries
has fluctuated, but with a secular downward trend. In the 1930s
depopulation was of grave concern, particularly in Europe, although
fertility rates still were at about replacement. In the 1970s and 1980s
fertility has come to be sharply and seemingly permanently below
replacement; worries about depopulation have resurfaced and with
them growing calls for pronatalist policies. This advocacy results
mostly from domestic concerns, such as the difficulties posed by an
unbalanced population age structure. But not infrequently the pronatalist positions contain a tinge of fear that a falling population will
result in diminished world standing and power. From arithmetical
necessity, if the native population is not to fall in the rich countries,
their fertility must rise by more than one-fourth. The only alternative
is permanent and sustained immigration from third world countries,
which are the only source of people available. This is not likely to be
an attractive alternative for the rich countries, although it may be to
some degree unavoidable: it is perceived as diluting the nation's
cultural and ethnic identity and as a certain source of social conflicts.
As the masking effect of the baby-boom generation slips by, and
population decline becomes manifest, it seems certain that pronatalism in the rich countries will become stronger. On the evidence from
its present forms, this position is likely to be ideologically linked in
the West to conservative political views which stress national power
and traditional values of folk, family, and female roles. Ironically, it
is in the socialist states of Eastern Europe that pronatalism has been
most vigorously pursued.

Although in the past many poor countries have ignored or opposed population control policies, within the last decade most of them have shifted to active policies of fertility reduction and have welcomed international assistance to this purpose. But stresses will abound in a world in which poor societies try to lower their births while rich ones try to raise theirs and fend off immigrants. The neo-Malthusian global simplicities of limited resources in the face of a growing world population will not do: over his lifetime, the extra child produced by policy in a rich country would consume many times over the quantity of resources saved on the child averted by policy in a poor country. Moreover, it does not help that the rich countries (with the exception of Japan) are predominantly white, while the poor countries — as these things are reckoned — are predominantly colored. Already some in the developing world have claimed that racism lies behind the rich countries' fervor for world population control, and there have even been accusations of attempted genocide. Wild as these accusations may be, the sad likelihood is that they will become endemic. Symmetrically, one may expect in the rich countries instances of demagogy — based on racism and supported by pseudosciences — on the themes of the dying of the race, the laxity of morals and the abandonment of traditional values, the proper role of women and the decline of the family. From either side these will play a role in domestic and international politics, and one can only hope that it will be a limited one.

Even without the poison of racism, this demographic asymmetry ensures abiding economic and political tensions. Some analysts have suggested dire scenarios where the better-off, low-fertility peoples may face tragic choices, sometimes called "triage" or "life-boat ethics," of withholding help from poor peoples sinking into Malthusian quicksands from the weight of their progeny. But short of such doomsday visions, and in spite of worries about deindustrialization, it seems likely that for the medium term labor will be relatively scarce in rich countries and overabundant in the others. The economic consequences for the world economy will be large, and can already be seen to some extent. Economic logic says that wage differences should widen in favor of the rich, but that comparative advantages for certain industrial activities should shift toward the poor countries. This suggests that the rich countries will maintain their lead in material well-being, but be continually subject to painful industrial and labor dislocations as certain types of production migrate to the third world. The geography of this shift of economic activity will not be random: it will concentrate in developing countries where conditions are economically and politically most favorable, and these countries will experience accelerated economic growth. This can be seen already in what the development literature calls the "newly industrialized countries" (NICs), such as Korea, Taiwan, and Singapore in Asia, and Mexico and Brazil in the Western hemisphere. The rapid economic growth of these nations has been matched by a sharp decline in their fertility, particularly the Asian ones. Thus the NICs are intermediate economically and demographically between the rich and the poor, blur the distinction between North and South, and promise to introduce further variants and surprises to the processes of worldwide demographic interactions.

In one or another way each of the essays in this volume touches on some kind of migration, although they do so in very different ways. A principal conclusion emerges, however: because of the magnitudes involved, migration from South to North may, if it occurs, have a large demographic impact for the low-fertility industrialized countries but would only have a trivial effect on the aggregate demography of the poorer countries. To cite the numbers, the poorer nations as a whole had a total 1982 population of 3.4 billion, and were growing at 2.1 percent for an annual increase of 71 million (calculated from World Bank, 1984). This yearly population increase in the third world is one-tenth of the total population of the industrial market economies (723 million), and it is obvious that however many immigrants the rich countries took in, it would make no basic difference to the demography of the third world. This is not to say that the poorer countries may not experience indirect effects from remittances, cultural transmission, or brain drains, or that such migration might not be meaningful for particular small developing countries. It is to say that the potential population consequences of immigration are large for the rich countries, but for most of the poor ones emigration will be only one factor, and a minor one, in the context of other exchanges which include capital, technology, goods, and services. It must be noted that the several authors in this volume differ considerably in their assessment of the social and economic consequences of these movements.

A second common theme, unanticipated when the essays were commissioned, emerges strongly in this volume: the crucial role which nation-states play in today's demographic processes. Since World War II, with the dissolution of the Western empires, almost all of the human population has become sorted and organized — not always neatly — according to the principles of territoriality and citizenship which characterize the nation-state. A hundred or so new nations have been forged out of former colonies, while the former seats of empire have traded most of their imperial transnationalism for a narrower domestic identity.

Nations have often perceived their interests, rightly or wrongly, in ways that have had profound demographic consequences. Some policies have been aimed directly at demographic issues, such as pro- or antinatalism or the encouragement or blocking of immigration; but many policies adopted for nondemographic reasons may have important demographic consequences, as when such ordinary matters as housing, education, or female labor policies have unanticipated effects on fertility. Sometimes actions which bear directly on population are formulated with other goals in mind, as when minorities are expelled or immigrants are barred on account of notions of national identity. Sometimes such actions have reached extremes which defy human sensibilities and mock the mild categories of social scientists, such as the genocidal and eugenic breeding programs of Nazi Germany and the starvations and resettlements of the Stalinist Soviet Union earlier in this century, and in more recent times the horrors of Cambodia, the excesses of China's Cultural Revolution, and South Africa's sustained villainy toward those whom it does not define as white.

The essays in this volume are loosely organized into two sections, the first providing historical background and structural insights. William McNeill paints a broad canvas of interacting populations in the premodern world. These interactions were transacted through migration, trade, conquest and dominion, disease, technology, the introduction of new food crops, and even genetic adaptation. The perspective of this historical sweep lets us see more clearly aspects of our own times often obscured from us by their very closeness. Toward the end of his essay, McNeill reflects that some recent developments in the rich countries may signal an end to the barbaric and historically regressive notion of the equivalence of the nation with the folk and a return to the civilized patterns of the deeper past, for which he coins "polyethnic lamination."

Similarly, in considering the long history of alien labor in Western development, Aristide Zolberg provides a valuable perspective for the understanding of some of the essays in the second part which deal with current South to North migration. Too often this is seen as an unprecedented phenomenon, but Zolberg traces its long history, from the period of recruitment of African slaves from the fifteenth to the nineteenth centuries, to that of indentured labor (primarily Asian) in the nineteenth and early twentieth centuries, to the free migration of labor from the eighteenth century to the present. He makes clear that the economic forces, social conflicts, and policy dilemmas of today are variations in this long process.

Hedley Bull considers the different perspectives of rich and poor countries on population issues, contrasting the third world's insistence in linking population control with economic development and social justice to the neo-Malthusian viewpoint often found in the rich countries, as evidenced at the United Nations World Population Conference held in Bucharest in 1974. He notes the growing presence of the third world in global affairs, economic, political, and even military, and matches this to the evolving sense of moral responsibility in rich countries for conditions in the poor ones. He outlines the ideal of a world cosmopolis, where the rights and needs of an individual anywhere in the world would count as much as those of any other, but recognizes that the world is divided into sovereign nation-states and urges them to develop institutionalized cooperation on population and other issues and to promote the idea that states can behave not merely as custodians of the interests of their own peoples but also as the agents of the common interests of mankind.

In the final essay of this section, I develop a theme raised in each of the previous essays: that of the varied and changing social definitions of the identity of populations. In particular I note the emergence of citizenship in a nation-state as the dominant *de jure* identity and its conflicts with older forms of identity such as race, tribe, language, and religion, as well as with the supranational organization of power and allegiances in former and current empires. I explore the consequences of evolving identities for the demographic processes of political and economic migration and of births and deaths.

The second section concentrates on various aspects of migration and other international flows resulting from economic, political, and mixed causes. In the first essay, Juergen Donges places international economic migration in the context of trade policies and the movements of other factors of production in an increasingly integrated world economy. Comparative advantages have shifted among the developing and the industrialized countries, particularly for labor-intensive production, and have had major consequences for the international specialization of production. The industrialized countries have found it painful to make the structural changes needed to adjust to these shifts, and out of domestic political considerations, and for short-term economic convenience, they have sought to avoid them through various combinations of importing labor or protectionism. In the prosperous 1950s and 1960s the economies relied mostly on imported workers, but when economic difficulties and chronic high unemployment began to develop in the early 1970s, the governments shifted to policies of trade restriction and subsidies. This has rigidified international trade, hindering growth in the developing countries and recovery in the industrialized ones. Donges calls for the industrialized countries to lead in liberalizing and rationalizing international economic policies, so that the global market may function efficiently in the interest of recovery and sustained economic growth.

Hans-Joachim Hoffmann-Nowotny considers the social and cultural dilemmas facing northern Europe, which stem from its labor-importing policies in the prosperous 1950s and 1960s. The foreign workers were to be temporary and disposable, but it is clear that they or their descendants will forever be a significant part of those societies. Max Frisch epitomized the issue: "We called for labor and human beings came." How are these newcomers to fit into the host society if they will not go home? Will they be a permanent underclass, victims of prejudice, discrimination, and exploitation? Such an outcome would not only hurt the newcomers, but act as a poison at the very root of the host liberal societies, which are based on the intrinsic worth of the individual and the equivalent worth of individuals. Must the host countries assimilate the immigrants culturally, or is a culturally plural economic integration possible which allows the immigrants' continued ethnic identity? Hoffmann-Nowotny reviews the recent experience and political debates in Europe, and casts doubt on the feasibility of cultural pluralism, comparing the attempt at integration without assimilation to the search for the philosopher's stone. This conundrum faces each of the rich countries, with the exception of Japan, which has been adamant in rejecting immigration and exporting capital and technology precisely in the interest of preserving its ethnic and cultural integrity. American readers will recognize many of the themes of their own political and intellectual history in Europe's current situation, and European readers may hear echoes of the reactions elicited by comparable international (but intra-European) migrations in the last two centuries.

Myron Weiner also touches on the dilemmas raised for rich countries by economically induced immigration, but he concentrates in the second and major part of his paper on the significance of this migration for the migrants, their families, their communities of origin and destination, and for the sending countries. He contrasts the earlier rationales and expectations of senders and recipients with what has actually happened, and analyzes competing interpretations of these results. In the first part of the paper he considers induced or forced emigration from third world countries based on political factors, such as the expulsion of political dissidents or of cultural and ethnic minorities for the sake of greater national homogeneity, and the forcing or encouraging emigration as a means of putting pressure on neighboring states.

Politically induced migrations are Francis Sutton's theme, as he looks at the tragic issues of exiles and refugees. Earlier in this century this seemed mostly a problem of Europe and the Middle East, but now the bulk of this phenomenon occurs within the third world. The rich countries' geopolitics are often responsible for these displacements, directly or indirectly, but most of the population movements occur within the third world and the rich countries experience them demographically only marginally and selectively in the sense of their hosting large numbers of refugees. The treatment of these people in the West will depend on the shared sense of affiliation or antipathy, derived from political, ethnic, cultural, and historic circumstances; the degree of confidence which receiving countries have of their strength to absorb the refugees and to deal with the international consequences; and the depth of a broader concern for equity, humanitarianism, and international responsibility. To these three determinants, basically characterizing the attitudes of the Western receiving countries, a fourth might be added: the effects of foreign policy pressures across the membrane dividing poor from rich nations, as when Thailand demands that Western countries admit more Vietnamese boat-people for resettlement. Sutton reviews national and international efforts to anticipate and deal with the problems of refugees and the limited progress which may be possible. The magnitude and tragedy of these issues will not likely abate in the near future, but Sutton argues that we can do better than we have.

The last essay of the volume deals with international human communities. In it Orlando Patterson explores the complex system he calls the circum-Caribbean region, which extends along a giant curve from North America, through Central America, to the northern coast of South America, and embraces the bouillabaisse of the Caribbean islands. Patterson portrays this region as a flowing field of forces consisting of capital, culture, ideologies, power, weapons, drugs, and peoples — these last being migrants, dual citizens, short-term experts, tourists, and so on. The picture which emerges is far more complex than that of center and periphery which has been so widely accepted, particularly in Latin America. In contrast with the other authors in this volume, Patterson argues that, at least in this region, the compartmentalization of populations into nation-states has been giving way to a more fluid situation, where national identities are confounded by affiliations transcending national boundaries.

In all, the intent of this volume and its essays is to explore the interactions among diverse human populations, particularly among those of rich and poor nations. They interact in more complex ways than those depicted in the ecological models of animal populations. The ecological interplay among nonhuman populations, based on prey-predator, symbiotic, or commensalistic relationships, is complex enough in its own right, but human population interactions are transacted along additional lines. These are, fundamentally, the dimensions of culture, institutions, and ideas; and, evolved from these, the more purposive constructs of material or political interest, and the more evocative ones of hope and hatred.

I

History and Structure

ONE

Migration in Premodern Times

William H. McNeill

IT IS SAFE to assume that when our ancestors first became fully human they were already migratory, moving about in pursuit of big game. The rapidity with which hunting bands occupied all the continents (except Antarctica) in about 50,000 years attests to this propensity. No dominant species ever spread so far so fast before. Our ancestors broke through climatic and geographical barriers with comparative ease because the invention of clothes and housing allowed them to sustain a tropical microclimate next to their almost hairless skins, no matter what conditions prevailed in the environment at large.

Tools, language, and disciplined cooperation in the hunt made it easy for advancing human bands to outwit rival predators. Moreover, as our ancestors left tropical Africa behind and moved into temperate zones, they shed most of the parasites and disease organisms that had helped to maintain ecological equilibrium within humanity's cradleland. A population explosion resulted, sustaining the rapid occupancy of the principal land masses of the earth.

Once that great migration had been completed (ca. 8000 B.C.) a global crisis confronted humankind. Population growth could no longer be accommodated by finding new, unoccupied hunting grounds. Intelligent humans responded by intensifying their food search; and in many different places the possibility of expanding natural populations of edible plants was systematically explored. Where suitable plants existed, agriculture began; the enhanced food production, however, came together with the intensification of infection that resulted from a more sessile existence, which meant that for the ensuing few thousand years human population growth and an expanding food supply remained approximately even.

Much early agriculture was itself migratory — slash and burn. As a result, both wheat and barley traveled across the whole of Eurasia within 5000 years, moving east and west from their initial locus of domestication in the Near East. Other forms of agriculture were more closely tied to special environments — for example, rice to seasonally flooded ground — and therefore spread more slowly. In the New World maize had to undergo a lengthy biological evolution before agriculture became productive enough to sustain entire communities. This retarded cultural evolution kept Amerindians significantly behind the pace of Old World developments until modern times.

The next major historical-ecological horizon dates from about 4000 B.C. when, in favored locations, human communities learned to build sailing vessels capable of crossing open water and to navigate well enough to get back to home port, at least most of the time. This made off-shore islands like Crete available for human settlement, and gave fishing and long-distance trading far greater importance than before. Initially, though, these new possibilities were important mainly in the Mediterranean, with its summer trade winds, and the Indian Ocean and South China Sea, where monsoon winds made navigation easy.

More important for human life as a whole was the development of another specialized lifestyle: pastoral nomadry. This dated from about 3000 B.C. It required human populations to establish enzyme mutations that allowed adults to digest milk. Domesticated flocks and herds, too, underwent biological change registered in the bones that archaeologists study. Once these adaptations had occurred, human herdsmen could kill off all but a tiny breeding stock of male newborns and substitute themselves as consumers of animal milk.

Pastoralists, of course, were also migratory, because the concentrated flocks and herds on which they depended — sheep, goats, cattle, horses, and later even camels — ate the herbage faster than it grew and had therefore to move to new ground every few days or weeks. That kind of mobility meant that once the biological adaptations and skills required for successful nomadry had been achieved, the broad grasslands of the Eurasian steppe and the equally extensive savanna lands of Africa and the Middle East were quickly occupied by pastoralists whose rapidity of movement and superior diet gave them a clear military advantage over more sessile and (often) protein-deficient cultivators.

The emergence of seafaring populations along the coasts of quiet seas, and of nomadic communities in the heartlands of Eurasia and Africa, meant that even when the plow made fully sessile agriculture normal on suitably well-watered soils after 2000 B.C., there still remained a mobile element among Old World populations that kept each part of the ecumene at least loosely in touch with the rest. Under these circumstances, important innovations could and did spread very widely and rapidly whenever the superiority of the new was clearly apparent. Eurasia's lead over other parts of the earth in technical skills resulted from this circumstance.

The increased variety in ways of life had as its initial result the creation of what we commonly call civilization. Sumerian-speaking seafarers from the south settled in the flood plain of the Tigris-Euphrates about 4000 B.C. and subjected the previous inhabitants to their rule. In the next millennium rulers and subjects proceeded to elaborate the earliest known civilization, developing wheeled vehicles, bronze metallurgy, writing, monumental buildings, irrigation, and many other new skills. A dozen or so Sumerian cities, each with about 20,000 to 50,000 inhabitants, were the first conglomerations of this magnitude.

Civilization differed from other forms of society in allowing specialization of occupation among relatively large numbers of persons. Specialists quickly developed higher skills than were attainable when everybody farmed or hunted most of the time and engaged in other forms of activity only occasionally. The fundamental differentiation was between rulers and ruled, for it was this distinction that allowed a few to collect taxes and rents in kind from the majority and then use such unrequited income to sustain themselves and the gods, as well as artisan specialists and soldiers. Trade goods for distant exchanges came mainly from artisan workshops, where specialists' skills produced goods precious enough to bear the high cost of transport.

The advantage of civilization lay in the superior skills that specialization guaranteed, and the enhanced wealth that division of labor permitted. Its weakness lay in the alienation that normally prevailed between rulers and ruled. Common interest, though real in the very long run, was hard to recognize in view of the immediate collision between tax collectors and taxpayers. Moreover, early civilizations usually exhibited ethnic differences between rulers and ruled, which reinforced and widened the social distance between them.

Ethnic diversity was in turn largely a function of military specialization that allowed some groups to dominate others. Professional warriors were used very early — by 3000 B.C. — and since they were armed and armored with metal, which was lacking in uncivilized communities, such troops could expect to prevail in most encounters with barbarians. This gave civilized communities a capacity to expand, sometimes by direct conquest. More often, civilization spread by contagion, as neighbors acquired the military and other skills needed to hold threatening civilized neighbors at bay. Over the long haul civilized social structures expanded despite innumerable local setbacks and temporary breakdowns of the social hierarchies sustaining early civilization. Evolution toward civilized complexity occurred in the New World some 2000 years later than in Mesopotamia. Not surprisingly, Amerindian peoples never caught up and were radically vulnerable to Spanish conquistadores and the diseases the Spaniards brought to America after 1500 A.D.

Once civilized societies had taken root in the Far East, in India, and around the eastern Mediterranean, as well as in the Middle East (that is, by about 2000 B.C.), the resulting social diversity complicated and at the same time structured subsequent patterns of human migration. Details are infinitely complex. Yet one can hope to discern a few overall, organizing tendencies.

Four possible forms of migration may occur within an ecumene already occupied by human populations whose diverse skills and social organization defined the carrying capacity of the landscapes they happened to occupy. These are: (1) radical destruction and replacement of one population by another as a result of systematic exercise of force; (2) conquest of one population by another, leading to symbiosis of two previously diverse communities on the same ground; (3) infiltration by outsiders who are to some degree acquainted with existing populations and do not displace existing rulers; (4) importation of individuals or even of whole communities that had been forcibly uprooted from their initial place of residence by slave raiders and traders.

Of these, the first was and remained characteristic of barbarian societies — societies organized on kinship lines in which nearly every family did the same sorts of things as every other family, save perhaps for a few chieftains and priests. Such societies had little use for foreigners, except for a few itinerant smiths who made iron tools and weapons available to the barbarian world of Eurasia and Africa after about 1000 B.C. Occupation of a given territory involved exclusion of others, though fictitious kinship, solemnized by special rituals, could and did expand in-group boundaries beyond biological limits.

Pastoralists of the steppe were the most important early communities that conformed to these specifications. Struggles over pasture lands were endemic and ever recurrent among them. Victory for one tribe or tribal confederation required survivors among the defeated to flee elsewhere. Invasion of agricultural lands was one possibility for defeated steppe communities; assault on some neighbor within the grasslands was the only alternative, since both the northern forests of Eurasia and the tropical rain forest of Africa were too inhospitable to allow survival of more than a scattered few.

Constant turmoil thus prevailed within the Eurasian and African grasslands. In northern Eurasia a definite geographical gradient asserted itself. Any group seeking to expand or fleeing from an aggressive neighbor preferred to go where grass was richer and temperatures somewhat less harsh. Dispersion from Mongolia, where conditions were the most severe, therefore took the form of sporadic migrations east, south, and west. In the savanna lands and hot deserts of Africa and southwest Asia, Arabia played a very similar role, for that land, too, represented the most severe landscape within which nomadry could flourish and therefore became a cradle whence streams of emigrants moved west across Africa as well as north into the Middle East.

Nor did nomadic migration stop where grass gave way to cultivated fields. On the contrary, the superior nourishment and superior mobility of the nomadic bands made them always able to exploit any weakening of civilized frontier guard. When such weakening occurred, successful raids snowballed into conquest. In this way, Semitic speakers supplanted Sumerians in Mesopotamia by about 2000 B.C. To the north, first Indo-European tribesmen, then Turks, and finally Mongols spread their languages and political dominion far and wide across most of Eurasia, while Semitic tribes, originating in Arabia, did the same in North Africa, both north and south of the Sahara.

Such conquest, however, involved a break with the nomadic way of life and brought the tribesmen into the circles of civilization, with its mixing of diverse populations and systematic differentiation of occupations. Civilized populations had their own distinctive migratory patterns that intersected the nomad movements. These two currents, if we knew more about them, would explain a great deal of the political and cultural history of the world. But statistics are absent, so impressionistic description is all that historians can supply, at least so far.

Basic to civilized society was the fact that cities became seats of intensified infection — so much so that urban populations were incapable of sustaining themselves biologically. This changed only in the second half of the nineteenth century, when public health measures and the advance of scientific medicine made it possible for the first time to interrupt the cycles of infection for a wide variety of communicable diseases within dense population settlements.

Before then cities had to import people from the hinterland, as well as food and raw materials, in order to survive. Consumption rates for food and raw materials were relatively constant, but deliveries were often interrupted by political upheavals and difficulties of transport. Sporadic food shortages, together with the erratic outbreaks of lethal epidemics, made for sharp fluctuations in urban deaths. In a bad year, half of the population might die in a matter of weeks. In a good year, births might equal or exceed deaths. But on the average, population decay prevailed. Even in more recent times, when statistics do become available, the gap between urban births and deaths was substantial. In eighteenth-century London, for example, the shortfall averaged 5,000 per annum, or about 1 percent of the city's population. Urban deaths were probably higher in more ancient times, because fluctuations in food supply had been much reduced by improved transport in eighteenth-century Britain.

Cities, the seats of civilized skills and specialization, were demographic sink holes, so civilization itself could persist only if rural populations normally produced a surplus of children over and above what was needed to maintain the rural work force and its production of a taxable surplus. Family regimens making early marriage almost universal could assure this result, and it is clear that the moral codes of all Eurasian civilizations did inculcate such a regimen for the majority, despite the praise of celibacy associated with Christianity, Buddhism, and Manichaeanism. In view of the natural and manmade disasters that afflicted rural communities — crop failures, epidemics, and plundering raids, or any combination of the three — the rural demographic balance obviously had to be such as to guarantee rather rapid growth in normal times. Otherwise, speedy demographic recovery in rural areas and maintenance of decaying urban populations would be impossible. This, in turn, meant that after no more than a single generation of normal harvests with no political or disease disaster, villages could expect to see more children coming of age than the local supply of cultivable land could easily support *in situ*. The regular appearance of this sort of surplus, at least in some rural localities, was a condition of overall stability. Any deviation would swiftly deprive the cities of that influx of eager apprentices from the countryside that was needed to keep urban skills alive across the generations.

Obviously, an exact balance between supply and demand for labor was impossible to maintain, especially in a world where unforeseen disaster was a recurrent reality. Periods of acute manpower shortage were probably as important a spur for early civilized history as periods of surplus. Shortages provoked raids to capture slaves for the least attractive occupations of civilized society. Much of the early war was of this character. Heavy population losses arising from military operations were at least partially offset by wholesale enslavement of the defeated. Often this involved forcible migration from some remote periphery toward the center of urban civilization. The Jewish prophets who mourned their lost Zion beside the waters of Babylon may remind us of this pattern of forced migration; and the general importance of slavery in the ancient world, of which Karl Marx made so much, is further testimony of the frequency with which voluntary recruitment into urban centers fell short of desired levels.

When the imbalance was in the opposite direction, too many rural children came of age and crowded into cities, overflowed provincial towns, and provoked various kinds of public disorder until political disaster again cut the population back to or below the carrying capacity of the land. Hellenistic and Roman Palestine illustrated this condition vividly, and the Gospels and the Book of Maccabees have made that overcrowded matrix familiar to us. Because modern times have also seen prolonged and massive population growth, we are likely to take rural surplus for granted. A better perspective would recognize that rural population growth and cut-back alternated irregularly with periods of shortage more threatening to the continuance of early civilizations than periods of surplus.

Once in a while another response to population growth in the rural hinterlands of civilized societies became possible. Whenever civilized methods of agriculture could get more from the soil than existing fringe populations were able to produce, migration to the frontier made sense. And when rural manpower surpluses existed, extra hands could migrate away from the crowded center and take up land on the frontier, thus extending the civilized body-social.

The Chinese occupation of what is now central and southern China is the most conspicuous and best documented example of such civilized pioneering. It was a result of the superiority of Chinese rice paddy agriculture to any less labor-intensive use of land in the Yangtze valley and further south. The taming of northern Europe to the plow between 300 and 1300 A.D. is second only to China's southward expansion in historical scale and importance. It arose from a juxtaposition of an expanding Germanic rural population with a new technique: the use of moldboard plows. These plows created an artificial drainage system in even the flattest landscapes of northern Europe, and thereby allowed grains, native to semi-arid habitats, to flourish on previously waterlogged soil.

As historic China was shaped by water engineering and rice paddy cultivation, so historic Europe was delineated by migrants whose way of life depended on the moldboard plow and the social organization of work its operation dictated. The emigrants traveled from the plains of northwest Germany, the British Isles, northern France, northern Italy, and east along the Baltic and Danube to establish the frontier states of Prussia and Austria. Far less is known about comparable expansion in the Middle East and Central Asia, where Iranian engineers, by inventing underground water conduits, checked evaporation losses and thus expanded the areas of irrigation markedly, beginning some time before the Christian era. Even greater ignorance attaches to North Africa and India, where it is known only that areas under cultivation did sporadically increase under circumstances presumably analogous to those prevailing in China and northern Europe.

What one needs to conceive, therefore, is a basic human circulation within civilized bodies-social that sporadically carried some families toward the periphery where they expanded the area under cultivation, and a contrary, more continual movement toward urban centers, where recruitment from the hinterland was necessary to sustain human skills and numbers. These were the really massive flows, analogous to currents in earth's magma, that direct the motion of tectonic plates. As collisions of tectonic plates provoke geological spectaculars — mountain ranges, earthquakes, volcanoes — so also in human affairs, it seems likely that political spectaculars like the rise and fall of civilizations rested on these basic currents of human migration.

First among the factors producing such macromovements was the military. As I have already said, nomads by dint of their way of life enjoyed a systematic military advantage over agricultural populations. The result was sporadic conquest from the time of Sargon of Akkad (ca. 2250 B.C.) to the Mughal and Manchu conquests of India and China in the sixteenth and seventeenth centuries. Across those three millennia, the middle reaches of the ecumene experienced recurrent conquest by nomads or by the heirs of nomads who had abandoned pastoralism for the richer reward of shepherding humans, substituting taxes and rents for harder-won milk and fleeces.

But as Ibn Khaldun was perhaps the first to point out, the conditions of life that faced successful nomadic conquerors were not conducive to the maintenance of their power. Alienated subjects were prone to rebellion, and their superior numbers meant that such rebellions, inspired by heartfelt native reaction against alien rulers' exactions, could and often did spread like wildfire. Moreover, tribal discipline and moral cohesion among the rulers were certain to diminish once the daily exercise of tending herds and moving from pasture to pasture ceased to govern their lives, while the epidemiological perils of urban living eroded their numbers.

These factors conspired to produce speedy decay of purely nomadic empires. Those that lasted more than about a century had to bring in members of the subject populations into the ruling group to strengthen and prolong their power. But even in the long-lived empires other, slower processes — often related to the inability, after prolonged peace, to find satisfactory niches for what had become an excessive rural population — came into play, provoking civil war and opening the way, as often as not, for a new invasion from the grassland.

Disease and famine associated with such catastrophes sharply reduced rural and urban populations, often far below the level needed to staff the least attractive jobs. The surviving poor also benefited from the fact that social upheavals always pruned back personal claims on tax and rental income, swollen in times of stable administration above any really functional level. New dynasties often began their careers by exacting rather less per capita from a sharply diminished tax- and rent-paying population, and then saw both population and the tax and rent burden creep upward as time passed, until a new social crisis broke out.

In the context of these political rhythms the nomads, by advancing their camps to or just outside the cities of the civilized world, constituted a slender and sporadic countercurrent to the migration of peasants toward the frontiers. Its political-military importance was quite out of proportion to the numbers involved. Only Japan and westernmost Europe were far enough removed from the Eurasian grasslands to be almost exempt from the rhythm of nomadic conquest; and they not completely. Elsewhere in the Old World, political history turned mainly on these events.

The dynamics of these military migrations had another important effect: the tribesmen of the steppe and savanna lands of Eurasia and Africa acted like the molecules of a confined gas to transmit advances in military technology and related skills from one end of the ecumene to the other in very short periods of time. The "instantaneous" diffusion of stirrups in the fifth century A.D. is a well-known example of this phenomenon; the spread of gunpowder weaponry in the fourteenth century — a change that eventually helped destroy nomadic military superiority — is another. The overall effect was to ensure that Eurasians maintained an easy military superiority over other, more isolated populations. The modern expansion of Europe was vastly assisted by this fact.

Although at first less significant numerically than the military, the mercantile was a major factor shaping these population movements. Before about 1000 A.D. only a tiny handful of people made a living by moving long distances with goods for sale. Still, such groups carried knowledge and skills across commonly unbridged barriers and had much to do with the spread of civilization onto new ground. If some itinerant trader happened across a potentially valuable resource at a distance from his home, he was sometimes able to show local chieftains and men of authority how to start up a new mine or produce some other commodity for export. In this way local social hierarchies, analogous to the more elaborate ones of civilized cities, sprang into existence even at great distances. In favorable circumstances, closer and closer ties with the metropolitan center could bring a more active exercise of the full range of civilized skills to such communities without political annexation or conquest. Southeast Asia illustrates this pattern best. The spread of urban life through the western Mediterranean in the first millennium B.C. offers another example of what could happen through trade.

In these and other instances, long-distance traders moved back and forth between regions of high and low skills, and in doing so tended to spread skills and knowledge more uniformly, within limits set by geography and by the social organization of existing populations. Being more knowledgeable than nomadic tribesmen, they carried a good deal more than military technology from place to place. For example, the spread of religions was a byproduct of ancient trade. All of the world's higher religions, from Buddhism to Islam, were initially propagated along the trade routes of the Old World partly by merchants and partly by itinerant holy men whose pattern of life approximated closely that of merchants, although their stock in trade was salvation rather than more tangible commodities.

Whether sporadic or tenuous, these military and mercantile patterns of migration were therefore important in shaping the world's high culture and politics. They also circulated diseases from one part of the civilized world to another. The establishment of regular caravan routes and shipping between China and the eastern Mediterranean lands about the time of the Christian era was probably the conduit for destructive epidemics that broke out in both the Roman and Chinese empires in the second century A.D. epidemics that killed off so many of the inhabitants as to disrupt city life and precipitate the collapse of both the Han and Roman empires.

Civilization recovered, of course, both in Europe and China, as survivors developed resistances to the new disease patterns that had come to prevail. In the fourteenth century, when the Mongol empire was at its height, Eurasia suffered another bout of exposure to a major disease: the bubonic plague. Yet the plague did not suffice to disrupt European or Islamic society and seems to have had even less effect on China. A single new disease, even one as lethal as plague, was not enough to reduce population so sharply as to endanger urban continuity. It required a battery of new diseases, one following hard on the heels of the other, to produce the sort of disaster that had come to the Roman and Chinese worlds in the first Christian centuries, and to cause the even more severe catastrophe that destroyed Amerindian civilizations after 1500, when European explorers brought their own as well as African tropical diseases to the New World.

The group that suffered most severely and persistently from the plague was, in all probability, the nomadic tribesmen of the Eurasian steppe itself. For the bubonic bacillus apparently spread throughout the grasslands in the fourteenth century, establishing permanent foci of infection in the nests of burrowing rodents. This put nomads at risk as never before, and there are clear signs that drastic depopulation of the Eurasian steppe ensued. Moreover, long-distance commerce had linked more closely all of the regions of the Old World, assuring that no considerable population would long escape exposure to the diseases circulating within the system as a whole; in their contacts with others the nomads were thus newly exposed to a variety of diseases to which the others had acquired some degree of immunity. As a result, the millennial migratory current that had carried waves of so many nomadic invaders onto agricultural ground ceased to flow after the fourteenth century with anything like its accustomed force; by the sixteenth century, encroachment on the grasslands by pioneer settlers became the dominant trend instead. Gunpowder weaponry allowed civilized states to counter nomadic arrows more successfully than before, but it was the profound demographic shift that had forwarded the change by emptying out some of the best pasture lands of Eurasia in advance of settlement.

The increased importance of interregional and transcivilizational commerce was part of a more general commercial transformation of society that altered human relationships fundamentally after about 1000 A.D. and inaugurated a new phase of civilized history. It affected patterns of migration by greatly expanding the scope of infiltration, on the one hand, and enslavement, on the other. As conquest of one population by another was the hallmark of early civilized history — the basis on which most and perhaps all civilizations arose — so infiltration and enslavement became the special characteristics of migration into civilized societies during this second, commercialized phase of civilized history.

Today market exchanges govern everyday lives almost completely. We no longer produce what we consume, but instead get the necessities of life by purchase and sale. This now so much a matter of course that we have some difficulty in remembering how recent, and, historically speaking, exceptional this mode of life actually is. Before about 1000 A.D., about 90 to 95 percent of all families produced everything they needed to sustain life, and very rarely bought anything made by someone else. In cities this was of course not so; but cities were the exception. In the countryside self-sufficiency was the rule, and the market scarcely mattered. Taxes and rents sustained the cities, but returned nothing to the countryside except protection from another, perhaps even more ruthless, predator.

To be sure, in a few places where transport was unusually cheap, rural populations had been able to enter into urban exchange networks. This became true in part of the Aegean coastlands, for example, where selling olives and wine in exchange for grain imported from across the seas sustained the bloom of early classical culture. But even in that favored landscape, this commercial system proved precarious and never penetrated inland. Moreover, citizen-farmers who entered the market as autonomous buyers and sellers gave way by the second century B.C. to great estates staffed with slave labor; and the cities of the Roman empire drew their sustenance from rents and taxes extracted from rural populations that had too little left over after paying their dues to landlords and publicans to be able to buy and sell much of anything on their own account. So even in the Mediterranean lands, where commerce was favored by geography, the involvement of the agricultural majority in market relations remained exceptional in ancient times, however important the exceptions were in shaping our cultural heritage.

In Europe, the medieval revival of commerce was associated with improvements in ship-building and navigation that cheapened water transport markedly and made seafaring a year-round business for the first time. Winter storms no longer halted shipping; even the northern seas presented manageable risks. This technical advance sustained and undergirded the remarkable upthrust of commerce that transformed medieval Europe from 1000 onward.

Simultaneously, an even greater change affected China in unexpected and radical ways. There the water engineering associated with rice paddy cultivation created — incidentally, as it were — a network of canals and canalized rivers that cheapened internal transportation very greatly. Eventually, even small differences in local costs of production allowed boatmen to transport goods of common consumption across scores and even hundreds of miles from regions of low to regions of high prices, and still make a profit. This opened up all the advantages of specialization of labor that Adam Smith was later to analyze so persuasively in *The Wealth of Nations*.

To be sure, it took time for commercial skills and organization to take root in Chinese society; but during the eleventh century a tippoint came when millions of ordinary peasants began to enter the market as a matter of course, buying and selling to secure an optimal assortment of goods for their own consumption. About mid-century taxes were commuted into money, and this greatly accelerated the shift from rural self-sufficiency to market organization of mass human effort. The resulting specialization of labor exploited differences of soil, climate, and human skills more rationally than ever before. The efficiency of rural production increased dramatically. All of society, in a sense, became urbanized by becoming commercialized; and the fundamental advantage that civilized social structures had always enjoyed over undifferentiated communities was enormously magnified.

A rough index of the resulting increase of wealth and productivity is the fact that China's population under the Sung dynasty (960–1279 A.D.) doubled, while Chinese skills surged far ahead of all other parts of the civilized world. Marco Polo's report of what he saw in Cathay is eloquent testimony to China's lead over the rest of the ecumene at the end of the thirteenth century; fifty years later, an equally well-informed Muslim, Ibn Battuta, confirmed the Venetian's report.

When everyday activity of ordinary people, that is, of the peasant majority itself, came to be keyed to buying and selling in the market, older social hierarchies altered considerably. A new form of power — money — entered the scene. Landowners, military commanders, and government officials had to cope with new competitors: bankers and merchant capitalists who ordered human activity not by the old straightforward method of issuing commands and compelling obedience by punishment and threat, but by taking advantage of human greed and need. They merely offered and withheld credit, niggled over prices, bought cheap and sold dear, while keeping a sharp eye out for new and suspect ways to make money.

Nearly everyone regarded such behavior as immoral, and in better governed parts of the world capitalists were kept carefully in check. This was conspicuously the case in China, for example. In the Indian and Muslim lands, military and bureaucratic managers dealt with them more crudely: by capriciously confiscating private accumulations of wealth, or by asking such heavy bribes that large-scale commercial integration of societies over which they presided was stunted. Throughout Asia, therefore, market relations escaped inhibiting official attention only among the artisans and peddlers. But from the eleventh century onward, China's massive commercialization proceeded by way of the same ancient virtuosity with which Middle Eastern bazaar dealers chaffered over prices while concealing their wealth from tax collectors. Thereafter, the activities of Chinese and Middle Eastern merchants and peddlers gained for the market far greater control over ordinary human activities than it had in earlier times.

The almost uninhibited impact of the market, however, was initially concentrated in Europe. In that remote, ill-governed and politically fragmented part of the ecumene, capitalists could play one local ruler off another and transfer themselves and their wealth wherever protection costs were least. Sovereign and independent city states governed by merchants and artisans arose in favored parts of the continent in the eleventh century, and the richest of them played the military and diplomatic roles of great powers for the next four hundred years. To get loans, territorial rulers and lords of high degree in the rest of Europe granted lavish economic rights and privileges to capitalist entrepreneurs; and although such deals were as often as not broken off, and although European bureaucrats and kings, like their Asian counterparts, often resorted to confiscatory taxation, those who did saw commerce flee their domains while neighboring realms prospered.

Europe's political fragmentation, in other words, allowed a loose market in protection costs to sustain itself, even in territories not directly governed by men of the market. As a result, by the sixteenth century the greatest states of the age found themselves irretrievably entangled in a web of credit and commerce spun by European businessmen. A more secure *modus vivendi* emerged in the seventeenth century, when rulers and officials of Europe's strongest states decided that forwarding the interests and activities of merchants and bankers was sound policy, because it enlarged tax revenues and thus permitted the maintenance of larger armies and navies.

The greater scope for private pursuit of profit improved economic efficiency and eventually allowed Europe to outstrip China and become the world's leader in technical skills, especially those requiring large-scale investment, such as ship-building, mining, and metallurgy. Enhanced wealth and power brought Europe the means for domination of the world. That predominance inaugurated the distinctive modern period of world history — an era which in all probability is now closing.

The effect of the commercial transformation on migration was as profound as on other aspects of human activity. First, it facilitated the entry of a variety of strangers into civilized communities. Persons coming as merchants and traders, along with their attendant caravan and seafaring personnel, were only the opening wedge. In a commercially articulated society, any stranger possessing an exotic skill could hope to make a living by selling his particular goods or services. The limits to this sort of specialization were extremely elastic. New services and occupations, introduced initially by strangers, often came to be conventionally assigned to outsiders, being deemed beneath or above an ordinary person's capacity. Consequently, humble roles, like garbage collector and restaurant keeper, as well as highly respected professions, were often permanently assigned to strangers and outsiders. Variegated trade and skill diasporas thus arose in every civilized land. Sometimes these diasporas disappeared after a few generations, when the relevant skills had been acquired by persons of local birth, or when descendants of the original immigrants assimilated themselves into the society. But some diasporas were

very long-lived, either because the skills involved were somehow
repugnant to the society, or because a continued connection with
some distant land was necessary for the maintenance of the pertinent
activity.

A circumstance that often acted to maintain a trade or skill diaspora
for long periods of time was when some conspicuous cultural mark-
ers — usually canonized into a religious code of behavior — separated
the newcomers from the rest of society. The role of Jews in Christen-
dom and Islamic lands is especially noteworthy, of course, although
there have been other religious sects and diasporas that resembled
the Jewish case: Parsees in India, Greeks and Armenians in the
Ottoman, Romanov, and Hapsburg empires, Nonconformists in sev-
enteenth- to nineteenth-century England, Old Believers in Russia,
and the like.

Such people infiltrated other societies peaceably by providing
goods and services otherwise unavailable. Mistrust and dislike often
surrounded them; toleration was only halfhearted. Money lenders,
especially those involved in giving and withholding credit from poor
people who had little experience with the market, were obvious
targets for popular violence. Yet local pogroms and more systematic
holy wars against infidels and intruders might destroy or drive away
a hated group, but they did not often succeed in permanently eliminating the kinds of services such strangers provided. The reason
was that outsiders performed an important function in the community as a whole, connecting it with the world's trading network.
Doing without such connections was costly, and few communities
were really prepared to revert to local self-sufficiency, with all the
constrictions of supply and demand that this implied. So exposure
of diaspora peoples to sporadic crowd violence became a cost of
doing business in marginal communities. Soon after popular outbreaks of violence damaged or destroyed storehouses and workshops, and their owners, the old relationships usually resumed, *faute
de mieux* on both sides.

Missionaries, teachers, and foreign experts who deliberately set
out to impart new knowledge and skills to local personnel constituted
an important variant of the diaspora pattern. Such persons came
sometimes invited, sometimes not. Their ability to transmit what
they meant to impart to the host society varied enormously. Often
the most significant interaction took place on an unintended level.
Still, religious missionaries, secular teachers, and especially medical
and military experts commonly had far greater impact on the host

societies than the trifling number of such migrants would suggest. However imperfectly their purposes were achieved, the simple fact that they set out to change people's minds and habits meant that they made more of a difference than other strangers living in diaspora were likely to do.

Despite the many frictions and failures resulting from the mingling of diverse groups of peoples, it is clear that the overall effect of the diaspora phenomenon was to improve skills and increase wealth at the cost of diminishing the coherence of the society. Civilization itself paid that cost to achieve that result. From the beginning, alien populations had met and mingled in the seats of civilization. The enhanced scope for such intermingling that the commercial transformation of society brought about in the second millennium of the Christian era thus represented no more than an intensification and enlargement of the diversities of skill and culture that were characteristic of civilization itself.

Similarly, the scope for involuntary migration incidental to the commercial transformation was no more than an intensification of older aspects of civilized social dynamics. Economically unrequited and at least partially forcible collection of rents and taxes was the way early civilizations had sustained specialists. Rural populations were not only usually enslaved in law, but the legal practice of taking from them part of what they had produced lowered their status to that of slaves. Slavery, both ancient and modern, differed inasmuch as it operated with the context of a commercial system, so that slaves themselves, the food they ate, and the goods their labor produced all alike entered a market. That difference was not trivial; yet we should remember that the appropriation by some of the product of others' labor was the unjust price of all early civilization.

Slave migration affected far larger numbers of persons than ever entered willingly into trade and skill diasporas, but since most forms of slavery did not encourage biological reproduction, the traces slave migrations left behind are fewer than historians' recent efforts at head counts might lead one to expect. As we saw above, in ancient times recruitment of slaves from afar allowed cities to replenish their numbers without depopulating tax-paying villages near at hand. Middle Eastern cities seem to have been especially active, in ancient as well as modern times. Between the ninth and nineteenth centuries, they drew slaves from the north in vast numbers — Turks and Russians mainly — and imported enormous numbers from Africa.

Slaves were usually wanted for domestic service in private households. Some became wives and concubines; others served the great and mighty as bodyguards, and some usurped power and became rulers themselves. The slave dynasty of Delhi and Mamelukes of Egypt are well-known examples of this surprising twist that enslavement sometimes took. Ottoman rule, manned by slaves from Balkan villages of the mountainous wild west, was an even more remarkable example of how the promotion of slaves to the political apex of society could be institutionalized.

In all these cases, slaves originated in regions beyond the borders of the state over which they presided, or else came from backward localities where failure of commercial development made ordinary taxes uncollectible. Middle Eastern cities, in other words, organized their hinterlands into a closely administered inner zone from which came food and other supplies, and a remoter circle from which came the manpower (and also animals for transport and slaughter) needed to sustain the urban complex. This sort of differentiation was made possible by the commercial transformation of society, which rationalized human relations by geographical specialization. It gave particularly dramatic and visible form to the longstanding pattern of human recruitment into urban hierarchies.

The Mameluke regime lasted in Egypt until Napoleon invaded in 1798, but the Ottoman system wore itself out, interestingly, when changes in demography within the empire's heartland began to provide a reserve of candidates eager for admission to the privileged ranks of society. Such persons were no longer content to see outsiders monopolize the top administration and were willing to accept nominal slavery if that was the price of power. As this occurred during the latter half of the seventeenth century, when the Old World was drifting away from slavery, the peculiarities of the Ottoman policy became residual. Older, less formalized patterns of urban recruitment resumed their sway.

The privileged roles assigned to slaves and strangers in Islamic society perhaps reflected the depth of alienation of rulers and their diverse urban subjects and rural tax-paying populations. To exercise power securely in their environment, princes desperately needed trustworthy agents and subordinates. Men utterly detached from their social origins and dependent entirely on status within a militarized slave hierarchy constituted a more coherent and dependable group than any alternative body from which officials might be drawn. Military discipline and *esprit de corps,* supplemented by the power of bureaucratic ambition to direct the behavior of men eager for promotion, gave such structures surprising stability — more than people who have never served in an army or experienced the group bonding inherent in military life may be ready to believe. Emotionally vibrant forms of sectarian religion offered the only alternative; and that, too, frequently occurred in Islamic lands, most notably in Iran.

Domestic slavery also existed in China, India, Europe, and Africa, although it never had the political and military significance that it attained in the Muslim world. Whether these various slaveries increased in importance after the commercial transformation of society is impossible to tell in the absence of any sort of statistical indices. Indeed, historians have been so preoccupied by the transatlantic slave trade that they have paid little attention to other kinds of slavery. We therefore do not know enough even to guess at the overall importance of domestic slavery in non-Muslim Eurasia.

On the other hand, we do know that slaves working outside the household did become much more numerous and more important economically as the commercial transformation proceeded. Plantation agriculture and mining were the two activities most often staffed by slaves. The link was so prominent in the seventeenth and eighteenth centuries that we tend to equate slavery with this particular organization of labor. Yet even at the height of the West African slave trade, it is not certain that more Africans crossed the Atlantic to work on plantations and mines in the New World than continued to filter into the Muslim world as domestic servants. The numbers involved in both flows was substantial; about eight million moved in each direction between the seventeenth and nineteenth centuries.

Together with white indentured servants, who also crossed the ocean in comparatively large numbers, African slaves constituted the overwhelming majority of immigrants to the New World before 1840. Only persons of wealth could pay the cost of passage for themselves, and few of them wanted to leave home. Most of those who crossed the ocean before steamships transformed conditions of transatlantic travel did so at someone else's expense and against their own will.

Those who paid the cost of transport for slaves and indentured servants did so because other sources of labor were unavailable in the New World. That in turn was largely due to the inadvertent destruction of Amerindian populations by sudden exposure to unfamiliar Old World diseases. Isolated populations always ran that risk on first contact with civilized, disease-experienced populations, but in earlier ages such contacts had usually come by stages and affected relatively small populations at any one time. But the opening of the oceans after 1500 meant that enormous territories and large populations, of which the Amerindian was by far the greatest, were suddenly put at risk. Not one but dozens of epidemics followed fast one on the other, each compounding the death-dealing damage its predecessors had wrought.

The result was to empty out fertile lands on a scale never seen before. The "open" frontier of American history was one result. Similar emptying occurred in northern Siberia, southernmost Africa, and in Australia, New Zealand, and other islands of the Pacific. A great frontier was thus created by the global homogenization of diseases. Europeans were uniquely able to respond to the opportunity that this demographic disaster created, since they alone controlled transport and possessed information about conditions overseas. Slave populations suffered heavy death rates and often failed to reproduce themselves in new places. By contrast, even small initial settlements of European freemen multiplied rapidly in temperate climates. This provided the manpower for the westward movement of early American history. Canada, Australia, South Africa, and Brazil, together with Argentina, had similar histories. In the tropics, however, where African diseases flourished, Europeans faced crippling disease attrition. There, Africans fared better. As a result, the Caribbean eventually became predominantly black, while adjacent semitropical lands came to be populated by varying blends of black, white, and red, with a significant addition of yellow from nineteenth-century Asian coolie gangs.

Improvements in transportation in the mid-nineteenth century cheapened ocean travel and made it far safer than before. This coincided with a growth of rural population in most of Europe that taxed the absorptive capacity of cities. The result was a vast exodus overseas, totaling about 46 million between 1840 and 1920, which dwarfed all earlier migrations. Because the migration was so huge and because it occurred recently, we are prone to take it as the norm. Yet the conditions that permitted such an intercontinental outpouring were exceptional when measured against the circumstances of the deeper past. All three — the depopulation of lands of in-migration, opening fertile land for occupancy, and the upsurge of numbers within the disease-experienced centers of civilization in the Old World — were without earlier precedent and are unlikely to recur. It is therefore quite unwise to suppose that patterns of migration that prevailed for eighty years (1840–1920) constitute a pattern for humanity, and important to insist on the atypicality of this period.

In closing, I would like to suggest that the barbarian ideal of a homogeneous ethnic nation is incompatible with the normal population dynamics of civilization. The fact that Europe's achievement of high civilization between the ninth and thirteenth centuries coincided with a swarming of population in northwestern Europe, and that modern Western expansion and nation-building also coincided with population growth of exceptional character, meant that throughout the nineteenth century Europeans were able to combine the barbarian ideal of a single ethos — a nation of blood-brothers — with the reality of civilized specialization and urban living. To be sure, the blood-brotherhood of European nations was largely fictitious, but a real cohesion of language and culture was achieved within each nation's boundaries that far exceeded civilized norms.

Only since World War II have European nations begun to experience the ethnic mingling that was once usual in civilized lands. Population losses due to war, or at least a reproductive rate inadequate to fill available jobs, and recruitment from ethnically diverse peripheries, again prevailed in post-1950 Europe and America. Consequently, polyethnic lamination — the clustering of different groups in particular occupations in a more or less formal hierarchy of dignity and wealth — is again asserting itself, in the USSR as much as in Germany, France, Britain, and the United States.

This change constitutes a reversion to the civilized pattern of the deeper past, when the world's great empires were ruled by small groups — their members often recruited from a multiplicity of ethnic backgrounds — presiding over hierarchies of specialized occupations, each of which tended to be dominated by a particular ethnic group. Such social arrangements do not accord well with liberal theory, which recognizes no significant differences among citizens. When such differences do in fact exist, theory gets into difficulty. Surely the gap between theory and practice is growing among us with respect to migration and the status of ethnically diverse immigrants. It is time we thought about it carefully. Acquaintance with migration patterns of the deeper past will help us to do so with better results than are likely without a world-historical perspective of the sort hastily sketched here.

T W O

Wanted But Not Welcome: Alien Labor in Western Development

Aristide R. Zolberg

INTERNATIONAL labor migrations took place long before individuals were uprooted by the great transformation wrought by the industrial revolution in Europe, and the expansion of the international capitalist economy to a global scale. Throughout the long era of demographic scarcity, one of the signal benefits of imperial domination was the possibility of expanding economic production by exploiting alien labor. Work could be exacted from the population of a conquered territory in the form of *corvée* or by skimming; alternatively, workers were forcibly taken from the subject society to where imperial authorities and entrepreneurs thought they would be more useful, in some other possession or even in the metropolitan center itself. Engaging like their imperial predecessors in primitive accumulation, Europeans followed suit in the course of their own rise to global paramountcy. Despite the profound transformations Western societies have experienced in the intervening period, international labor migrations have continued to play a significant role in their economic development down to our own times.

This essay examines the successive ways in which the West has organized the procurement and profitable use of such manpower from the earliest phase of its expansion to the present. Allowing for a considerable amount of variation, each epoch can nevertheless be characterized by a particular pattern involving mode of procurement, preference for certain places of origin and individual characteristics, as well as sectoral allocation and mechanisms of labor control in the place of destination. Albeit reflecting prevailing material and social conditions within the societies of origin and of destination, these patterns should not be thought of as narrowly determined; rather, each of them represents an imperfect and unstable solution — one among several possible — to the problems that imported labor inevitably brings to the hegemonic society.

Of particular interest in this respect is that imported labor tends to be alien in the deep sense — that is, not merely foreign, but representing for the receiving society an undesirable "otherness." This is by no means happenstance, as it is precisely the alien character of the labor that makes its importation profitable in the first place; and it is also the case that the people involved remain alien afterward as a consequence of the role to which they are confined in the receiving society. It follows that by using alien labor a hegemonic society tends to foster an increase in its own heterogeneity, an outcome that commonly gives rise to severe political strains pertaining to issues of societal identity and cohesion.

The patterns to be considered include African slavery (fifteenth to nineteenth centuries); Asian indenture (nineteenth and twentieth centuries); and free migrant labor, involving the movement of disparate groups from a variety of peripheries to industrial societies (eighteenth century to the present). An analytic case study will illustrate each pattern, highlighting the crystallization of a particular form under epochal circumstances. Overall, the essay adumbrates more formal diachronic comparisons, a task that must be reserved for a larger work. In the conclusion, I shall briefly highlight the dilemmas Western Europe and the United States face today as a consequence of the choices they made earlier in this sphere.

Colonization and the Importation of Slaves

The institutionalization of plantation slavery in the West. Whereas from the very beginning slaves constituted the dominant category of labor in European colonies, they were a marginal category in Western Europe in the medieval period. The prevalence in Europe itself of serfdom, a more limited form of bondage than slavery, has been attributed to a demographic decline around the end of the first millennium, which fostered labor scarcity and gave peasants some bargaining power in relation to lords. In addition, coercive supervision of the sort slavery entails was probably inefficient in relation to the varied tasks carried out in the manor economy (North and Thomas, 1973, p. 20). In keeping with this, and reflecting as well the dispersal of sovereignty that was a central feature of feudalism (Anderson, 1974), by the ninth century Europeans had developed cultural prohibitions against the enslavement of their own kind. Loyal Christians were deemed to possess human rights incompatible with the absolute degradation slave status entailed, and respect of these rights in turn constituted the foundation of legitimate authority (D. Davis, 1967). But as these prohibitions did not apply to *external* populations, the knights fighting in the Iberian *Reconquista* enslaved captured Muslims for their own use, as did conquering Anglo-Saxons with resisting Celts in the British Isles. Europeans also acquired external populations for trade, particularly captured pagan peoples from beyond the Elbe — known ever since as "Slavs" in most European languages — who were moved through Germany and France for resale in Muslim Spain (Verlinden, 1970).

In the course of their expansion at the beginning of the second millennium, Europeans also launched colonies for the production of commodities they lacked. Such undertakings made sense where land was a geographically fixed factor of production, as in the extraction of minerals or the cultivation of crops limited to particular climates, including sugar-producing establishments located on frost-free islands of the Mediterranean.

European crusaders encountered sugar in the Holy Land, where the Arabs who had brought it from the East organized production on a plantation basis, combining the growing of cane with the extraction of molasses by the use of pressing mills, and using imported slaves as the manpower (Deer, 1949). This unusual combination of primary and secondary economic production, which Europeans took over without significant modifications, was probably dictated by constraints inherent in the production of sugar under prevailing technological conditions. Mills must be adjacent to the fields because of spoilage; the construction of mills required capital; and the high fixed cost of the machinery entailed in turn the organization of a large plantation to produce sufficient cane. The result was a specialized market-oriented enterprise, rarely encountered in medieval Europe, which precisely met the conditions under which supervisory costs might be "low enough to make it economically feasible to hold slaves rather than serfs" (North and Thomas, 1973, p. 20).

As honey was the only sweetening then produced within Europe itself, sugar rapidly caught on as a much sought-after luxury. By the thirteenth century Venetian entrepreneurs were exporting it from Palestine and Syria to Western Europe; when the area was conquered by the Turks, production was launched on Cyprus, where it underwent further development into a more capitalist form and, by the

fifteenth century, included the local finishing of sugar loaves. Concomitantly, the island became an important slave market. Similar
enterprises emerged in Crete and Sicily. The Mediterranean slave
trade to supply these plantations, involving mostly population from
the Black Sea area but also some black Africans acquired from Arab
traders, reached a peak in the fourteenth and fifteenth centuries, as
indicated by the recording of over 10,000 slaves sales in Venice alone
between 1414 and 1423 (D. Davis, 1966, pp. 42–43). Throughout this
period, Europeans also operated the sugar industry established by
the Arabs along the southern coast of Iberia, for which they obtained
black slaves from West Africa by way of the trans-Saharan caravan
trade (Parry, 1974, p. 84).

Was the fact that the slaves used in these colonial undertakings
were generally *imported* an incidental consequence of labor scarcity
in particular locations, or was importation an integral component of
the system? Charles Verlinden, the authority on European medieval
slavery, firmly inclines toward the integral view. When a large labor
force was needed, slaves were necessarily imported because the dis-
ruption occasioned by the wholesale enslavement of indigenous populations was incompatible with the political order required for the
success of the colony (Verlinden, 1970, p. 46). Other considerations
support this interpretation. A confrontation between an immigrant
minority aspiring to the status of masters, unfamiliar with the local
terrain, and an indigenous population at ease on its own turf, and
hence able to defend itself or alternatively to escape, would foster
extremely high supervisory costs. In contrast, the uprooting of people
and their resettlement in an unfamiliar environment creates a situation of extreme disorientation that permits the exercise of totalitarian
control by a minority. Control is further facilitated by making slaves
clearly distinguishable from nonslaves, a goal commonly achieved
by branding; but importation can also serve this objective by bringing
in a group that is culturally, and in some cases also physically, distinct
from both natives of the colony and immigrant masters.

Importation provides narrowly economic advantages as well.
Whatever the actual costs of purchase or capture may be, the importation of external labor means that the receiving economy does not
incur the opportunity costs of alternative uses of that labor, and the
costs of reproducing it are borne by the society of origin.

Conversely, where the use of external labor made economic sense,
slavery was the most likely form in which to organize the importation. In the absence of an international market in *labor*, whose insti-

tutionalization is conditional upon the existence of a money economy in the societies of origin and destination, the necessary transactions could only occur as a trade in *persons*. In such an exchange, the seller must be compensated in a single transaction for the total labor potential of the person being traded; concomitantly, the purchaser must pay for this all at once, as well as for the costs of transport and of relocation which, under preindustrial conditions, tended to be quite high in relation to a person's total labor potential. In order to recoup his investment, the buyer must retain control over his purchase after the transaction is completed.

The Atlantic system. In the fifteenth century the Portuguese and their Genoese associates performed a feat of entrepreneurship of classic Schumpeterian stamp, combining two distinct activities, trade and colonization. They were able to enhance the value of a newly available and plentiful trading commodity — African slaves — by creating a demand for it as a factor of production in newly founded colonies devoted to the manufacture of another commodity — sugar — for which a very large market already existed in Europe.

The Portuguese ventured southward into the Atlantic in order to gain access to West African gold without passing through the intermediary of Muslim traders. To complement this factor, from the fourteenth century onward the European colonial system was threatened by Turkish advance into the eastern Mediterranean. The search for new colonial sites was therefore an additional motive for the growing European interest in the southern Atlantic, where the existence of some frost-free islands was known, and that of many others suspected. Moreover, West Africa was also reputed as a source of slaves, who had long constituted an important share of the total value of Portuguese trade south of Morocco. In order to avail themselves of the material benefits slavery afforded, westerners cast African blacks in the role of permanent nonsubjects, absolute outsiders dwelling in the heart of darkness, and whom they might therefore condemn with impunity to social death (Patterson, 1982).

Madeira rapidly emerged as the most successful of the new colonial ventures; with additional sugar plantations in the Azores, the Cape Verde islands, and Sao Tome, Portuguese production soared to such an extent that the price of sugar in Europe dropped by half between 1470 and 1500, an outcome that prompted Portugal to restrict exports and provided the incentive for others to seek locations for launching colonies on the Madeiran model, as Castile did shortly afterward in the Canaries (Duncan, 1972, p. 11; Morison, 1974, p. 16). In the first quarter of the sixteenth century, slave imports into the Old World averaged 1,700 per year, of whom 70 percent were destined for the recently established island colonies (Curtin, 1969).

Considered in this perspective, the discovery and colonization of America accelerated and extended an established process. Since America turned out not to be the Indies, once the Castilians appropriated available gold, they had little choice but to engage in mining and other forms of colonization. Of the various experiments, cattle ranching for the production of hides and sugar plantations emerged as most promising. Familiar with the Madeiran trade, Columbus himself probably introduced sugar cane into the New World on his second voyage. Sugar thus spread from the Canaries to Hispaniola, and thence to Puerto Rico, Cuba, and Jamaica, as well as most of the tropical coastlands of Spanish America; on the Portuguese side, it was but a short skip from the Cape Verde islands to Brazil.

The prospect of riches and power quickly drew a substantial flow of Castilians to the New World, which in the context of the times was nothing short of a mass migration (Mörner, 1976, pp. 766–767). The obvious source of labor for the new undertakings was the immense manpower reserve provided by Middle America and its adjacent islands, which at the time of first contact were highly populated, owing to a much higher agricultural productivity than had been achieved in Europe (McNeill, 1976, pp. 176–180; Klein, 1967, p. 129). In keeping with prevailing legal doctrines derived from the *Reconquista*, resisters captured in the course of what were self-evidently just wars could be enslaved. As in Africa, native authorities were willing to sell men; and it was easy for Europeans to pretend that these too had been procured in the course of just wars. Local Amerindians enslaved in this rough-and-ready manner initially provided the sole source of labor for the mines, sugar plantations, and cattle ranches that sprang up on Hispaniola and Cuba in the early years; some natives were even exported to the Old World (Verlinden, 1970, p. 24).

In 1503 natives of America who submitted to Castile were declared free and not liable to *servidumbre* (slavery). Although they were subjected instead to a form of feudal serfdom similar to the one imposed earlier in the conquered Muslim territories and the Canaries, with obligations that included tribute in labor as well as in kind (Parry, 1966, p. 60), in the initial period colonists were unable to exploit the Amerindian labor to which they had secured entitlement under Spanish law, because they were unable to deprive the native population of its economic self-sufficiency. Even before the great epidemics erupted, the shortage of labor was so acute that the crown considered importing manpower from Spain. But Castilian landlords in turn successfully resisted attempts to organize a substantial emigration of tenants and laborers. Hence as early as 1510 the crown ordered the *Casa de contratación* to send 150 blacks to Hispaniola to be sold to the colonists for work in the gold mines (Newton, 1937, p. 62).

The demographic catastrophe that subsequently befell the Amerindian population exacerbated the labor shortage, providing further stimulus for the Atlantic slave trade. Initially hampered by the requirement of conducting all transactions by way of Seville, the expansion of slave imports resulted largely from smuggling; but following the union of the Spanish and Portuguese crowns in 1580, Portuguese slavers were authorized to trade directly between Africa and Spanish America. Numbers rose from about 500 a year in the second quarter of the century to 1,000 in the third and 1,500 in the last, totaling about 75,000 for the century as a whole. In the same period the Portuguese also carried 40,000 to their own sugar plantations in Brazil. In the seventeenth century emigration from Iberia to the colonies was even more severely restricted, and 850,000 slaves were imported into Spanish and Portuguese America (Curtin, 1969; Klein, 1967).

Other Europeans faced even more acute manpower problems when they in turn sought to colonize America in the seventeenth century. Getting started after the demographic catastrophe had taken its toll, they could not launch colonial undertakings without resorting to massive labor importation from the very beginning. The situation they faced has been formalized by economists into a model of labor procurement under conditions of "free land," whose main proposition is that in an agricultural economy where land and labor are the only factors of production, "free land, free workers, and a leisure class of non-working landowners cannot exist together" (Menard, 1977, p. 357; Domar, 1970). Take a group of people who assert ownership of a certain amount of land in an unpopulated area where land is available for the taking: any free workers they import will naturally seek to avail themselves of the opportunity to launch agricultural enterprises of their own; wages will be driven up, and the original landowners will be left with no surplus to appropriate. This path leads inexorably to the formation of an economy consisting for the most part of self-sufficient family farms. Alternatively, if landowners are to obtain income beyond what they can produce with their own hands, they must impose restrictions of some sort on the labor force.

These alternatives correspond to the contrast in development between New England or New France which, despite their many differences, became European *settlements* (that is, overseas extensions of European societies), and French and British *colonies* in the south and the Caribbean (undertakings organized around the production of a specialized staple for export), which relied from the very outset on restricted labor. With the African slave trade still under firm Iberian control, English entrepreneurs had no choice but to transplant a labor force from Europe under indenture, usually for a seven-year term. This labor was integrated into colonial trade more generally as a commodity whose price was subject to market fluctuations, and whose ownership was protected by the state. The system was crucial for the settlement of the Caribbean islands, which received twice as many English emigrants as the mainland in the second quarter of the seventeenth century. Around mid-century, besides indentured servants the arrivals included convicts and political exiles or prisoners taken in the English civil wars, among them a large number of Irish Catholics "barbado'd" by Cromwell (Smith, 1971). Overall, between one-half and two-thirds of all white immigrants to the southern mainland and Caribbean possessions of the British Empire during colonial times came under some sort of bondage (Galenson, 1981).

African slaves were available to English colonies from Dutch interlopers early on, but the supply was not assured, and their purchase price — which represented transport costs plus a lifetime of labor — was higher than for whites. D. Galenson has demonstrated that slaves tended to replace indentured whites where the demand for labor was particularly strong, because under such conditions whites could choose their destination and bargain for more attractive terms of indenture, while slaves could not; and slave traders chose their markets by the prices offered for their cargoes. By and large, the productivity of labor was highest in the sugar colonies, where slave imports accordingly grew fastest (Galenson, 1981, pp. 172–177).

Changes also occurred on the supply side. Toward the end of the seventeenth century, in the face of a growing demand for labor at home, the emigration of English servants came to be an issue of competition between England and its colonies for the same labor; as in Iberia, the home country devised regulations to render exit more difficult (Menard, 1977, p. 379). Concurrently, in 1660 England organized the Royal Africa Company which, with the backing of naval power, quickly secured direct access to the African source of slaves and hence significantly reduced their cost to British colonies.

Accordingly, in the last quarter of the seventeenth century the British Caribbean imported over 6,000 slaves a year, so that by 1710 slaves constituted over 80 percent of the island population (Curtin, 1969, pp. 119, 125). The flow of white servants to the southern mainland colonies peaked in the 1660s, and the proportion of blacks in the population rose from 5 percent at that time to 21 percent in 1700. Overall, despite their belated start, British colonies imported about 264,000 Africans in the seventeenth century. As the shift from whites to blacks accelerated, the distinction between servants and slaves was formalized as well, and new legal institutions were devised to operate a system of slavery.

Similarly, within the French empire slaves began to replace indentured white servants in the Caribbean after the introduction of sugar in the 1640s. Much as England conquered Jamaica and then went on to displace the Dutch on parts of the African coast in order to procure their own slaves, so within a decade France occupied the western coast of Hispaniola (later Saint-Domingue, then Haiti), and in 1677 wrested the Gorée slave entrepôt on the coast of Senegal from the Dutch. By 1700 France's West Indian colonies had received between 35,000 and 50,000 white settlers — many more than Acadia and New France combined — but had also imported 156,000 slaves (Poussou, 1970, pp. 53–54).

Notwithstanding changing relations of economic and political power among European states, in the eighteenth century Europe collectively continued its ascent to world hegemony. Mercantilist theory counseled a concentration of investment in true colonies, operated with alien labor. In keeping with this, slaves arrived in the Americas at an average rate of 55,000 a year for 1701–1810, totaling over six million, nearly two-thirds of the entire Atlantic trade from its beginnings in 1451 to its termination in 1870 (Curtin, 1969, p. 268). After Portugal, which brought 1.9 million to Brazil alone, came Britain and France, with 1.7 and 1.3 million respectively. Forced to relinquish the *asiento* (contracting) to foreigners, and without direct access to the African source, Spain was now a distant fourth; nevertheless, its slave imports rose to nearly 600,000 during this period, twice the number of the preceding century. Similarly, the Dutch introduced close to half a million slaves into the few colonies they retained in the Caribbean.

Whereas until 1700 the European and African migrations to America were of the same order of magnitude, after the turn of the century Africans vastly outnumbered whites. In the British West Indies the ratio of black to white arrivals rose from approximately 1.5:1 in the seventeenth century to 11:1 in the eighteenth; in the French West Indies, from approximately 4:1 to 27:1.

Substitutes for Slaves

In many of the regions where slavery had prevailed, including the sugar colonies of the West Indies, when slave-owning proved no longer practicable economic entrepreneurs resorted to the importation of Asians under indenture. Asians were used in the same fashion in the launching of new colonial undertakings throughout the expanding European empires, including those in Asia itself. The pattern, which shared many of the characteristics of slavery, was no mere temporary expedient in the course of a transition to free labor: initiated in the 1830s, the practice lasted until well into the twentieth century, and involved the relocation of many millions. A slightly different version of the basic pattern emerged in the late nineteenth century as the principal mechanism for labor procurement in southern Africa, where it prevails into the present.

Historical reality challenges the terms of reference of the protracted debate between idealists and materialists over whether the end of slavery in the British Empire is attributable to heightened moral sensibility or to the shifting functional needs of capitalism. In the peripheral regions of the Western-dominated international capitalist system, bound labor remained the most economically rational form for many purposes; and the newly developed moral sensibility of British elites must be qualified, for it did not interfere with the institutionalization of what some, at least, denounced early on as "a new form of slavery" (Williams, 1980; Anstey, 1975; D. Davis, 1975; Tinker, 1974).

The emigration "push" from Asia was itself fostered by the incorporation of that continent into the European-dominated world economy. In the Indian case, the growing supply pool was attributable to the character of British policies, which "introduced another element of uncertainty, another complex web of parasites and exploiters of the village (e.g., the new officials of the British raj), a considerable shift and concentration of ownership, a growth of peasant debt and poverty" (Hobsbawm, 1962, p. 197). Since India was also undergoing a systematic deindustrialization, no domestic labor market arose to absorb the displaced rural population, which early in the nineteenth century was recruited to man the new European plantations of Southeast Asia. The emigration rapidly grew in size, spilling even beyond the British Empire. One estimate for the period 1830 to 1870 suggests a total of well over a million for British and French plantations alone (Tinker, 1974, p. 115); a more comprehensive count of emigration to the West Indies, South Africa, and Ceylon gives 2.7 million for the period 1834 to 1913; but as many destinations are left out — including large importers such as Mauritius and Malaya — the overall total was probably even higher.

In China the initial "push" was triggered by growing rural poverty, itself attributable to a slight increase in the rate of population growth. The subsequent competition for scarce land led to higher rents — as in Ireland or India — and to a concurrent enlargement of the upper class, which resulted in a greater squeeze on the peasantry. Political upheavals such as the Opium Wars and the Taiping Rebellion contributed to the push as well. Starting in the first third of the nineteenth century, the emigration of labor overseas was organized by Chinese entrepreneurs in response to demand from the newly launched plantations of British Malaya and Dutch East Indies. Although emigration remained officially forbidden, imperial authorities did not have the capacity to enforce the prohibition (Bastid-Bruguière, 1980, pp. 582–586, 591–593). The arrival of Western shipping in the South China Sea following the opening of treaty ports in the 1840s expanded the size of the traffic and its domain.

The bulk of the emigration continued toward Southeast Asia, but in the thirty-year period starting around 1845 about half a million left for the New World as well. Of these, at least 100,000 went to the United States and another 20,000 to American-owned sugar plantations in Hawaii; 80,000 to 100,000 were shipped to work the guano deposits on the offshore islands of Peru, with an estimated survival rate of less than one-third; and about 150,000 ended up in the sugar plantations of Cuba as substitutes for slaves (Boyd, 1970, p. 48). For a brief period in the 1860s, Britain also organized government-supervised emigration from Hong Kong and Canton to its West Indian colonies, following the Indian pattern. Overall, two to three million Chinese were living abroad by 1876, and eight to nine million in 1908, ranging as far afield as South Africa and the islands of the Indian Ocean. One can therefore hazard the guess of a total emigration from India and China to other parts of Asia or overseas of the order of 20 million for the "long nineteenth century," a total much larger than that of African slaves in the eighteenth, and approximately half the size of the great Atlantic migration of Europeans in the nineteenth century.

Given the high cost of relocation in relation to earnings (which the workers could not meet on their own), the imperfectly monetarized structure of the sending economy, and the receiving economy's continued reliance on a coercive element in labor organization, the migration was organized as a trade in persons on the basis of long-term labor contracts that entailed various forms of bondage, for which "indenture" serves as the generic term. Although by all reports conditions to which Asian workers were subjected were as harsh as any encountered under slavery, indenture did not entail "social death" and did specify a limited time; formal arrangements — albeit often violated in practice —usually provided for returning the workers to their country of origin. Like slaves, however, indentured workers were members of a distinctive racial group ineligible for membership in the receiving community. As with the slaves, the physical and cultural distinctiveness of the workers facilitated supervisory control. It is noteworthy that the plantations of Southeast Asia, albeit located in densely populated regions, were operated mostly with imported labor, Indian as well as Chinese, in keeping with the logic followed in importing slaves.

As with slaves, the alien character of imported workers did not matter a great deal in colonial possessions, where Asians became one more ethnic-economic group within emerging plural societies; but it generated severe tensions among the handful of Pacific locations that were simultaneously colonial undertakings and settler societies aspiring to autonomous development — the West Coast of the United States, British Columbia, Australia, and New Zealand. A comparison of the two situations sharpens our understanding of the basic pattern and of its limiting conditions.

Indians in the British Empire. In the late eighteenth century, when pressures arose in Britain and elsewhere to abolish the slave trade, plantation economies — with the singular exception of the American South — required a constant replenishment of their labor supply. The partisans of abolition thus expected that the end of the trade would undermine slavery itself; mirroring this, the planters generally opposed abolition. Britain's decision in 1807 to abolish the trade supplying its own plantations and to prohibit further slave imports was facilitated by wartime conditions and an oversupply of sugar;

but the effects of this decision — a declining supply of labor — were keenly felt after the end of the Napoleonic wars, when industrialization, rapid population growth, and a rising standard of living stimulated a proliferation of colonial plantations throughout the world's tropical and subtropical regions, in response to a vast expansion of the European market for commodities such as sugar, tea, coffee, and later rubber.

Initially, the British West Indian colonies struggled to grow sugar with the available manpower, seeking unsuccessfully to increase it by way of natural reproduction of the slaves. To make the continuation of slavery itself more palatable to public opinion in Britain, they enacted "melioration laws"; but after 1823, the scandalous contrast between these nostrums and West Indian reality induced British abolitionists to insist on outright manumission. This was achieved ten years later amidst the surge of reformist sentiment that also brought about signal changes in British constitutional structure. News of impending freedom triggered off a slave rebellion in Jamaica, which in turn "proved the decisive factor in precipitating emancipation" (Green, 1976, p. 112).

The morality of emancipation was to be vindicated by a demonstration that sugar production could thrive under conditions of free labor; but because conditions in some of the larger islands approximated those of the "free land" model, it was expected that slaves would desert the plantations to engage in subsistence farming (Green, 1976, pp. 115–116). To forestall a critical labor shortage that would ruin the planters, the emancipation law maintained the apparatus of coercion by way of an extended period of mandatory "apprenticeship," during which, in keeping with established practices, the masters would retain the ex-slaves' wages (Green, p. 119). But some planters came to believe that apprenticeship provided an opportunity for the Colonial Office to exercise oversight in the sphere of labor relations, and felt they might be better off with outright emancipation. Other factors too contributed to this result as slaves in Antigua and Bermuda were manumitted without restrictions in 1834, and apprenticeship was terminated elsewhere in 1838, two years ahead of schedule (Green, p. 159). Where the ratio of population to unused land rendered squatting and subsistence agriculture possible, slaves indeed deserted the plantations in droves. This was the case in Jamaica, Trinidad, and Guiana, the three largest British West Indian producers, whose total exports declined by nearly half between 1830 and 1840 (Tinker, 1974, p. 24; Bolland, 1981, pp. 591–619).

The labor crisis of the West Indies provided an opportunity for Mauritius, a British Indian Ocean colony situated approximately 1,000 miles from the nearest point on the African mainland and 2,000 from the Indian subcontinent. Although the island's original Dutch and French planters had imported most of their slaves from Africa and Madagascar, they had acquired some from India as well, as did the French of nearby Bourbon (subsequently Réunion), until the government of India prohibited the traffic in 1789 (Tinker, 1974, p. 44). When the British conquered Mauritius in 1810 there were about 6,000 Indian slaves on the island; and local authorities later imported convicts from India and Singapore for use in public works as well. In the late 1820s, seeing an opportunity to sell more sugar on the British market, the Mauritius planters expanded production by importing slaves illegally from Africa and by recruiting workers in India, from which they also imported provisions to feed their workers (Tinker, 1974, p. 12; Cumpston, 1953, p. 12).

Although conditions for Indians cannot have been very different from those of the Atlantic slave trade, this migration did not evoke British concern because it was considered an internal affair. However, after the government of India learned in 1830 that workers were being exported to neighboring French Réunion as well, it required that a declaration of voluntary emigration be filed before a magistrate, with contracts limited to a maximum of five years and compensation specified in advance. Migration under indenture — which had been a common practice for Europeans until the early decades of the nineteenth century — was thus newly legitimized for the British Empire and rudimentary institutional mechanisms arose to regularize the traffic (Tinker, 1974, pp. 14, 41, 61).

The regulations governing the traffic to Réunion were generalized for all Indian emigration in 1837. The following year, Mauritius devised an ordinance which "laid down terms for the Indians which included residual elements of the slave laws" but was deemed acceptable by the Colonial Office. Its most important feature was *penalization of vagrancy*, a characteristic device of colonies in the post-slavery epoch that prevented ex-slaves or indentured immigrants from taking advantage of "free land" conditions to engage in subsistence agriculture and thereby withhold their labor from the market. The system was an instant success. Over 25,000 Indian "coolies" were imported within the first two years; exporting 36,559 tons of sugar in 1840, Mauritius now emerged as the leading producer within the British Empire (Tinker, 1974, pp. 17, 24, 61).

The importation of indentured labor beckoned as a solution for the West Indies as well. The problem there was that the most convenient source of manpower was Africa itself, but, unlike in India or China, there were no processes at work there as yet to drive people to seek cash wages. Moreover, the Colonial Office, sensitive to a public opinion at home and abroad in whose eyes African migration was inextricably linked with slavery, prohibited recruitment on the African coast. In 1837 John Gladstone, a well-connected Guianese proprietor — he was the father of the future Liberal leader, then a Tory Undersecretary for the Colonies — secured the enactment of an Order-in-Council authorizing the importation of Indians under the Mauritius system for a three-year trial period (Cumpston, 1953, pp. 18–39). However, the venture was quickly denounced not only by *The British Emancipator* but even by *The Times*, which objected that the transportation of bound Indians halfway across the world heralded "a new slave trade." The agitation spread to India as well, where hearings gave wide publicity to the coercive practices of recruiters, carried out in collusion with the police. In May 1839 the government of India prohibited all emigration for manual labor outside the subcontinent.

Free traders at this time were fully committed to the preservation of the British Empire, but sought to render it economically efficient. One leading suggestion envisaged government-sponsored relocation of labor from one part of the Empire to another so as to maximize its productivity and make more efficient use of land. The main concern was to move English paupers and the "surplus" Irish from the British Isles to Canada and Australia. In 1840 a Whig government established for this purpose the Colonial Land and Emigration Commissioners, a remarkably precocious mechanism for manpower planning at the level of the empire as a whole. Later in the same year, a new Conservative government entrusted to this body the additional task of organizing the movement of acceptable indentured labor to the sugar colonies (Hitchins, 1931). Because the Colonial Office and the Indian government remained set against transportation of Indian coolies to the West Indies, their emigration was restricted to Mauritius. Under the new system, 35,000 coolies — including some Chinese — were shipped there in the first year.

In 1842 the West Indian planters prevailed on the government to authorize recruitment in Sierra Leone, where the Royal Navy had been depositing Africans liberated from captured slave runners. The scheme was designed in part to reduce the costs of operating that colony, which had been established in the late eighteenth century as a place for settling American slaves manumitted for loyal service to Britain in the War of Independence. Although for the most part these had originally settled in Nova Scotia, many had ended up as paupers in London. The colony's black British subjects engaged in subsistence agriculture and petty trading, requiring occasional handouts from the government but producing no revenue for its operations. It was reasoned that the experience of plantation labor would lift idle freedmen to a higher plane of civilization, as well as stimulate the colony's economic development. To avoid charges that Britain was acquiescing to a revival of the slave trade, the workers were to be transported in government ships (Cumpston, 1953, p. 74; Tinker, 1974, p. 81; Asiegbu, 1969).

However, the African scheme turned out to be a dismal failure. White merchants and traders in Sierra Leone discouraged an emigration that interfered with their attempts to develop a local market; missionaries objected on humanitarian grounds; settled subsistence farmers had no incentive to engage themselves for work overseas; and recently liberated slaves refused to be subjected to a new deportation. On the West Indian side, the trickle of newly imported Africans tended to merge into the population of Creole ex-slaves, deserting plantations at the earliest opportunity; ironically, the same somatic distinctiveness that had facilitated control of African labor now rendered this difficult. As of 1845 the traffic was not heavy enough to justify government transportation, but the use of private trading ships rendered Britain even more vulnerable to the charge of hypocrisy when it prosecuted foreign slavers (Asiegbu, 1969; Green, 1976, pp. 265–276).

Meanwhile, as Britain accelerated its transformation into a producer of industrial goods, the tacit coalition of industrial capitalists and workers on behalf of free trade was steadily gaining ground; but the Peel government that undertook in 1844 to reduce the duty on sugar imported from free-labor countries *also* finally authorized West Indian planters to import Indian coolies. The prospect of government loans to defray import costs was held out as an incentive to the planters to accept prescribed conditions (Cumpston, 1953, p. 84). By the end of the year, when foreign sugar began entering Britain at the lower rate, Jamaica had secured authorization and funding for 5,000 coolies, Trinidad for 2,500. Guiana followed suit in 1845 (Tinker, 1972, p. 81).

Two years later the Whigs eliminated the remaining discrimination against slave-grown foreign sugar. The Secretary of State — an ardent abolitionist who had resigned in protest twelve years earlier when the government stopped short of unqualified emancipation — acknowledged that under the new conditions British sugar planters could survive only by drastically reducing labor costs, and that this in turn required restricting the workers' freedom of choice. To this effect, he suggested the imposition of a monthly tax of 5s on immigrants during the time they were not under contract as a penalty on "idleness," as well as a stamp duty of 40s on the initial engagements with a given employer (Cumpston, 1953, p. 108; Tinker, 1972, p. 83). This gave the colonies license to convert the tax into a fine enforced by imprisonment. The government also indicated its willingness to accept the planters' perennial demands for long contracts and harsher laws prohibiting vagrancy and squatting (Cumpston, p. 139).

With the settlement of the issue of free trade and the establishment of a credit system under imperial guarantee, the sugar colonies disappeared from the British political agenda. The antislavery movement shifted its concerns to domestic issues. The African experiment was terminated in the late 1850s, when the development of the economic resources of Britain's new acquisitions in Africa required their labor to be retained for local use (Asiegbu, 1969, p. 151). Altogether, only about 36,000 Africans were transported to the Caribbean in the postslavery period, as against over 400,000 Indians (Green, 1976). Governmental supervision of the traffic in coolies, designed to protect the empire's Indian subjects, in effect legitimized the institutionalization in the sugar colonies of what Lord John Russell had denounced at the very outset as "a new system of slavery" (Tinker, 1972, p. iii). Regulation became largely a matter of administrative negotiations in which the permanent officials of the Colonial Office, charged with the protection of colonial labor in very distant places (including India after 1857), carried little weight. The outbreak of the Indian Mutiny in 1857 abruptly soured British feelings about their Asian fellow subjects (Tinker, 1974, p. 241); deteriorating conditions in India, which had contributed to the Mutiny and were further exacerbated as a consequence of it, fostered a growing pool of Indians available for overseas recruitment. Attributing India's troubles to overpopulation, the political managers of the empire welcomed the opportunity to export these troublesome surplus subjects to where they might be more usefully occupied, much as they did with the Irish or French Canadians.

The Indian labor migration expanded steadily in geographical scope and numbers until the early part of the twentieth century, without significant modification of the system. The demand for labor in plantation-based industries — not only sugar, but also coffee and tea, and later rubber — grew apace in response to the steadily enlarged consumer market for such commodities in Europe and North America. The end of the remaining European slave trade and of plantation slavery generated additional demand for Asian substitutes. Within the British Empire, the flow of Indian emigrants shifted direction. Demand for them in the West Indies declined and Mauritius reached a plateau shortly after 1870. But the traffic rapidly expanded in the plantations recently launched in southern Africa (Natal), and especially in Ceylon and Malaya — which lay closest to the source of labor — after completion of the Suez Canal reduced their distance from the European market. Fiji, North Borneo, and East Africa were added later on as well. The supply at its disposal was so very large that the British Empire even became a labor exporter, offering Indian coolies to France, the Netherlands, and Spain as an inducement to relinquish African slavery.

Notwithstanding the organization of the flow as a return migration, wherever Indians were brought as indentured workers, some remained to form permanent Indian communities, often occupying a niche in the economic transactions between former masters and slaves or between colonial officials and natives. In the second half of the century, the British cane-sugar industry sought to resolve the crisis triggered by the growing competition of continental beet sugar by encouraging peasant agriculture, in which Indian smallholders were to play a major role (Tinker, 1974, pp. 31–39). Accordingly, Britain reversed the return requirement in favor of a policy designed to accelerate the transformation of coolies from sojourners into settlers; this was implemented by imposing a minimum quota of women for each shipload, ranging from an initial 25 per 100 men in the late 1850s to 40 a decade later. In this manner, as the stream to the West Indies and to Mauritius ebbed, the Indian coolies slowly evolved into racially distinct Creole communities.

Chinese labor in the United States. Drawn to California like everyone else by the discovery of gold, by 1860 the Chinese numbered between 35,000 (according to the U.S. census) and 47,000 (according to local estimates). It was an overwhelmingly male population, approximately two-thirds of whom engaged in mining, with the remainder performing a variety of household services normally provided by women, most prominently laundry and food preparation for other miners (Coolidge, 1909, p. 498).

The accessibility of alluvial gold and the ease of filing claims made gold mining in the early days akin to the situation of "free land"; and it is in this connection that the Chinese emerged as a controversial group. *Mutatis mutandis*, California reenacted the colonial debate between advocates of a free agrarian society and promoters of plantations. Independent American miners insisted claims should be allocated to individual operators, in the manner of homesteads, and opposed the use of slave or Chinese contract labor, which capitalists advocated for the launching of large-scale mining operations. Reflecting these alignments, in 1852 the California legislature *almost* enacted two opposite measures: one to exclude the Chinese outright, and the other to render ten-year labor contracts enforceable in state courts (Barth, 1964, pp. 133–136; Janisch, 1971, pp. 5–10).

The legislature did enact a heavy tax on foreign miners, whom Americans viewed as intruders deserving no share in their recently acquired Eldorado. Most independent foreign miners — among them, many French and Latin Americans — were violently expelled. The Chinese fared somewhat better because they possessed mediating organizations able and willing to negotiate mutually advantageous economic arrangements with the dominant group, and the taxes they paid constituted a substantial part of state income in the 1850s. Over time the Chinese came to specialize in exploiting claims abandoned by American miners who had moved on to newly discovered deposits (Barth, 1964, pp. 133–136, 148–149; Janisch, 1971, pp. 5–10).

Transformation of the Chinese into mass labor occurred in the early 1860s, when fierce competition between the Central and Southern Pacific to complete a line across the Sierras generated a huge demand for labor gangs. Recruitment of local white miners was prohibitively expensive; transportation costs from Europe or from the East Coast were of course very high; and the onset of the Civil War caused an abrupt decline of immigration from Europe while military requirements caused a manpower shortage in the United States as a whole. Hence China was the obvious source of recruitment. Given their marginal position in the mining sector, many local Chinese abandoned the mining camps for the railroads, where they provoked little resentment because white workers were concomitantly upgraded to supervisory positions (Saxton, 1971, p. 60). In addition, Chinese merchants and American firms in San Francisco began supplying groups of laborers directly from China. Agents of the Central Pacific started recruiting in the mountain districts of the Pearl River Delta, much as their counterparts for eastern railroads had been doing in Europe (Barth, 1964, p. 117).

The question whether Chinese immigrants to America were free agents or slavelike coolies arose as early as 1852, when Chinese passengers transported in an American vessel complained of mistreatment, staged a mutiny, and killed the captain and some of the crew. The issue was quickly integrated into the ongoing national controversy over slavery and became central to the debate over the desirability of Chinese immigration. Whatever their motives, those who did not want the Chinese insisted that they were coolies; in response to this, opponents of exclusion went to great lengths to show that the "coolie" label was generally inappropriate — a position adopted subsequently by well-intentioned liberal historians (Kohler, 1936; Coolidge, 1909, p. 41).

It has recently been established beyond doubt that most of the Chinese who came to be United States were *indentured*; that they were *sojourners* rather than immigrants; and that the flow was a *trade*. There were three types of arrangements: indentured emigrants who slid into debt bondage to Chinese merchants in the process of obtaining passage; laborers who entered into contracts directly with foreign importers and Chinese middlemen; and finally coolies proper, that is, individuals who had been tricked or coerced into an extreme form of contract, sanctioned by the use of violence. In Barth's view, "The variations among the three types were less important than the basic enslaved nature of the indentured emigrants, contract laborers, and coolies alike" (Barth, 1964, pp. 50, 52, 55). Because under American conditions the coercive mechanisms involved were not sanctioned by law but operated mostly within the Chinese enclave, the involuntary aspects of labor contracts were hidden from the view of the general public and of white employers, who in any case had an interest in averting their eyes from them. It should be noted, however, that the merchants could prevent the Chinese workers from returning home until all debts were paid off, a form of control whose exercise required the acquiescence or even active collaboration of American employers, steamship companies, port authorities, and local law-enforcement officials.

In the face of domestic criticism and the Chinese government's demands for better treatment of emigrants as a condition for the expansion of trade relations with the West, a law was enacted in 1862 to prohibit the transport of involuntary Chinese passengers in American vessels and to subject all U.S. ships departing from China to inspection by an American consul. Although by virtue of this all Chinese arriving in the United States were henceforth officially certified as "free," Barth suggests that in effect the act left matters unchanged (1964, p. 76).

While this was going on in California, after the end of the Civil War Southerners stumbled upon the same device that West Indian planters used three decades earlier, namely importing "another racial group engaged in menial labor in order to bring recalcitrant freedmen to terms" (Barth, 1964, p. 188). Chinese sugar workers were brought in from Cuba as early as 1867 to man plantations in Louisiana; and although many Republicans howled this was slavery, Secretary of State Seward reassured them they had come voluntarily (Miller, 1969, p. 150).

Despite mounting agitation in California for Chinese exclusion, in 1868 the United States government imposed on China a treaty designed explicitly to facilitate the massive procurement of Chinese labor. The active role played by a capitalist-minded Republican administration, on the morrow of the Civil War, in the importation of bound workers who were members of a distinctive racial group ineligible for membership in the American body politic, is a revealing episode of American history, equivalent to the contributions of the British Liberals to the institutionalization of Indian indenture.

Briefly, this is how it came about. In the face of the war-time manpower shortage, the United States had relinquished its traditional laissez-faire on behalf of an interventionist immigration policy. In 1864 Secretary of State Seward secured adoption of a law that eased the massive recruitment of European labor by making labor contracts enforceable in U.S. courts; U.S. employers — or brokers acting on their behalf — would thereby be able to advance the travel costs of European workers, with the assurance that the debts incurred by the immigrants would be worked off after their arrival. The measure passed with little or no opposition. However, when an attempt was made to bolster the system by imposing penal sanctions on workers who violated their contract, radical Republicans and organized labor denounced the proposal as tantamount to bondage. Opponents explicitly charged that European contract workers would be no better off than Chinese coolies. Accordingly, the law was repealed in March 1868.

In the very same month, however, Anson Burlingame, the retiring U.S. Minister to China, arrived in Washington as head of a diplomatic mission to the West on behalf of the Chinese Empire; and in July, Secretary of State Seward himself wrote the terms of a treaty designed to facilitate Chinese emigration to the United States, which Burlingame immediately signed on behalf of the Chinese Empire — lacking any specific mandate to that effect and without consulting the Chinese authorities (Hsu, 1980, pp. 73–74; Davids, 1973, I, xxiii–xxiv, 49).

The document asserted the right of the Chinese to expatriate themselves and to immigrate freely into the United States, but specified that the right of entry should not be construed to entail the right to acquire American citizenship by naturalization, in keeping with the law of 1802, then still in force, which limited naturalization to "free and white" persons. Hence it is reasonable to infer that the architects of the Burlingame Treaty envisaged future Chinese arrivals as segregated sojourners — in today's language, "guestworkers" rather than immigrants. The treaty also restated the terms of the 1862 law forbidding involuntary immigration, and in addition committed China to prohibit involvement of its subjects in the coolie traffic. The latter must be seen as a perfunctory provision designed to forestall charges that the treaty fostered a new form of slavery.

The linkage, by way of Seward's active involvement, between the Burlingame Treaty and the failure of the attempt to establish a system of contract labor on the Atlantic side suggests that development-minded American leaders envisaged Chinese labor not merely as a solution to California's short-term problem, but as a device for augmenting the nation's manpower more generally. The treaty's effectiveness was reflected in a rapid escalation of recorded Chinese arrivals, from an annual average of 4,300 for the 1861–1867 period to 6,707 in 1868, 12,874 the following year, and 15,740 in 1870. With intervening fluctuations numbers rose to 20,292 in 1873 and 22,781 in 1876. When completion of the transcontinental railroad made it possible to move the Chinese inland, interest in procuring this labor became nationwide. The promoters of a Chinese Labor Convention held in Memphis in July 1869 spoke of bringing in several hundred thousand workers to the cotton fields; but the scheme was aborted because impoverished Southern planters could not afford it (Barth,

1964, p. 195). The following year, however, several hundred Chinese were recruited for work on the Alabama-Chattanooga railroad.

There were thoughts of using the Chinese as industrial labor as well. For example, the editor of *The Nation* wrote in July 1869 that prejudice and prohibitory legislation notwithstanding, American capital would continue to seek Chinese workers because they "will work harder and for less wages, and are more tractable" than Irish or Germans (Armstrong, 1962, p. 93). In California tensions between white and Chinese workers were exacerbated when the transcontinental railroad was completed in 1869, as this brought about a massive influx of white workers from the East Coast — mostly recent Irish immigrants — while surplus Chinese railroad workers were dumped on the labor market, facilitating rapid industrialization of the mining sector (Young, 1970). In the early 1870s the Chinese constituted only about 9 percent of the state's total population, but as nearly all of them were adult males, they amounted to one-fifth of the economically active manpower and probably one-fourth of all wage earners (Saxton, 1971, p. 10).

Employers on the East Coast were remarkably quick in availing themselves of the Chinese as a weapon in industrial confrontations. In 1870, shortly after the transcontinental line was completed, a contingent of seventy-five Chinese shoemakers under three-year contract was brought all the way from San Francisco to North Adams, Massachusetts, to break a strike staged mostly by Irish and French Canadian Knights of St. Crispin; later in the year, two carloads were brought to the Passaic Steam Laundry in New Jersey in order to discipline a work force made up of immigrant German and Irish girls recruited at Castle Garden; a similar episode was reenacted two years later at a cutlery in Beaver Falls, Pennsylvania (Barth, 1964, pp. 203–207). Although the practice remained limited because of its high cost and was abandoned at the onset of the Panic of 1873, when white workers became more tractable, the issue of Chinese immigration became a major grievance of organized labor until well into the twentieth century. Demands for exclusion were voiced in the annual congresses of various state and national labor organizations, including a convention of Negro workers in 1869 and the International Workingman's Association in 1873 (Miller, 1969, p. 196; Thorud, 1982, pp. 105–123; Saxton, 1971).

California remained at the forefront of the struggle. In the 1870s white immigrant workers launched a radical labor movement which gained considerable power in the municipal politics of San Francisco and at the state level, but its substantial achievements on behalf of white workers were jeopardized by the availability to employers of the Chinese alternative. The ultimate outcome was a trade-off whereby the movement turned toward "business" unionism, with organization restricted to skilled crafts, in exchange for being allowed to exclude the Chinese from the West Coast industrial labor market (Saxton, 1971, pp. 59, 71, 113–137, 138–140). The issue did not simply pit white workers against employers. The use of Chinese labor, which required overhead capital, gave larger industrial enterprises an edge over small manufacturing and mining operations; and because Chinese entrepreneurs were more efficient than Americans in exploiting coolies within the confines of the enclave economy, they competed successfully in certain mass-production sectors, particularly cigar-making and garment-manufacturing. Small white businessmen thus joined the exclusionist camp, leaving the railroad and mining "monopolists" as the only advocates of the Chinese (Miller, 1969, p. 183; Saxton, 1971, pp. 105, 209).

Anti-Chinese racism was also growing at the level of general opinion, fostered by well-publicized events such as the massacre of American missionaries in Tientsin (1868), a coolie revolt in Peru (1870), and the outbreak of famine in China (1879), which raised the specter of the swamping of America by a tidal wave of starving humanity comparable to the Irish of an earlier generation, but whose size would be commensurate with a population of four hundred million (Miller, 1969, pp. 151, 159). It was also becoming quite evident that southern and eastern Europe would suffice to supply the escalating needs of American industry for cheap, unskilled manpower.

Within this climate, the advocates of Chinese labor were driven to the defensive, and it became easier for the exclusionists to achieve their objective. In December 1874 President Grant recommended congressional action to exclude Chinese brought by "headmen" against their will, singling out women imported for "lewd and shameful purposes" as the worst abuse of the coolie flow. A law enacted in the next session constituted the first national measure to control immigration directly. In 1880, a mere twelve years after imposing on China a treaty providing for free emigration, the United States dictated a modification of that treaty whereby it could one-sidedly restrict Chinese immigration (Davids, 1979, pp. xiii, 108–109, 124–125). Two years later Congress prohibited the importation of Chinese contract labor for a ten-year period; the prohibition was renewed for another decade in 1892 and again in 1904, and was made applicable to Hawaii as well when the islands were annexed in 1898. It was presumed that Chinese seeking to enter the United States were coolies unless they could prove otherwise, and the authorities assumed that most Chinese in the United States were illegal entrants. All persons of Chinese origin, including not only business visitors but also U.S. citizens by virtue of birth, were subject to harassing identity checks and liable to deportation, unless they could produce a certificate to the effect that they were *not* coolies or proof of U.S. birth.

Beyond this, for the remainder of the century legislators made half-hearted attempts to undo the effects of the original importation policy by fostering the departure of the Chinese, paralleling efforts in the earlier part of the century to return former slaves to Africa. As a result of these measures, the Chinese population of the United States, which peaked at 107,488 in 1880, declined to 89,963 by 1900; in California, a high of 75,132 in 1880 diminished to 45,753 twenty years later (Coolidge, 1909, p. 501).

As the Chinese presence waned, other nationalities took their place. Mary Coolidge remarked in 1909 that "the history of general labor in California since about 1886 is the story of efforts to find substitutes for the vanishing Chinese" (Coolidge, 1909, p. 384). In the last decades of the century California discovered its vocation as the homeland of agroindustry, an updated version of the colonial plantation system, for which a massive supply of cheap "stoop" labor was required. Given the opportunities available in industry, such work did not attract the "new immigrants" from southern and eastern Europe. Initially, the demand was met by Chinese already in the state or introduced surreptitiously. As of 1886 they constituted seven-eighths of the state's farm labor (Coolidge, p. 370). In the face of the steady increase of anti-Chinese sentiment, Californian farmers in the 1890s steadfastly opposed exclusion; when they were unable to secure additional Chinese field and ranch hands, they turned to Japan and the Philippines (Boyd, 1970, pp. 49–51). The experience of the Japanese, initially wooed and later excluded, largely paralleled that of the Chinese. Meanwhile, efforts to prohibit Asian immigration altogether met with success in an absolute prohibition in 1924.

Foreign Migrant Workers in Industrial Societies

In contrast to most of the colonies, the industrializing societies of Western Europe and North America had no shortage of labor. They were in the throes of a demographic boom, and the commercialization of land ensured that most adult males, as well as many women and children, must sell their labor on the market in exchange for cash wages. Indeed, one consequence of the "great transformation" in Europe appeared to be a population surplus; from the 1820s onward this triggered massive relocation overseas and ensured a plentiful supply of labor on the other side of the Atlantic, which in turn fostered the rapid emergence of industrial capitalism in the United States (B. Thomas, 1973).

Yet even as they were still experiencing massive emigration, countries such as Great Britain and Germany also employed considerable alien labor from their respective peripheries. Although conditions differed profoundly from those prevailing in the colonies, here also the workers were culturally distinct; deliberate attempts were made to forestall their permanent settlement; and their mobility within the labor market tended to be more restricted than that of the natives. By the turn of the twentieth century foreign migrant labor played a significant role in every one of the industrial economies, including the United States. Once again, variations of the basic pattern can be accounted for by differing national configurations, within which two elements were especially significant: the role of the state in relation to economic development and the organization of the indigenous working class at the relevant time. The effect of these factors will be clearer from a comparative look at Britain, Germany, and the United States. I shall focus on the historical origins of the migration pattern around the turn of the twentieth century.

The Irish in Britain. The flow of Irish workers to Britain in the mid-eighteenth century strikingly foreshadows the dynamics of transnational labor migrations from peripheries to developing centers in the industrial epoch (Clapham, 1933, pp. 596–604; Kerr, 1942–43, pp. 365–380; Hobsbawm, 1969, pp. 309–312). By way of "push," Ireland experienced a Malthusian crisis long before the tragic Great Hunger of the 1840s. The island's population, estimated at two million around the end of the seventeenth century, rose to five million by the time of union with Great Britain in 1801 and reached 6.8 in 1821, approximately one-third of the total population of the United Kingdom (Beckett, 1973, pp. 173, 244, 272; Mitchell, 1976, p. 21). Successive tallies in the early nineteenth century indicated a rate of population growth on the island itself of about 2 percent a year; but if emigration is taken into account, this must be revised upward to 2.5 or 3 percent. Such a rate of growth, similar to that of the United States or Canada at the time, was not inherently catastrophic; what made it so here were the economic and political structures imposed on southern Ireland following the fall of the Stuarts in 1690, when as punishment for supporting the defeated monarch, most of the land remaining in Catholic hands was seized and the Penal laws implemented with the utmost severity. The bulk of the country's land passed into the hands of English absentee owners who had little incentive to improve their holdings, given mercantilist policies that precluded the development of commercial agriculture for export. Investment was in fact unnecessary to produce substantial income because proliferating tenants generated a growing demand for land, with resulting raises of rent. The population increase was largely attributable to the introduction of the potato, which vastly expanded the caloric yield of available land. But rising rent made it necessary for families to find additional cash income to keep the land from which they eked a subsistence. The Irish survived by organizing their households as units of production, combining subsistence agriculture on rented parcels with cash-producing activities such as home crafts (weaving or lace-making), and reduced their numbers by seasonal or perennial migration to Britain (Kerr, 1942–43, p. 179). Permanent emigration originated around 1740, when an outbreak of famine in Ireland coincided with a construction boom in London.

This pattern of economic adaptation arose contemporaneously in Flanders and other parts of Europe where similar conditions prevailed; it is also encountered in such widely differing locales as Quebec in the nineteenth century and Turkey, Mexico, and much of southern Africa in the twentieth (Zolberg, 1974; Portes and Walton, 1982). To maintain itself, the pattern requires large families, and within the family unit, sufficient authority to ensure that the progeny will continue to make an economic contribution to the parental household until well into adulthood. Poverty itself thus provides an incentive for the achievement of greater fertility. But this solution, albeit rational in the short term and at the level of the individual household, exacerbates difficulties over the long term and renders the society as a whole more vulnerable to catastrophic economic events, such as the Irish potato famine of 1846.

While English carpenters, masons, and bricklayers effectively defended their claim to a monopoly of their trades, "the native unskilled labourers had no power to enforce any such claim; and so the Irish peasant workers, who crossed to seek their fortune in the spring, often found employment all summer as builder's labourers" (Clapham, 1933, p. 597). The movement expanded further with the rapid growth of British industry in the 1775–1820 period and was vastly facilitated when steamship service began between the two islands in 1816. Over time the Irish became more exclusively urban, displacing Scottish and English workers from marginalized occupations such as handloom weaving. Sizable settlements emerged in the industrial boom towns Glasgow and Liverpool, which were the principal ports of entry, as well as Manchester, with additional concentrations in the two capital cities, London and Edinburgh.

One of the major advantages capitalist economies derive from the use of foreign migrant labor is that such labor can be disposed of when not needed. However, it stands to reason that the migrants themselves, acting in their own interest, would seek to reduce their disposability. Disparities in the United Kingdom's welfare system — Ireland did not have a Poor Law of any kind, whereas the Irish born in English localities thereby acquired a right to assistance — provided an incentive for Irish migrants to relocate permanently. By the time Engels studied Manchester, nearly one-fifth of its inhabitants were Irish, but they constituted half of the needy poor, with similar proportions in Glasgow and Liverpool (Clapham, 1933, p. 598).

The relocation within Britain itself of part of the "disposable industrial army," which was highly vulnerable to unemployment, further exacerbated the maldistribution of private benefits and public costs. In good times the benefits of migrant labor flowed into the pockets of the manufacturers, but in bad times the costs were passed on to local authorities — and beyond them to the taxpayers. Because under the old Poor Law parishes were not obligated to assist outsiders, the Irish "who were found moving about in search of work or of alms were treated as vagrants and transported from county to county until they arrived at the sea" (Clapham, 1933, p. 599). The buck was finally passed on to seaboard counties, which had no choice but to ship the migrants back to Ireland at local expense.

Despite the contributions of Irish labor to the development of British industrial capitalism, the migration deepened long-standing prejudices toward Ireland and its people among all ranks of British society. At the level of elites, in the years following the Napoleonic wars, the Irish migration came to be identified as one of the principal causes of increasing English pauperism, and hence of the rising burden imposed on relief institutions under the Poor Law (Thompson, 1963, p. 430; Jones, 1973, p. 11). The growing enclaves of permanent settlement in British cities, where distinctive religion, speech, social behavior, and occupational specialization rendered the Irish extremely visible, encouraged the negative stereotyping of the Irishman as the simian "other" of Victorian culture (Curtis, 1971, pp. 29–57). Compounding the nightmare was the fear that the Irish flow would foster emigration of the English, Scots, and Welsh, and hence result in the "irishization" of Britain itself.

Containment of the Irish in their home island was not immediately feasible; they were free British subjects who could come and go as they pleased within the United Kingdom. In any case, this was hardly a politically desirable solution as long as Ireland itself remained unmanageable. From a political rather than an economic perspective and no matter whether they stayed home or crossed the Irish Sea, too many Irish arrived in the British Isles; and there were many more of them than landlords or employers could possibly require. As one of the innumerable commissions appointed to deal with the Irish Question concluded, "The Irish . . . have practically decided, that emigrate they must, — the only question for us to determine, is, whether it shall be to England or America" (Johnston, 1972, p. 143). The British decision in the late 1820s to encourage Irish emigration overseas can thus be seen, in part, as British *immigration* policy.

Marx is eloquent on the reactions of the English working class around the middle of the nineteenth century:

> Every industrial and commercial center in England now possesses a working class *divided* into two *hostile* camps, English proletarians and Irish proletarians. The ordinary English worker hates the Irish worker as a competitor who lowers his standard of life. In relation to the Irish worker he feels himself a member of the ruling nation and so turns himself into a tool of the aristocrats and capitalists of his country *against Ireland*, thus strengthening their domination over himself. He cherishes religious, social and national prejudices against the Irish worker. His attitude toward him is much the same as that of the "poor whites" to the "niggers" of the former slaves states of the USA. The Irishman pays him back with interest in his own money. He sees in the English workers at once the accomplice and the stupid tool of the *English domination in Ireland*. . . . This antagonism is the *secret of the impotence of the English working-class*, despite their organization. (Hechter, 1975, p. 15)

In effect, by the middle of the nineteenth century, the southern Irish had become industrial Britain's informal "guestworkers," moving to and fro without any restriction whatsoever in response to market conditions for their labor in the two islands. The Irish invasion of Great Britain peaked in 1861, when 806,000 Irish-born were counted on the island, after which numbers waned to 632,000 in 1901; at this time, nearly one-fourth of all persons born in Ireland were living in the United States (Thomas, 1973, pp. 73–75). But the migration continued throughout the twentieth century despite the dramatic changes in the political relationship between Britain and Ireland. In the 1950–1961 period about 750,000 Irish moved annually in each direction, leaving a yearly increment in Britain of thirty to forty thousand. In 1971 there were 681,110 Irish-born in Britain, and approximately 1.2 million British-born with at least one parent born in Ireland. It is estimated that the British population of recent Irish descent amounts to about 10 percent — a much larger proportion than constituted by the "blacks" (Asians and West Indians), in comparison with whom the Irish immigration is now considered to have entailed relatively low social costs (Rees, 1979, p. 69). In fact, at a time when Britain has drastically restricted immigration, the Irish remain entirely free to enter the country.

Poles in imperial Germany. Throughout the nineteenth century Germany was mainly an emigration country, second only to the United Kingdom in the overall size of its flow, directed mostly toward the United States. Emigration began tapering off around the 1870s, when the onset of rapid industrialization created an internal labor market for the country's vast rural populations. Contemporaneously, foreign labor made its appearance on the scene as a solution to the crisis of German agriculture.

In the face of competition from American and Russian grain, in 1879 Germany erected high tariff walls ("the marriage of iron and rye") behind which the East Prussian Junkers, who constituted the political backbone of the regime, undertook to transform their great estates into capitalist enterprises. Success of the undertaking was predicated on the availability of a plentiful supply of cheap labor; but the recently freed peasants — mostly ethnic Poles incorporated in the course of Prussia's eastward expansion — were drawn to the industrial sector. Polish peasants from contiguous provinces of the Russian and Austro-Hungarian empires immigrated to fill the need of the agricultural sector (Nichtweiss, 1959, p. 29). Jewish traders and craftsmen-shopkeepers from the same regions followed their traditional clientele to Germany.

Both components of the Polish immigration, Roman Catholic peasants and petty-bourgeois Jews, came to be viewed by Bismarck and the political authorities of the empire as serious political issues. The arrival of a mass of Polish peasants posed a problem that must be understood in relation to the *Kulturkampf* of the 1870s, whereby Bismarck sought to challenge the traditional autonomy of the Roman Catholic church and affirm the political hegemony of Lutheran Protestantism (Craig, 1978, p. 71). Not only did the newcomers enlarge the Catholic camp; this immigration also complicated the task of "germanizing" Prussian Poles, who constituted the empire's largest ethnic minority. Amounting to only 6 percent of the total population, they concentrated in the eastern provinces of Prussia, when local rural districts often had a Polish majority while German culture remained by and large confined to the towns. The persistence of cultural diversity among the lower classes came to matter more at this time because of mass armies and universal suffrage; in 1873, after a century of relative laissez-faire, the Prussian government decreed that German alone should be taught in the elementary schools (Dawson, 1908, pp. 467–494). But the Poles resisted education in German because they feared assimilation into a Protestant culture. The ensuing controversy over the language of education stimulated the formation of a Polish nationalist movement, paralleling contemporaneous developments in Canada or Belgium. Over the last two decades of the century the Poles became subject to a tug-of-war between elite segments. After repeated hesitations for fear of offending the czar, in March 1885 Bismarck ordered all provincial departments of Prussia to prevent the further entry of Poles and to expel all those already in the state. Although Bismarck later insisted that there was no religious motivation for this action, the measure was in effect enforced only against Catholics and Jews; Protestant Poles were specifically exempted (Young, 1951, pp. 184–185; Neubach, 1967). Altogether between 30,000 and 40,000 persons were expelled over the next eighteen months. This was coupled with a policy of internal colonization, whereby the state purchased Polish-owned estates for resale "to German settlers of unquestioned national and political integrity" (Dawson, 1908, p. 476).

However, as economic recovery set in and the labor shortage grew, spreading beyond the border districts to industry as well as agriculture, German landlords — including the new colonists — actively sought to obtain a change of policy while simultaneously exploring alternative sources of imported labor, including Chinese coolies (Nichtweiss, 1959, p. 38; Dohse, 1981, pp. 29–81). In 1890, notwithstanding the continued opposition of the Prussian Ministries of Education and of the Interior, the Caprivi government opted to allow

German employers in the border provinces to recruit Poles under contract in both industry and agriculture for an experimental three-year period. A major condition was that these workers must be out of the country between November 15 and April 1 — a period known as the *Karenzzeit* — so as to prevent their settlement; and for the same reason, they could not be utilized as household servants. Jews were specifically declared ineligible for such contract labor (Schofler, 1975, p. 25). Reenacted in 1894, the organized migration of contract workers for a limited period under the aegis of the state constituted a rudimentary version of the German and Swiss guestworker system.

The solution remained controversial. For instance, Max Weber commented in 1896 that the Poles were good for capitalism but harmful to the national interest: "The dynasty of the Kings of Prussia has not been called upon to rule over a rural proletariat without a fatherland and over wandering Slavs alongside small Polish peasants and depopulated latifundia . . . but over German peasants alongside a class of large landowners whose workers know that they will be able to find their own future independence in their homeland" (Dibble, 1968, p. 109). But despite efforts to reinstate the 1885 prohibition or to organize the recruitment of less objectionable substitutes, the contract system became firmly institutionalized. Later on the Karenzzeit was shortened, and Poles were declared eligible for agricultural work throughout Germany; as their numbers grew, regulatory mechanisms proliferated as well, with special care to prevent foreign Poles from forming ethnic political organizations and joining labor unions (Dohse, 1981). Even so, the proportion of foreigners in the German labor force rose from about .8 percent in 1880 to 3.4 in 1907, of whom about two-thirds were Poles. With some modifications the contract system was reinstated by the Federal Republic in the late 1950s, with guestworkers now coming from a variety of Mediterranean countries. The 1907 level was equaled again in 1963 and then rapidly exceeded (Wirtschaft und Statistik, 1965, p. 93).

The U.S. back door. One constant in the pattern of foreign migrant labor in the United States comes up as early as 1909, when Coolidge comments that "while the Immigration service makes desperate efforts to catch a few Chinamen crossing over without certificates, the pauper Mexican Cholos, by the hundreds, freely come and go under contracts of labor" (1909, p. 330). As the century progressed, migrant workers from south of the border emerged as an ever more prominent feature of the economy, spreading within the agricultural sector from California to the Southwest more generally, then spilling beyond the fields into the country's manufactures, and later yet into its growing service sector. The Mexicans were but the most prominent of numerous transamerican migratory flows in the twentieth century, which also brought Caribbean workers to the fields of the Southeast, and included a very substantial movement of Quebeckers to the lumber camps and factories of New England — one that was strikingly similar to the Irish migration toward the industrial areas of Britain, but largely ignored by U.S. historians of immigration.

Despite intermittent attempts to regularize these flows along the lines of the German system, laissez-faire generally prevailed thanks to a combination of two distinctive features of the American configuration. Despite a tendency toward growing restrictions on movement across international borders, the United States, unlike the other industrial countries, retained some elements of its initial character as a "nation of immigrants"; and second, organized labor successfully defeated early attempts to institutionalize importation under contract, thereby in effect foreclosing the massive use of this device except under exceptional circumstances of national emergency. As a result, an immigration policy tradition developed that was founded on a differentiation between two segments — the main gate and the back door — that is, *immigration* from Europe and *labor migration* from the Western hemisphere. The latter process came to be institutionalized in the form of illegal border-crossing, organized by American employers or specialized entrepreneurs, with the benefit of benign neglect by the authorities (Zolberg, 1978).

In the days of sail, the transatlantic passage was arduous and costly; for the European lower classes such a voyage was usually a one-way trip. Concomitantly, immigration from Europe was the equivalent in the United States of rural to urban migration within European industrializing countries. As the American economy gained momentum in the years after 1815, labor-hungry employers attempted to organize immigration in a manner akin to indenture, advancing the costs of relocation in exchange for a long-term work obligation. But such practices — and in particular the "redemptioner" system used to procure Germans — raised strong objections from European states and from many Americans, who associated literally bondage with racial inferiority and freedom with being white, excluding any form of long-term contract sanctioned by public authority. As it was, by the mid-1830s the supply of labor had become self-sustaining as a result of chain migration financed by relatives.

Opposition to the use of contracts to procure workers abroad emerged early on as a rallying issue of organized labor. American workers scored a signal victory in 1868 when the Congress repealed the immigration law enacted four years earlier at Seward's initiative. However, the issue returned to the fore twenty years later, when the steadily decreasing cost of transportation — by this time, railroads were available at both ends of the journey and fast steamships with a much enlarged carrying capacity plied the Atlantic itself — rendered economical a traffic that amounted to long-term commuting between Europe and the United States. Concurrently, employers quickly availed themselves of the newly established transatlantic telegraph to shape immigration according to their precise needs, most notoriously for recruiting Europeans with specific skills to replace striking Americans.

Contemporary observers believed that the contract feature, combined with the temporary nature of their residence, rendered these "birds of passage" significantly different from previous waves of European arrivals, and socially much more objectionable. To a contemporary audience, the following description — admittedly hostile, as it was provided in 1884 by a congressional committee advocating the prohibition of immigration under contract — undoubtedly evoked the notorious coolie trade, with which the report repeatedly made explicit parallels:

> This class of immigrants care nothing about our institutions, and in many instances never even heard of them; they are men whose passage is paid by the importers; they are ignorant of our social conditions, and that they may remain so they are isolated and prevented coming into contact with Americans. They are generally from the lowest social stratum, and live upon the coarsest food and in hovels of a character before unknown to American workmen . . . They, as a rule, do not become citizens, and are certainly not a desirable acquisition to the body politic. When their terms of contract servitude expires, their place is supplied by fresh importations. The inevitable tendency of their presence amongst us is to degrade American labor and reduce it to the level of the imported pauper labor. (48th Congress, 1st Session, H. of R. Report No. 144, Feb. 23, 1884: 2)

A similar note was struck by T. V. Powderly, leader of the Knights of Labor and future Commissioner-General of Immigration, in one of the earliest recorded statements of organized labor on the subject of U.S. immigration policy: "These imported men show no disposition to become citizens of this country, but, on the contrary, seek to obtain a certain sum of money, which they consider a competence, and with it return to Italy or Hungary." He deplored the willingness of such people to live under conditions unacceptable to American workmen, and concluded: "These men are brought into competition with skilled as well as unskilled labor, and it is fast becoming as bad as the competition of the Chinese in the West" (Report No. 144, 1884, p. 8).

In response to these representations, in 1885 Congress enacted a law prohibiting immigration under contract. However, the law turned out to be quite ineffective, because formal contracts were drawn up rarely. In the absence of institutional obstacles, the pattern of immigration denounced in 1884–85 continued to develop. A differentiation emerged within the transatlantic flow between the traditional pattern of familial relocation and settlement, and "birds of passage" who came to work for a limited period (Piore, 1979, pp. 141–166). Overall, for the fiscal years 1908–1910, European aliens departing from the United States equaled 32 percent of arrivals; but for "new immigrants" from southern and eastern Europe alone — excluding Russian Jews — the proportion of returnees rose to 38 percent of landings (Piore, 1979, p. 149). The flow of labor migrants was largely governed in each group by loose contracts enforced through social sanctions paralleling the Chinese practice: the European variants were covered by the single name of the "padrone" system, borrowing from the Italian version (Nelli, 1964). The differentiation between permanent and temporary migrants facilitated the institutionalization of segmented labor in American industry (Gordon, Reich, and Edwards, 1982; Piore, 1979).

Despite the 1885 contract prohibition, when World War I brought immigration from Europe to an abrupt halt while simultaneously stimulating a huge demand for American goods, Congress authorized the government to organize the recruitment of contract labor from neighboring countries, including the Caribbean islands as well as Mexico and Canada. After the war the United States deliberately undertook to reduce the contribution of immigration to its societal development. When entry through the main gate became severely restricted, the back door took on its full significance as an economic mechanism (Zolberg, 1978).

After 1924 ordinary immigration was limited to an annual quota of 150,000, but, notwithstanding vociferous objections by restrictionists, no numerical cap was imposed on immigration from the Western hemisphere. Although this population was subject in theory to qualitative restrictions (such as a literacy requirement), in effect laborers from Canada (mostly Quebec), Mexico, and the Caribbean could enter freely at the bidding of U.S. employers. The workers were meant to be temporary, but there were no institutional mechanisms for distinguishing them from ordinary immigrants if they stayed — except the stigma of their illegality. In the Great Depression, those who did not leave voluntarily were rounded up and dumped pell-mell across the border, much as British parishes had done with the Irish a century earlier.

Migrants from the Americas continued to play an important role in the United States in the subsequent half-century; but arrangements for their utilization have varied considerably. After the outbreak of World War II Congress once again enacted a law allowing the entry of temporary labor, mostly from Mexico, under a system of government-supervised contracts known as the *bracero* program. Although the program was terminated at the end of the war, the flow itself continued; but the migrants were now illegal "wetbacks." At the outbreak of the Korean War the United States again legalized the recruitment of braceros, but the flow of undocumented workers responding to the stepped-up demand outpaced the growth of contract workers under the official program. By the mid-1950s such workers were employed as far north as Minnesota, and were often found outside of agriculture. Although the Korean emergency ended in 1953, the bracero program lasted until 1964, when it was finally terminated under pressure from U.S. organized labor. In its last five years, as the number of contract workers was reduced, the flow of the undocumented — estimated on the basis of reported arrests — nearly doubled.

Laissez-faire subsequently prevailed once again in the form of lax policing of borders and an absence of control over the penetration of the U.S. labor market by undocumented border-crossers. Although the energy crisis of the 1970s and the protracted recession of the early 1980s stimulated the formulation of legislative projects designed to dam the tide of illegal aliens, most of the proposals provided sufficient loopholes to ensure the continuation of labor migration; and in any case, there is good reason to doubt the effectiveness of the proposed measures in the face of the conjoined contrary interests of U.S. employers and of the labor migrants themselves.

Conclusion

The economic advantages the use of foreign migrant labor affords the receivers are well established (Kindleberger, 1967; Castles and Kossack, 1973; Piore, 1979; Freeman, 1979; Portes and Walton, 1982; Burawoy, 1974). At the most general level, the availability of an external labor supply tends to reduce the price of wages in the receiving economy below what it would be in its absence. Should the capitalist economy be structured into segments characterized by unequal levels of development — be they distinct regions within a country or separate states — a less developed one can function as a sort of manpower storage facility, enhancing the elasticity of the labor supply in the more developed one and reducing the costs of storing this labor when not needed. This effect is well captured by the term "conjuncture-buffer," coined in post-World War II West Germany with respect to guestworkers. Moreover, acceptance of a lower standard of living, and especially participation in a household economy that ekes out part of its subsistence in a rural region of the country of origin, enables the migrants to sell their labor below what is established as an acceptable minimum in the more developed segment. Migrants are often also more docile than native workers, because more vulnerable to political control. A number of analysts, beginning with Marx, have also pointed out that employers benefit as well from the divisive consequences of competition between ethnically or racially distinct workers — a pattern Bonacich has termed "split labor" (Bonacich, 1976).

The institutionalization of a migratory flow of free wage labor at the international level is predicated on a low-cost movement of people among states participating in a common transnational market economy, but which have different internal conditions making for significant variation in market conditions for workers — a type of structural differentiation commonly known as "core" and "periphery." The costs of movement are determined by some combination of proximity, cheap transportation, and low transaction costs. Historically, the introduction of steam transport on both land and sea between states participating in an international capitalist economy governed by the gold standard was a major turning point in this respect; but the possibilities have been vastly expanded in more recent times, as cheap air transport has brought Yugoslavia close to Australia, while superhighways have brought Stuttgart within easy reach of Istanbul, or Tapachula of Chicago.

Although the migrant workers are free in contrast with slaves and indentured labor, their actual freedom in the country where the work is performed usually is significantly constrained. Admission is often contingent upon a limited contract, which reduces the foreign worker's access to the labor market of the receiving country and his ability to compete with natives; and political regulations may restrict the possibility of organizing for collective bargaining. Alternatively, entry and employment are surreptitious, making the worker extremely dependent on the employer's will. Moreover, as in earlier comparable forms of labor recruitment, this pattern includes institutional barriers erected by the receiving country which prevent the incorporation of the workers into the population at large. Such barriers constitute an important structural element of the pattern; without them many of the advantages of alien migrant labor would disappear.

Under contemporary conditions in liberal regimes the migrants no longer suffer formal status distinctions by way of racial or ethnic categories; although discrimination does occur in practice, the most important mechanism of exclusion consists of legal obstacles to the establishment of permanent residence and the acquisition of citizenship — often carried into the second generation. Alien workers in affluent societies are thus still wanted but not welcome.

THREE

Population and the Present World Structure

Hedley Bull

THE VIEW that the growth of the world's population must be curbed is sometimes put forward in the Western countries as if there already existed a world society and a world authority able to give effect to its wishes, in disregard of the actual economic, political, and legal structure of world affairs. We should be cosmopolitanists in our values, but when prescribing steps to control the size, the rate of growth, or the geographical distribution of the world's population, there is need to take account of the context in which these issues arise. This contextual view must consider the unequal distribution of the world's wealth and resources, the changing distribution of power among nations or states, the obligations and interests of the rich countries toward the poor, the bearing of migration on population policy, the relation between population and development, and especially the system of sovereign states, which provides the prevailing form of universal political order and along with it our chief agreed ideas of legitimate conduct in international relations.

Population and the Distribution of Wealth

By the early 1970s predominant opinion in the Western countries, which (we are inclined to forget) in the early postwar period had been for the most part strongly pronatalist, had come to favor efforts to curb the unprecedented growth of the world's population, especially in developing countries. Spokesmen in the Western countries began to express a neo-Malthusian concern about the pressure of population on finite resources — exemplified by the first Club of

Rome Report — and to discuss the religious and other social inhibitions to the worldwide adoption of birth control.

The pressures emanating from the West for a global strategy to curb rapid population growth were inevitably directed primarily at the developing countries of Asia, Africa, and Latin America. It was not only that most (perhaps nine-tenths) of the world's population growth was taking place in these countries, but that, according to strong conviction in the Western countries, it was the failure of the developing countries to control the expansion of their populations that was most responsible for nullifying efforts to raise their *per capita* incomes through development assistance. Indeed, there was a growing belief that population policy was the key to the development of poor countries, as reflected in President Johnson's remark in 1965 that five dollars spent on population control was worth one hundred spent on economic assistance, and in the rising sums the Western countries devoted to assistance in population programs. At the same time by the early 1970s, faced by recession and mounting unemployment, the countries of Western Europe, North America, and Oceania were taking steps to curb the immigration from poorer countries which they had permitted and even sought during the labor shortages of the 1950s and 1960s, when economic growth was the order of the day. Change in their economic condition reinforced the Western countries' conviction: if population pressure within the poor countries could not be relieved by emigration, it must be reduced at its source.

When the representatives of the developing countries were confronted with the Western case for a global strategy to curb population growth, most notably at the World Population Conference at Bucharest in 1974, their responses (although by no means uniform) proved to be mainly negative. First, some third world nations, led by Argentina, Brazil, and Algeria, adopted explicitly pronatalist positions, if not in relation to the world as a whole then at least for themselves. They did so on substantially the same grounds as the Western countries used to justify it in the late nineteenth century and earlier in the present century, when Malthusian ideas had been in decline and population growth was seen as linked to industrial and agricultural advances. A growing population is proof of a nation's vitality and a mode of capital formation; people are producers of resources rather than mere consumers of them; a rapidly growing population is a youthful one, better equipped to assume the task of development; in competition with adversary nations, advantages are held to lie with a nation whose population is large and growing; external attempts to limit a nation's population growth are a form of "demographic containment."

Some third world spokesmen pointed out that the pressure of population on resources has to be reckoned in terms of consumption per capita as well as in total numbers; given the vastly greater consumption per head of energy, food, and other raw materials in the rich countries, the disequilibrium between population and resources might be attributed less to the rapid growth of population in the developing countries than to the levels and growth of consumption of the developed countries. Population growth might be slow in the rich nations, but one birth in the United States, it has been said, is the "ecological equivalent" of twenty-five in India.

Third world spokesmen also argued that population control should be regarded as an outcome rather than as a precondition of development. The historical experience of the Western countries themselves, it was argued, indicated that the decline in fertility came not before but after the transition to industrialization and its attendant social forms. It stood to reason that advances in mass literacy, in education (especially of women), in social security, in liberation from the conditions of peasant life (in which large families are a deep-rooted tradition, and are regarded as sources of labor, security in old age, and social prestige) provide the conditions in which birth control becomes widespread. The economic development of poor countries would itself be "the great contraceptive" that would bring birth rates down.

Third world spokesmen argued that if their countries were to be regarded as "overpopulated" now or in the future, this also raised questions about migration. A classic means of relieving the pressure of population on resources is, after all, to allow it to shift to where adequate resources are. This means had been available to the peoples of Europe in the era of demographic, democratic, and industrial revolutions, when the surplus populations of that continent had moved out across the globe. Why should the peoples of Asia, Africa, and Latin America now be asked to impose limits to the growth of their populations, while being denied entry into the rich pastures of the Western countries, or be admitted only on restrictive terms that often robbed them of the most skilled and educated among them, making development even more difficult?

Underlying third world criticism was an insistence that the question of control of the world's population must not be allowed to displace the question of the redistribution of the world's wealth and resources. The effort of the Western countries to focus attention upon the control of population was seen in this light by third world representatives at the Bucharest Conference. In 1974 the campaign for a New International Economic Order and a Charter of the Economic Rights and Duties of States was at its height. The proposed global strategy for controlling the population explosion, using such direct measures as promotion of contraception, raising the age of marriage, incentives to reduce family size, and such indirect ones as education, raising the status of women, and improving health care, would not by itself help to alleviate the inequality between developed and less developed peoples. "Zero population growth," proclaimed as an objective for the world as a whole, might imply the perpetuation of existing inequalities, at least if allowed to stand on its own; still more, perhaps, when it was coupled with "zero economic growth." To expect that developing countries make the same demographic transition that the advanced countries had undergone (from regime of high mortality and birth rates to one of low ones) seemed to imply, like Western doctrines of development through "stages of growth," that nations could undergo such changes in isolation from one another, without the necessary change in the international economic order. The suspicion that Western initiatives were an attempt to head off the campaign for the new international economic order must only have been confirmed by the brutal thesis, put forward by some in the West at that time, that if the developing countries should ever achieve standards of consumption comparable with those of the rich countries, an intolerable strain would be imposed on the world's resources.

It would be wrong to conclude from these responses that third world governments were or are hostile to the case for a global approach to population policy. Their defensive posture at the Bucharest Conference was in some measure tactical, attuned more to their wider policies in the North-South debate than to their attitudes to population matters as such. The doctrine that birth control is more a consequence than a cause of development has not inhibited China, India, Mexico, Thailand, South Korea, Hong Kong, Singapore, Chile, Colombia, Costa Rica, and many other developing countries from the pursuit of strong national policies to curb fertility, which have already had a striking effect in reducing the momentum of rapid population growth in the third world. The strict Marxist position that there is no global problem of overpopulation, only a problem of global economic and social injustice, is not that of most third world governments, whose theme at Bucharest was rather that solutions to the problem of overpopulation could only be found in the context of development.

Population and the Distribution of Power

It is not possible in practice to disregard the third world countries' insistence on linking control of population to matters of development and economic justice. Third world peoples can no longer be seen merely as passive objects of our oppression and neglect or recipients of our charity. In the course of the last half-century a massive shift has taken place in the distribution of power in the world toward the states, peoples, and political movements of Asia, Africa, and Latin America, however unevenly this has occurred as between one and another.

No doubt the countries of North America, Western Europe, and Japan still represent the dominant centers of wealth and technology in the world today, and along with the Soviet Union, the dominant centers of military strength. No doubt also the advances that have been made by third world peoples and movements since World War II still fall far short of their aspirations and of the goal of a world society in which wealth and power may be said to be justly or fairly distributed. But the third world's own rhetoric on the theme of continued domination by the Western powers or by the superpowers tends to obscure the changes that have taken place. By gaining control of sovereign states and of their political and administrative apparatus, third world leaders have indeed been able to promote the identity and cohesion of their people, to foster national economic development, and to assert local control of economic life against external influences. The idea that legal and political independence leaves peoples helpless in the face of a world economic system of dominance and dependence neglects the fact that it is through the exercise of state power and universally acknowledged rights of sovereignty that many developing states have been able to limit their involvement in the world economy or improve the terms of their participation in it.

In extending their influence third world peoples have benefited from the prestige of their numbers — the numbers not merely of their states but collectively of their peoples. It has been the fashion in Western thinking about international relations in recent decades to discount the importance of population factors, or at all events of sheer size of population, as a source of power. Neither the economies nor the armed forces of contemporary states are labor-intensive to the degree that would justify the treatment of population size as the crucial determinant of state power, as it was taken to be among European states in the eighteenth and nineteenth centuries. We recognize that today factors of technology and capital may be much more important than factors of population in determining the economic and the military performance of a modern nation; that where a nation's population is a significant consideration, its size may be less important than its cohesion, the level of its education, its competence in technology or the capacity of the nation's resources to sustain it; that for some contemporary states a large population is more of a liability than an asset; that in relation to economic, military, or other standards of performance, it makes sense to speak of an optimum rather than of a maximum size of population, however difficult this may be to estimate.

Nevertheless, our perceptions of the political weight or importance of a nation or state, and even of its rights, are determined in part by the size of its population. Nations as colossal as China and India are generally acknowledged to have an importance in world affairs that they would still enjoy, even if economically and militarily they were weaker than they are. A population of 100 million or more today is not sufficient to confer superpower status upon a nation, but it is widely thought to be necessary for this status. Given the ambitions of contemporary Brazil or Nigeria, it is not clear that their pronatalist policies are misconceived, even if they are not sufficient in themselves for the end in view.

The fear of superior numbers, especially when linked to differences of culture, of race, and of level of development, and reinforced by consciousness of a history of antagonism, is far weaker today among the Western peoples than it was at the turn of the century, when white Europeans, North Americans, and Australians spoke freely of the Yellow Peril. The change reflects not only the decline of belief in population as a factor of power, but also the weakening of racial exclusiveness owing to the processes of internal change by which all Western societies except South Africa have become multiracial societies. Nevertheless, it would be wrong wholly to discount this old fear. It focuses today as much or more on the threat posed by more populous countries to living standards and national cohesion than on threats to security. It is more noticeable on the periphery of the old white world (Australia in relation to Southeast Asia, Israel in relation to its Arab neighbors, South Africa in relation to black Africa, the Soviet Union in relation to China) than at its center. But though diminished, fear is still one of the unstated premises of Western concern about rapid population growth in the third world.

What is especially important in the present connection is that the significance of sheer population size is enhanced by the incipient cosmopolitanism in present-day thinking about world affairs. We believe that all human beings are equal in rights. We dimly perceive a world society of human beings possessed of these equal rights stretching over the globe, regardless of differences of race, sex, culture, or creed, their rights undiminished by state boundaries or rights or sovereignty. This perception is rooted in eighteenth-century visions of the rights of man to which both liberals and Marxists are heir, and which are proclaimed in UN protocols and conventions giving them legal or quasi-legal status. These instruments lack machinery for effective implementation and enforcement, and the actual practice of governments in many parts of the world is a mockery of them. Nor are there grounds for assuming that a groundswell is in progress that will lead inevitably to the dissolution of the system of sovereign states and the emergence of a cosmopolis or functioning world society. But the idea of a world society of equal human beings has a sufficient place in our perceptions of world affairs to have already had a profound influence on questions of right or entitlement.

When in the rich Western countries an assessment is made of moral claims to our position of power and wealth, three considerations have to be taken into account today that would not have had to be raised, say, half a century ago. One is what I have called the emergence of cosmopolitanist perspective, which invites us to consider the condition of individual persons across the globe rather than of states. A second is the progress of egalitarianism, which suggests at least a presumption in favor of an equal distribution of power and wealth (leaving aside for the present the question of what precisely this means). And a third is expanded demographic consciousness, which presents us with a clear picture of our dwindling numbers in the West. All of these considerations point toward the moral vulnerability of the Western countries' present position.

The Obligations and Interests of the Rich

Not only does the growing power of developing countries compel attention to the proposition that the control of world population be related to the development of poor countries; the rich countries' own sense of obligation, reinforced by a sense of their long-term interests, must lead them to the same conclusion.

The Western democracies, which by World War II were accepting the degree of responsibility for the basic economic and social welfare of their citizens implicit in the phrase "the welfare state," in the years since the war have come to recognize that this responsibility, although in diminished or attenuated form, extends beyond their citizens to mankind as a whole. Noncitizens were not thought, and still are not thought, to have the same claims upon the state as do citizens; they do not have legal rights but only moral rights to assistance from rich states, and even these moral rights are regarded as imperfect rather than as perfect, that is, they leave the state with some choice as to whether to respond to them or not. By itself the Western states' sense of moral responsibility would not have been enough to cause them to pursue the policies of development assistance they have in fact pursued; these policies also reflect the perceived interests of the Western countries. Moreover, the sense of moral responsibility that does exist toward poor people beyond the state's frontiers is not felt equally toward all of them; it is distorted by historical associations (for example, of former colonial powers and their dependencies), cultural links, and present patterns of connection. Nevertheless, this sense of responsibility is a real factor in world affairs. It is also a new factor. Although it has immediate roots in the responsibilities assumed by colonial powers for economic and social welfare in their dependencies in the last phase of colonial rule, and more distant roots in the antislavery movement and ultimately in the natural law tradition of a moral community of mankind, it is a sympathetic response to the greater recent awareness of poverty, suffering, and oppression throughout the world as a whole.

However, the sense of obligation that is felt in the rich countries not only does not always bring them into alignment with third world governments on matters of development assistance, but leaves them divided on a number of basic principles. The sense of obligation in the rich, Western countries is felt toward individual persons within the LDCs (less developed countries), more particularly toward those that are poor or suffering. Third world governments, on the other hand, place their emphasis upon the rights of poor states rather than on individuals.

It is, of course, hazardous to generalize both about Western and about third world policies. The policies that have been described, moreover, are not strict opposites: the transfer of resources to poor individuals within third world states has to be done through the agency of the governments of these states, and Western opinion generally recognizes that improving the lot of individuals requires the strengthening of the economic, social, and political structures. Nevertheless, there is a contrast of emphasis between a rich country's concern with the welfare of individuals, the relief of suffering, and the meeting of basic needs (none of which goals necessarily implies any change in the relationship between donors that are strong and recipients that are weak), and the third world's concern with the development of local structures, the transfer of resources to local governments, and the freedom of these governments to determine the uses made of these resources (goals which imply that the relationship of dependence between donor and recipient states will be brought to an end).

The Western sense of obligation thus does not imply an equalization of wealth or standards of living (any more than the commitment of Western countries to minimum standards of welfare for their own citizens necessarily implies commitment to a more equal distribution of wealth domestically). Many third world governments, by contrast, are committed — at least rhetorically — to goals of equality beyond the measures of redistribution necessary to meet basic needs. This does not mean that third world governments are committed to equal distribution of wealth among their own citizens (like Western governments, they vary widely in their practices in this respect), still less to any conception of an equal distribution of wealth among individual persons in the world as a whole. But it is part of the common doctrine of the third world coalition that existing inequalities should be removed between rich and poor countries in respect of degree of development and average per capita income.

Western and third world perspectives also differ on the ideological justification for a transfer of wealth and resources; whereas the Western thinkers place the emphasis on the present and future needs of third world peoples, together with the goal of harmony in the international community, the spokesmen for the LDCs sometimes emphasize a right of compensation for past exploitation. The doctrine of a right of compensation for exploitation during the past colonial or present neocolonial era involves a number of assumptions that are widely rejected in Western countries: that the wealth of the advanced industrial countries derives significantly, or in the past derived, from exploitation of non-Western countries; that the less developed status of the latter is a consequence of colonial rule or of neocolonial exploitation; that the alleged wrongs of past exploitation are to be singled out from the vast catalogue of wrongs done by nation unto nation throughout history; that the responsibility is a collective one, of colonialist or Western peoples as a whole, and not simply of those that were directly involved; and that the responsibility is passed on from generation to generation.

Third world governments frequently portray the present international economic order as the source of their underdevelopment, poverty, and need, while the Western governments emphasize local or domestic causes such as government corruption or inefficiency, political instability, social attitudes unfavorable to modernization, or lack of natural resources. For third world governments the international economic order serves as a scapegoat for local failures and difficulties, just as for the advanced countries the idea that the problems of the poor countries are brought about by local factors appears to absolve them from responsibility.

Finally, whereas opinion in the Western countries conceives of the objective in relation with the third world as a redistribution of wealth and the amenities of living that go with it, for third world opinion the objective is not so much the redistribution of wealth as the redistribution of power. For third world peoples and movements, an important part of what is objectionable about the present state of the world is their dependence on others, their vulnerability to the effects of decisions taken by outsiders. The poor countries do seek more power to resist outside forces as a means of securing a redistribution of wealth (thus the preoccupation that developed in the 1970s with the strengthening of third world "bargaining strength"), but they also seek it as an end in its own right. A redistribution of wealth is necessary ultimately because without it there can be no effective redistribution of power. For the Western countries, development assistance and transfer of resources are thought of as taking place within the existing structure of power; for the third world countries, a vital objective is to change the structure of power.

The sense of obligation that leads the rich countries to assist the development of poor countries is complicated, but not extinguished, by the above conflicts of perspective; on the other hand, it is reinforced by Western considerations of national or state interest. The interests that are advanced by development assistance have been variously and often unconvincingly described — at different times it has been said that the purpose of assistance was to make the recipients more impregnable to radical political change, or better markets for export. One interest that has been consistently pursued is the very simple and old-fashioned one of purchasing compliance and goodwill with subsidies, but this is not an interest that can explain or justify a permanent commitment.

The paramount interest of the Western countries in promoting third world development is, I would argue, the construction of a viable international order. No world order can have any prospect of enduring into the next century unless the countries which represent a majority of the states and most of the world's population come to feel that they have a stake in its continuance. To develop a sense of a stake in the system, they must have an adequate share of its economic rewards and adequate participation in the shaping of political decisions.

As the poor countries become richer and more powerful, the Western powers will be called upon to make uncomfortable adjustments (as in the retreat from colonial rule, neocolonial domination, or white supremacist privilege). They will have to distinguish between what is a timely concession to necessary and just change, and what may be weakness in defense of a vital principle (as in relation to third world acts of aggression, violations of human rights, or assaults on freedom of information). There is no guarantee that when third world countries acquire power and riches, they will use them to exert influence within the established international system rather than to pursue their objectives outside its framework. A world in which third world countries dispose of relatively more power and wealth is also one in which the countries of the Western world have relatively less power. As we might learn from the history of American policy, it is one thing to espouse the power and prosperity of other states as an ideal, but another to come to terms with it in reality.

Population and Migration

One way to relieve population pressure on the resources of poor countries may be through migration to places where resources are more plentiful. Some third world governments seek to encourage migration of their surplus population to Western countries, or to other areas in the third world such as the oil-producing states of the Middle East. Some, like Mexico, not merely demand entry into the United States for their surplus population, but speak as if entry were a moral right conferred by history or by present poverty. Such claims, moreover, do gain some recognition in those circles in the West in which there is sensitivity to global economic injustice.

From the point of view of the sending countries the benefits of this migration are clear enough. The migrants themselves escape from deprivation to a better standard of life, and if they have gone voluntarily, by their going at least show that they themselves believe that they will benefit. The families left behind may benefit from remittances, from no longer having to provide sustenance for the ones who have departed, and from reduced burdens of welfare. The sending country as a whole will have lost actual or potential labor, and in the case of highly skilled migrants may suffer the effects of the "brain-drain," but it may stand to gain from the export of unemployment, the acquisition of revenue and foreign exchange from remittances, and a safety valve for the release of social tensions. High growth rates like those following mass emigration from southern European countries in the postwar period and advantages like those derived by South Asian countries from migration to the Gulf area in the 1970s provide illustrations of these benefits.

Emigration from third world countries today has reached massive proportions, but does not in itself necessarily contribute to the goal of a just geographical distribution of population in relation to available resources, nor imply any demand for it. The causes of this emigration in the post-1945 era have been as much political as economic in nature: anticolonial wars (as in Africa in the 1960s and 1970s), the oppression and sometimes expulsion of minorities by newly independent states dominated by particular ethnic groups (as of the Chinese in Indochina, Asians in east Africa, non-Amharic–speaking peoples in Ethiopia), civil wars coinciding with foreign intervention (as in East Pakistan in 1971 or Afghanistan at present). The countries that have received the greater part of the migrants are not those of the West, nor indeed the oil-rich ones, but other poor third world countries (at present Sudan, Zaire, Somalia, Thailand, Pakistan, Jordan, Mexico).

The issues raised by these population movements almost invariably take us back to the perception that the present geographical distribution of population in relation to wealth, as between the West and the third world, is an unjust one. The great demand in third world countries for migration into the rich Western countries is fed by the urge to escape from poverty, oppression, and instability and by the lure of economic opportunity, liberty, and security in the West. It is facilitated and encouraged by the spread of information about the differences of conditions in different parts of the world, by the growth of social networks that facilitate the movement of migrants and their settlement in receiving countries, by the increasing ease and declining cost of long-distance transport, by the removal of barriers of racial and ethnic discrimination in the immigration and internal social policies of the receiving Western states, by the responsibilities recognized by Western countries toward migrants acknowledged to be "refugees," and by the inability or unwillingness of Western governments to cope effectively with illegal migrants. The fact that the Western countries receive only a small proportion of total emigrants from the third world reflects the barriers to migration rather than lack of pressure for it.

Even where entry into the Western countries is not directly at issue, these states are often expected — by themselves as well as by others — to assume the responsibilities imposed by their wealth and resources, especially when the migrants involved may be regarded as refugees. By long tradition refugees are a privileged class of migrants (if in other respects underprivileged), in respect both of their claims of entry into receiving states (the so-called right of asylum) and of their claims to just treatment after entry. But the concept of the refugee — a person outside his or her homeland, unable or unwilling to return to it because of persecution or well-founded fear of persecution — once applied principally to small numbers of individuals, usually political activists. In the twentieth century it has come to be applied to millions of people. Again, earlier in this century the refugees were mainly European; today they are chiefly African and Asian. Where once the persecution for which they were regarded as refugees was necessarily political in nature, today there is a tendency to speak also of economic persecution (meaning, moreover, not persecution by economic acts of the state, but rather the mere existence of economic conditions that fail to satisfy standards of human rights). It has even been suggested that for a person to be regarded as a refugee it may be enough that in the sending country there was an absence of positive rights, and that no actual infringement of positive rights is presupposed.

Along with refugees in the strict sense we have thus come to speak of de facto refugees, economic refugees, internal refugees, and crypto-refugees. The widening of the concept of the refugee reflects not only the extension of public sympathies in the rich countries to wider categories of third world emigrants believed to have been denied rights of one kind or another, but also a certain artfulness on the part of the emigrants themselves: the availability of refugee services tends itself to swell the number of refugees. The privileges enjoyed by designated refugees as recipients of special assistance in the West, compared with other migrants in third world countries and indeed with ordinary citizens of the home countries, have sometimes generated resentment.

As the concept has expanded to embrace new categories of migrant, the responsibilities of the international community toward third world emigrants are thought to have expanded also. The principal bearers of these responsibilities are the Western powers — the countries that have the strongest tradition of providing asylum to refugees. They have the most wealth in relation to their populations; in some cases (the United States, Canada, Australia, New Zealand, South Africa) they are accustomed to viewing themselves as countries of immigration; they harbor the chief international nongovernmental organizations active in this field and provide the bulk of the funds for the intergovernmental organizations. The responsibilities they are thought to have, in particular, are to be generous themselves in providing asylum to refugees; to provide generous assistance to "countries of first asylum," in cases where neither repatriation nor resettlement in third countries is an option; and to contribute by means of development assistance or transfer of wealth to changing the conditions in the sending countries that have led to the exit of the refugees.

The Western countries' acceptance of migrants from the third world has not made any great contribution to relieving the pressures of rapid population growth in poor countries. The number of migrants accepted by Western countries from the third world in recent decades has constituted only a tiny proportion of world population growth in that period. Although substantial numbers of refugees have been accepted for resettlement, the most notable example being the million or so Indochinese accepted in the United States, Canada, Australia, New Zealand, and European countries, the great majority of refugees in the world are in third world countries. While the economic growth of the European countries in the 1950s and 1960s was built in part on cheap immigrant labor (Commonwealth immigration in the

United Kingdom, guestworkers in West Germany and Switzerland), the recession of the early 1970s led to the virtual cessation of legal immigration, apart from acceptance of refugees. In the United States, Canada, and Australia the trend has also been toward restriction of entry. There is a new concern for developing tougher measures to control illegal entry, "interdiction of access," and measures to promote "return migration."

Yet in the receiving countries, pressures to relax barriers to third world immigration are still significant. A demand for cheap labor remains, especially in relation to work which local labor is unwilling to perform. This need is illustrated by employers' lobbying for Hispanic immigration into the United States. Political or ideological factors still operate in favor of particular immigrant groups, such as refugees from Cuba in the United States or from Vietnam in the United States and Australia. Campaigns are mounted by established ethnic groups, such as Indian and Pakistani communities in the United Kingdom, on behalf of particular individuals or families. In most Western countries the diplomatic requirements or relationships with particular third world countries operate to moderate what would otherwise be harsher policies (for Britain's relations with Commonwealth countries, for Australia with ASEAN states, for the United States especially with Latin American countries). But for the present the pressures to keep the doors closed are stronger. They include recession and the defense of jobs by organized labor; concern about the welfare burdens imposed by immigration; concern about social consequences, especially where (as in the case of Mexican immigration into the United States) the possibilities of successful integration are lessened by a "temporary migrant mentality," linguistic separatism, and alienation resulting from repression of illegal immigration.

The flow of migration from poor to rich countries — and more generally, all international migration — is impeded by the division of the world into sovereign states which claim the right and, by and large, possess the power to control the movement of persons across their frontiers. The right of individuals to leave their own country, or indeed any country, is asserted by liberal doctrine, proclaimed in the Universal Declaration of Human Rights and the 1975 Helsinki Final Act. In practice this right is on the whole respected by Western states, but in Communist states there is no right of exit, and in many non-Communist states outside the West exit is a privilege rather than a right. Conversely, freedom of entry into countries is universally denied as a legal right, even (indeed especially) by the Western democracies. It is generally recognized that a state has obligations to admit certain categories of persons, such as its own nationals, diplomatic agents, and representatives of international organizations. There is widespread recognition among Western, African, and Latin American countries of the rights of refugees to asylum; but this is not taken to entail a corresponding duty to admit them to one's own country; on the other hand, the positive duty not to return refugees to the country from which they have fled is widely recognized.

The right to determine the entry of persons into one's territory, and thus the character of one's population, is a matter of the deepest sensitivity for most states; it touches not merely on the prosperity and security of a community, but also on its identity and control of its own destiny. For some peoples, like the Japanese, the goal of preserving their social homogeneity has led to a virtual prohibition of permanent immigration. People like the Malays, the Fijians, or the Sinhalese under British rule that have lost control of their immigration policy have paid dearly for it, and people fight to win or to defend their sovereign independence partly in order to regain this control.

Migration is also impeded by failure of the sovereign state to accord immigrants equal treatment with established inhabitants or citizens. Again, liberal doctrine proclaims an ideal of the maximum interchangeability of civil rights as between one citizenship and another, and their conformity with wider standards of human rights. But in practice immigrants and other aliens are seldom accorded equality of rights with citizens, and indeed the rights of citizenship may vary between a core national group and peripheral groups, as in the British system of tiered gradations of nationality. In many countries deep social distinctions lie behind these distinctions in law as between natives, or sons of the soil, and immigrants, even those of long standing. These distinctions are not uncommonly expressed in the oppression of the migrants, which at its worst takes the form of mass expulsion or genocide.

It is sometimes suggested that the sovereign state's control of migration is breaking down in the face of a "tidal wave" of pressure from poor countries. This may be true of the U.S.-Mexican or U.S.-Caribbean cases, but these arise from special circumstances. The broad situation is that the Western countries, the most attractive targets for third world immigration, and the countries the most able

to contribute to a global equilibrium between population and resources, have used their sovereign powers effectively to stem the
flow.

Population and Development

The Western countries might respond to third world views on
population matters by intensifying their efforts to promote development in those countries which account for most of the world's growth
in population. Such a strategy might serve to check population
growth both by invoking the presumed contraceptive properties of
development and by making direct policies of population control
more widely acceptable in third world countries, while promoting a
more equitable distribution of wealth and resources over the world
as a whole. The means available for working toward such objectives
are those that have been debated for many years, and in some cases
implemented: improvements in the terms of trade for LDCs, such as
preferences for their manufacturers and funds to raise and stabilize
the price of primary exports; improved access to lending institutions;
transfer of technology; increased official aid and private foreign investment; schemes for income taxation of the rich countries or of
persons working in them; the proposed brain-drain tax.

Good reasons exist for questioning whether measures of this kind
would be sufficient to cause dramatic changes in the development of
poor countries, even if they were to be implemented on a massive
scale. It may be doubted that today's differences between countries
in wealth and level of development have much to do with the terms
on which they participate in the international economy. Domestic
differences in political stability, administrative efficiency, managerial
and entrepreneurial skills, and adaptability to change seem to account for the superior economic performance of those societies, especially in East and Southeast Asia, that are today moving out of the
ranks of the "less developed." Massive transfers of capital through
official aid or private investment can promote development only to
the extent that there is local capacity to absorb it or harness it to
developmental purposes. The very conception that what is at issue
between the North and South is "the distribution of wealth" is in
some measure misleading: some of the basic sources of the wealth
of nations cannot be distributed among them in the way that capital

can be; moreover, before wealth can be distributed, it has first to be produced, and proposals for arrangements to transfer wealth to poor countries have to deal also with the effects of these arrangements on the production of wealth, in which poor countries have a stake too.

There are special reasons for skepticism about redistribution of wealth through a brain-drain tax. Under this proposal skilled or professional migrants from poor to rich countries would pay a supplementary tax on their earned incomes, to be levied by their countries of origin, collected by the host governments, and transferred to a UN fund for development purposes. The advantages of this scheme, which has something in common with the exit tax imposed by the Soviet Union on emigrants, are that it would provide compensation to poor countries for the effects of the "reverse transfer of technology" they suffer as a consequence of the departure of highly skilled persons trained at their expense. It would also force rich countries to provide compensation for their interference with international mobility of labor in shutting their doors to unskilled migrants, and extend the principle of progressive taxation within poor countries across frontiers. On the negative side, the proposed tax would clearly infringe on the liberty of skilled migrants from third world countries, and handicap them in competition with others in the world labor market. It would discriminate against them within the host countries, and is likely to be in violation of antidiscrimination laws in the United States, the United Kingdom, and elsewhere. It would set aside the advantages which sometimes accrue to the countries of origin through remittances, the ultimate return in some cases of the migrants with their skills enhanced, and services which the migrants sometimes provide to the country of origin while still abroad. It would raise awkward questions as to what would count as a poor country and what as a rich country, which would be particularly hard to deal with for the very large professional migration which occurs among third world countries. Finally, it would tend to institutionalize distinctions between poor and rich countries, and between persons reared or educated in one or the other, distinctions that might otherwise become blurred, to the best interest of the international community.

If measures of development assistance are unlikely to be decisive in themselves, they may nevertheless contribute to the generation of wealth where local factors are favorable. Massive foreign investment of the kind proposed by the Brandt Report is technically possible and did play a vital role in the regeneration of Europe and Japan in the post-1945 era. What is clear, however, is that the Western countries do not at present have the inclination to undertake measures of this kind. The wellsprings of generosity of spirit toward the third world, and even of enlightened self-interest, have largely dried up in the West, and especially in the United States, during this long recession. The reluctance of the Western countries to face reductions in their living standards, always the basic factor making for a negative attitude toward proposals for an international redistribution of wealth, is felt more keenly at a time when these standards are already under threat. Further, the rich countries' reluctance to provide funds whose use they will not control has increased with mounting evidence of corruption and inefficiency in third world countries. Yet at the same time the successes of some third world countries in acquiring a degree of political and military power, or in competing effectively in international trade, together with the rhetorical assault that they have collectively mounted on Western positions over the last decade, have also left their mark on Western attitudes. The 1980s have seen a shift away from egalitarianism and welfarism and a renewal of faith in the operations of the free market in several major Western countries, and this has left them less than ever disposed to look favorably on proposals to interfere in the workings of international market forces. As the degree of hostility between the Western powers and the Soviet Union has intensified, the importance attributed to relations with third world countries has diminished, except insofar as they can be shown to be an aspect of relations with the Soviet Union.

Transferring wealth and resources to where the people are, like allowing people to move to where the wealth and resources are, is made difficult by the system of sovereign states, which claim and accord to one another the right to determine what is to be done with their wealth and resources, just as they claim the right to control their immigration policies. The developing countries may proclaim the rights of poor countries to development assistance and to a just share of the earth's resources, as in the Charter of Economic Rights and Duties of States of 1974, but the rich countries insist on their sovereign right to judge for themselves what their response to such proclamations will be. Nor are the developing countries in any position to dispute this, for they are themselves the strongest defenders of the rights of states to sovereign independence.

Population in Cosmopolis

A solution to the problem of world population would be easier to find in a world that gave up the constraints of the sovereign state system in favor of a cosmopolitan society in which individual human rights were paramount, except insofar as they were limited by a beneficent world authority charged with the responsibility to achieve control of population growth, just distribution of the world's wealth and resources, and guaranteed minimum standards of welfare. Labor would be free to leave countries or enter them and enjoy equal rights after entry, subject to the determination by the world authority as to what the proper geographical allocation of population should be (as once suggested by Albert Thomas, the director of ILO). Capital would be free to move to where it was needed, but required to do so if it did not; the world authority would impose taxation for redistributive purposes on the rich and ensure that the funds transferred to the poor were used for purposes of development. The rights of persons to control the size and spacing of their families would be respected but limited by the goal of an optimum size, rate of growth, and geographical distribution of the world's population.

The world we actually inhabit, however, is one in which we have to reckon with the constraints not simply of the sovereign state system but of the divisions in human society — political, economic, ideological, ethnic, historical — of which that system is merely an expression. Human rights are not implemented in practice not merely because of the claims of states to sovereignty, but more basically in many communities because of lack of will to respect them, agreement as to what they are, or even belief that they exist. Today, as much as long before modern notions of state sovereignty were conceived (the book of *Exodus* is instructive here), communities are determined themselves to control exit, entry, and the treatment afforded to aliens. In the world we live in capital is invested not where it is needed, but where it is profitable; rich nations are not willing to be taxed for purposes to which they have not consented, and poor nations in the first flush of independence are not willing to be told how they should spend their money; and in the unlikely event that a contemporary world authority were to be established, it would not necessarily be committed to individual human rights, minimum standards of welfare, and population equilibrium.

Yet from another perspective, in a divided world the system of sovereign states can play a positive role. This system, for all of its shortcomings, provides the possibility of coexistence or minimum order, in which diverse political communities respect one another's independence and spheres of jurisdiction, and without which the pursuit of more ambitious goals is not possible. It provides the basis for international cooperation, which through the UN system has reached unprecedented heights. But it does not imply (and should not be allowed to imply) the right of states and nations to disregard their responsibilities to one another and to the international community; whatever rights they have derive from the international community and are not held apart from it.

We can advance only by making use of the sovereign state system and its forms of institutionalized cooperation, inching forward toward solutions for these problems. Advances at the margin have in fact taken place: world population growth has slowed down, migration to the rich countries has had some impact, a shift of wealth and power to third world countries has occurred. Mention has been made of the growth in recent decades of a cosmopolitanist perspective. We should cultivate this perspective and seek to ensure that the policies of states are informed by it. The role of the UN system is crucial in this connection in spreading awareness, fostering debate, and building consensus. In matters of population, as in many others, it is worth promoting the idea that states can behave not merely as custodians of the interests of their own peoples, but also as the agents of the common interests of mankind, even in the face of much historical evidence to the contrary.

FOUR

Identity and Population

William Alonso

THE BALANCING equation of technical demography holds that the growth or decline of a population must equal births minus deaths, plus or minus net migration. But this is not always true. For instance the Indian (native American) population of the United States grew by more than 70 percent from 1970 to 1980; most of this growth owed not to the variables of the classic equation, but to the fact that more people chose to identify themselves as Indians to the census. Similarly, the Russian population gained over 600,000 members from 1959 to 1970 through the self-reidentification of people of other nationalities within the Soviet Union despite an internal passport system which, by listing it, inhibits changes in ethnicity (Anderson and Silver, 1983). Thus the qualitative factor of identity can confound the arithmetic certainties of quantitative demography.

We tend to take the categorizing of people into identities for granted, as if we were dealing with facts of nature, but identities are the changing products of the social, political, and economic processes of history. A man of mixed African and European descent may be considered white in the Dominican Republic, but becomes a Hispanic if he immigrates to the United States (only 7 percent of Hispanics listed themselves as black in the 1980 census), while a Caribbean immigrant of comparable ancestry but from an English-speaking island becomes a black. Only the social classification has changed, not the genotype. And the classifying system itself is subject to change, as did Louisiana's: under the French it had conformed to the Latin system (quadroon, octoroon, and so on) but has transformed itself to conform with the binary black-white American system. Comparably, the United States is now witnessing the social construction of "Hispanic" as an ethnic identity inclusive of very different kinds of peoples, much as a century ago the category "Italian" was applied to immigrants who thought of themselves as Calabrians or Genoese.

Race and ethnicity are not, of course, the only bases for the identity of peoples, and nationality, language, religion, territory, culture, caste, class, tribe, or combinations of these serve and have served as differentiators. To an outsider these distinctions may often appear to involve no significant differences, yet much of human history is a record of alliances and loyalties, of conflicts and hatreds, and of subjugations, persecutions, and exploitations based at least as much on the perceived affinities and dissonances of such identities as on material interests. History equally is witness to the changing nature of these identities, to transformations of the underlying issue of who *we* are and who are *they*.

The subject of the identities of peoples, which has concerned historians, philosophers, and ethnographers for centuries, is marvelously complex and subtle. This essay does not pretend to the larger subject, but only to examine the role of identity in demography, where it has been relatively neglected. It will look at the role of identities in actual demographic behavior (births, deaths, migration), at the evolving nature of identities, and the interplay of identities, demography, and policy, particularly in the interactions of rich and poor countries.

The Interplay of Fertilities and Identities

Keeping up with the Joneses. It is an overwhelming fact that the population of the poor countries is growing very fast while the fertility of the rich countries has for years been below replacement and shows no evidence of rising. Such native population growth as there is for the moment in the rich countries owes entirely to past baby booms, which provide them with a bulge in the prime reproductive ages; but in the absence of immigration, population decline in the rich countries is the likeliest prospect and has already begun to show itself in several European countries.

Several of these countries are considering or have already adopted pronatalist policies such as family allowances and labor legislation that compensates women for time lost in having children. More births are wanted for reasons of state, such as avoiding an excessive burden of old-age dependency upon a shrinking labor force, and maintaining the social and entrepreneurial vitality attributed to the young. But people are also expressing open concerns about the survival of the folk (outstandingly in West Germany) and about comparative economic and military power (outstandingly in France). In 1984 the European Parliament, worried about a weakened political role for Europe and a drop in its projected share of world population from 8.8 percent in 1950 to 2.3 percent in 2025, approved a resolution urging the member countries of the European Economic Community (EEC) to adopt pronatalist policies. While such policies in the rich countries are unlikely to be effective, one of the motives for them is higher fertility in the third world.

Pronatalism in the poor countries, or at least resistance to family planning, has often sprung from similar roots. Argentina and Brazil, for instance, wanted people to fill their expanses and to increase their military might (Domingo Faustino Sarmiento, a nineteenth-century Argentine president and philosopher, said that "to govern is to populate"). Until the mid-1970s Mexico's policies were pronatalist, partly in the belief that a larger population would be more powerful in face of the Colossus of the North. Until its adoption a few years ago of the world's most stringent population control policy, similar belief in strength through numbers (supported by quotations from Lenin) influenced China's laissez-faire natalist policies. Even now the idea of strength through numbers survives to some degree in China: under the new policy, minority peoples (Mongols, Hues, and others) are largely exempted from the population control program, partly for the geopolitical reason that most of them live along China's long frontier with the Soviet Union.

A similar phenomenon in miniature occurred in the island of Santo Domingo. The Dominican Republic rejected family planning until 1967 because of fears of being overrun by immigrants from Haiti. Joaquín Balaguer, who later became president, said in 1946:

> [The] Haitian population, for a biological reason, tends inevitably to flow over into the Dominican territory, which is much richer, much flatter, and much larger than their own . . . What were the consequences of this state of affairs? The Dominican Republic was rapidly becoming "Haitianized," and the common ties among the old Spanish part of the island were being destroyed. Voodoo, the national Haitian religion, a type of African animism of the worst origins, became the preferred cult of the entire frontier population. The Haitian currency, the *gourde*, replaced the national currency, even in the markets of the central region of the country. Dominicans living near Haiti — who were the most exposed to the denationalizing influences of our neigh-

bors — lost their sense of nationality, to the extreme where even today many families possess in their hearts an astonishing sentiment of ties to the country of Dessalines. The Dominican Republic was thus condemned to disappear, being absorbed by the Haitians, a race more prolific and homogeneous than our own; in another couple of decades the country would have been irreparably "Haitianized." (Warwick, 1982, p. 99)

Even after a birth control program was adopted in 1967, the zone bordering Haiti was specifically excluded because, according to then-President Balaguer: "There are zones in our territory which for deep historical reasons have to develop a sufficient population density so as to avoid absorption by the neighboring country. Our borders with Haiti must be increasingly populated by Dominican elements, and in these areas any practice aimed at reducing birth by artificial means will always be a senseless measure" (Warwick, 1982, p. 100).

Lowering the fertility of the Joneses. The dates of Balaguer's two statements are interesting in themselves. In 1946 he worried about the Haitians outbreeding and perverting the Dominicans, but not about Dominican overpopulation. Two decades later, he still worried about the Haitian influence, but the Dominican Republic had adopted a population control program. A brief look at world population history and policy will show the significance of the intervening period here and in other countries, such as Mexico and China.

There were people who worried about it, but before World War II world population growth had not been a salient issue. In the rich countries, especially in the late 1920s and 1930s, a marked decline in fertility touched off political and intellectual concern about depopulation. In the poor countries (many of them still colonies) long-term population growth existed, but it was an uncertain one: large countries, such as India and Mexico, could lose population to disease and famine through a whole decade. The perception of a world population explosion did not become widespread until the 1950s and 1960s, when population was growing in the rich countries because fertility was high, and in the poor countries not from higher fertility, but from a dramatic reduction in mortality brought about largely by advances in medicine, food production, and distribution, which had originated in the rich countries.

Some individuals in the developing world, such as Pandjit Nehru and Luis Muñoz Marín, had been concerned about overpopulation since the 1930s, but it was only gradually that opinion and resources were mobilized in Northern Europe and the United States, as a complex mix of economists, ecologists, feminists, sociologists, and other "ists" provided the intellectual base for the recognition of the problem and proposed programs of action. At first these programs were spearheaded by nongovernmental bodies such as foundations and the International Planned Parenthood Federation. The governments of the rich countries and international agencies joined more slowly, to some degree because of their internal politics (in much of the United States, for instance, abortion and the sale of contraceptives were illegal until the early 1970s), but when they did, they did so vigorously. By then fertility in the rich countries had collapsed, and the world population problem had become almost exclusively a problem of third world population growth. The rich countries, having raised life expectancies and thus the rates of population growth in the poor countries almost absentmindedly, set out with urgent purpose to lower their birth rates.

Many people in the developing countries saw matters differently. In some cases they were unpersuaded by the Malthusian scenario and the need for action in their particular case; often, they resented outside interference on matters involving deep social values, such as religion, sexuality, and the structure of the family. At a more global level, many in the developing countries and some theorists in the rich ones viewed population control as a neocolonial strategy of the rich countries to distract attention from the issues of third world development and a new world economic order. Many held a straightforward notion that population control was a racist attempt by the rich and light-skinned to keep down the numbers of the poor and dark. These more sinister interpretations were given weight by the many attempts by rich countries and their international agencies to coerce the poor countries to adopt the programs.

The United Nations Bucharest Conference of 1974 was the forum for a confrontation of these perspectives. The rich countries argued limited resources, capital-labor ratios, maternal and child health, and so on, while many of the poor countries retorted with the need for a new world economic order for third world development and claimed that "development is the best contraceptive." The confrontation was not resolved at that conference, but it is interesting to note subsequent changes in the position of the participants. China, which was one of the leading voices of the development-first position, by the late 1970s was adopting the one-child-family objective, and many other developing countries, such as Mexico, Brazil, and Indonesia, adopted new or stepped up existing programs of population control and family planning. By contrast, the United States, one of the strongest advocates of population control in 1974, advanced an official position at the second World Population Conference (Mexico, 1984) that economic development rather than population programs should have a higher priority for solving population problems, albeit in 1984 the American position on development was seen as emerging from dismantling controls and allowing free markets to blossom.

To some degree, then, the issue of population control in the poor countries has ceased to be always characterized by the attitude that "we" of the rich countries are trying to reduce the fertility of "them" of the poor countries. The basic logic of population policy has been largely accepted by poor countries as consonant with their own interests rather than those of some larger identity, such as the third world or mankind. The issue of group identity remains alive, however, within many nations with subpopulations of distinct identities, especially those with dual societies of rich and poor subnations (for example, the Soviet Union, South Africa, Israel, Singapore) and nations whose subpopulations are at comparable levels of development but which are in tribal competition (for example, Nigeria, Kenya). The dissonance between national and other forms of identity in the modern world will be a recurring theme in the following sections.

Empires and Shared Identities: The European Empires and Their Aftermath

Many of the demographic interactions between the rich and the poor countries are mediated by the structure of world power and by what I shall call the phenomenon of shared identities. Their historical antecedents are in the European empires and particularly in the British Empire, and afterward in the context of the hundred or so new nation-states created after World War II. The section after this one will discuss them in the context of the modern American empire.

The European empires. In Victorian times every citizen (or subject) of the British Empire had a migratory freedom which has disappeared today: he could take up residence in the mother country. It is worth considering why such a right should have existed then and why it no longer exists.

Empires can rarely rule colonies by force alone. Stability requires that the imperial country enjoy some allegiance or loyalty from the colonial population, or at least from its ruling elites. This usually involves the granting of powers and material privileges to client groups in the colonies; but it is equally important to develop a measure of perceived common identity between the metropolis and the colony through shared culture, formal education, language, customs, ceremonies, religion, and even sports. Britain in its imperial days had an instinct for this strategy. To this day many of its former colonies exhibit spit-and-polish Sandhurst types among the military, use English (often of the clipped variety) as an elite language, and enjoy cricket, golf, tennis, and tiffin. But the sharing of identity between colony and metropolis could not, of course, be total: to be useful, a colonial elite had to be able to function in its own society, or else it would become deracinated and ineffective. This molding was not totally one-sided, of course, and the British were themselves transformed as individuals, as a society, and as a culture by their interaction with Kipling's "lesser breeds."

The forms resulting from such dual identities can be touchingly odd at times, as are the white wigs on Nigerian judges or England's perennial losses in the Commonwealth games. The partial fusion of identities characterizes the subtle ebbs in the wake of empires and the love-hate relationships of colonies and colonizers. Britain and India still feel a special affinity for each other, as do the Dutch and Indonesia, France and Francophone Africa. They are somewhat like divorced couples who remain friendly, or become friendly again after the bitterness of separation, and still recognize the intimate echoes of their union.

It is in this framework that one must understand migration rights in the erstwhile British Empire and today's Cheshire-cat British Commonwealth. At its height, the empire ruled over one-third of the earth's population, and each person within its span was a subject of the queen-empress. A spiderweb of loyalties and obligations spanned these diverse peoples, different one from another as they were, both rulers and the ruled. The British were internally differentiated by class, religion, and regional ethnicity, and the subjects of Britain's empire varied along every conceivable criterion. Within this globe-girding panoply of peoples, the queen-empress was the common denominator for her subjects, and ultimate access to the ruler in her enchanted isle was both proof and promise of membership in this greatest of empires. The right of subjects to move to the hub of the empire demonstrated the legitimacy of the overarching system and confirmed their membership in it, much as did the extending of Roman citizenship to the barbarians in that other great empire.

Movement within the empire was also functionally useful. Of course, British civil servants and soldiers could move about as needed; and Britain was able to shift colonials (soldiers, workers, and trading minorities) from one to another colony when convenient. Members of local elites might make cherished visits to the mother country and educate their sons there, in both cases strengthening the bonds of identity. While an occasional colonial subject might take up residence in Britain, the circumstances of resettlement ruled out any prospect of massive migrations from the colonies to Britain.

But all of this was changed with the coming of today's "little" England. The European empires dissolved in the aftermath of World War II, and Britain no longer needed that high degree of shared identity with its former colonies, having ceased to rule them, although even today its residue remains useful for British commercial and diplomatic purposes. At the same time that the right to take up residence in Britain has lost its function, the demographic magnitudes have changed. From Britain's point of view it is no longer a question of wealthy visitors, students, and an occasional immigrant. Modern conditions make massive migrations possible and even likely: the East Indian merchants of Uganda, useful at the time of the empire, are expelled by that new nation and land in London; West Indians flee the poverty of their islands and stream to Britain. Moreover, third world populations, whose growth in numbers had been uncertain prior to World War II, are growing explosively.

Britain, of course, has by now become a middle-sized European country with a faltering economy and high unemployment. While it has occasionally sought foreign workers for special tasks, as when it recruited Jamaicans to drive London buses, Britain wishes its ex-colonials well but does not want them in Britain. It is not just a matter of economics or of a local sense of crowding; it is also a matter of who the British think they are. They have always had a strong sense of identity, in spite of internal class and regional diversity, and they have often shown an uncomplicated sense of racial and cultural superiority. To many British the new immigrants seem dark, poor, loud, threatening, and fertile, and their rejection has become a prominent political issue. The left fears their competition for scarce jobs with the British working class, and the right fears more squarely that these newcomers threaten British ethnic and national identity. Such matters are the relics of the empire, which the current nation-state inherited. As the banner carried by a dark demonstrator in London put it, "We are here because you were there."

It is not an easy matter to untangle matters of identity when disassembling a far-flung, multiracial empire. Consider the problem of Hong Kong, one of the few remaining colonies, with its several million British subjects of Chinese ancestry. Britain holds the territory through a 99-year lease from China imposed at the time of the Boxer Rebellion and due to expire in 1997. While it seems likely that a mutuality of interests between China and the capitalist nations will find a way of continuing Hong Kong's special role, the situation is unstable and many of the residents of that hothouse of entrepreneurial capitalism are making contingency plans to leave. Yet the one thing Britain cannot contemplate is granting residence to such a large number of Asians.

Such considerations dictated the convoluted revisions of British citizenship and immigration laws. Asians can obtain British passports, but these clearly state that they do not entitle the bearer to take up residence in Britain. But what about whites or people of mixed origins, and most particularly those with some British blood? Here the British have developed a concept of "patrials," which translates roughly to the descendants of Britons, and such people are given preferential treatment for immigration into Britain. In effect Britain has had to reinvent its rules for identity in adjusting from empire to nation, and has found many difficulties along the way.

The forming of national identities in the wake of empires. As the European empires ebbed after World War II, they bestowed independence to their former colonies as nation-states, either willingly and peacefully or after bloody struggle. Well over a hundred nations have been thus formed and re-formed in the last four decades, their original boundaries drawn more in accordance with the circumstances of European imperial possessions at the time of independence than on the basis of any coherent notion of local natural and social geography.

The territorial nation-state, as it evolved in Europe in recent centuries, equates a people with a territory and its governance. In fact the principle of one people, one nation was not always practiced there (one need only think of Bretons, Basques, Welsh, and Corsicans among others), but principle clashed with reality altogether in the forming of new nations. Their boundaries were carved arbitrarily and accidentally, usually bundling together very different and even antagonistic peoples that defined themselves variously as tribe, religion, language, and culture. Equally, these new boundaries often split people of other shared identities into different national identities on either side of the line. The new nations have struggled in various ways to match their social realities to these Procrustean beds of territorial nation-states, and some of the consequences have been wars, insurrections, massacres, massive migrations and expulsions, and the redefinition of many national boundaries.

To illustrate this process one need only think of the experience of the Indian subcontinent since its independence in 1947. It had been essentially a single British colony, embracing an extraordinary diversity of religious, ethnic, and language groups which lived together in relative peace and harmony under various degrees of independence and British rule. When full independence and consequently the removal of the British presence were imminent, it was as if the linchpin were removed from a wheel, and the various identities of the subcontinent flew apart. The major groups, Hindus, Muslims, and Sikhs, engaged in a complex and tragic conflict, leading to the partition of India and Pakistan and resulting in the migration of some 16 million people and something like a million deaths as these identities sought to sort themselves out geographically. Even so, this cataclysm did not settle matters, and aftershocks are still being felt. One need only recall the several Indian-Pakistani wars over Kashmir, or the bloody civil war that led to the creation of Bangladesh out of East Pakistan. The complexity that gives rise to conflict persists, for example, in the Indian state of Assam, which is inhabited by a majority with a distinctive culture, language, and identity. Over the past two decades millions of Bengalis have crossed the border from Bangladesh into Assam. The conflict between Assamese and Bengalis has produced riots, killings, and near-insurrections. Yet this is no simple conflict between two groups, as it is often portrayed. As the microscope enlarges the view, one can see a dozen or more groups, with cross-cutting identities (such as Hindu Bangladeshis and Muslim Assamese) which form shifting alliances. The conflicts in this region exemplify the tragic problems confronting many developing countries in preserving national unity and identity in the face of the diversity of religious, ethnic, caste, tribal, and language affiliations of their populations.

Adapting to the nation-state: creating identity, shifting boundaries, or moving people. Dozens of new nations around the world were suddenly faced with making the territorial nation-state the principal vehicle for the organization of their populations. In Europe, although regional ethnicities, religion, language, and other roots of group identity continue to function as sources of conflict, the ideal concept of the identity of the nation and the folk is well established. In the new countries, however, territoriality was overlaid on societies which lacked the historical roots of nationhood. And so these formerly colonized peoples, as they interact, are caught in the contradictions between the territorial definition of the nation-state and the other bases of their identity.

To resolve these contradictions the new nations typically pursue one or more of three principal strategies: (1) strengthening national identity; (2) redefining their territory; and (3) attracting or expelling certain groups. Their efforts will usually have distinct population effects, sometimes mild, but too often tragic. These consequences include dire migrations of thousands and millions, the direct and induced deaths attendant to international and civil wars, and the lowered reproductive capacity and life expectancy among the people blighted by these events. A thematic outline of these three strategies of adapting peoplehood to nationhood follows.

1. Most new nations, perhaps all, seek to reinforce the national identity and to weaken other affiliations; to form one people out of many. To do this they may use pomp and ceremony, reinterpretations of history, the unifying force of external threats, the adoption of a national language, the discouragement or suppression of non-national identities, the espousing of certain ideologies, and many other methods. Sometimes, when the goal of a single overriding national identity seems too distant, coalitions of diverse groups are sought. In such cases of enforced pluralism, national unity is legitimized by the very fact of the coalition, as a form of social contract. This had been the case in Lebanon before the delicate balance among its peoples so tragically fell apart.

One may hazard the hypothesis that efforts to impose national over other forms of identity generate opposing reactions to preserve the threatened identities. In social processes there is not the certainty of Newtonian physics, and so these opposing reactions may be greater or lesser than the action they oppose. The transition from the nationalism of the Shah to the Islamic reaffirmation of the Ayatollah Khomeini in Iran seems an instance of a greater reaction, while the extinction of Sumatran separatism within Indonesia seems an instance of a lesser one. Trying to kill one identity and build another is tricky business.

2. A second frequent result of the mismatch of peoplehood and

national identities is the reconsideration of national boundaries, either to adjust them or to reaffirm them. Some countries split apart (as did Pakistan), or successfully resist separatism (as when Nigeria held on to Biafra); the territory of others is taken by force (as in the Kashmir dispute), or attempts are made at forming transnational unions (as in the many efforts to create a pan-Arabic nation in North Africa and the Middle East). Attempts to match territorial extension to notions of population identity have not been limited, of course, to the new nations; one need only remember Hitler's rationalizations for annexing Austria and the Sudetenland, or be aware of the broad wave of separatist regional nationalities in Europe today. The struggles to preserve or change boundaries in the new nations are undoubtedly significant for the formal demographics of population counts, growth, and so on, but this is a trivial aspect. More important are the realities of actual population processes, such as dying or migrating, and in the longer run, the social transformations of subpopulations produced by national boundaries, by inclusion or by exclusion, and by defining the meaning of group membership.

3. A third major strategy of nation-building in the face of the contradiction between territorial nations and other forms of identity has been the induced immigration and forced departure of populations. Probably the outstanding instance in modern times is the Zionist movement, which has sought to gather into the nation-state of Israel the multitude of populations around the world which considered themselves Jewish by religion or ancestry. But Israel is not the only case; in a less dramatic manner many developing countries have tried to restore to themselves through immigration, or at least through renewed allegiance, residents of other countries who in a sense share their identity. This includes, for instance, China's courting of the overseas Chinese, particularly those with special skills. Many developing countries likewise try to attract back home those people who, through international educational or commercial success, have become deracinated. Such people are scarce, and they are prized. Rich countries too court their emigrés: France and Spain, for instance, have active programs to support shared identity with former colonies and emigrant enclaves, and look both to geopolitics and to attracting scientists, entrepreneurs, and other scarce human resources. The gathering of the tribe is the objective, and shared identity is the fundamental issue and bait in these cases.

Attracting immigrants of shared identity is, I suspect, far less frequent than is the expulsion of groups which are considered foreign to the national identity. Many of the new nations, soon after independence, have expelled important minorities. These minorities are nearly always better off than the bulk of the national population. They are typically a merchant-professional minority, such as the Chinese in Indonesia or the East Indians in Africa, or a landed aristocracy, such as the British in Rhodesia (now Zimbabwe) or the Dutch in Indonesia. The diaspora may help solidify the national identity of the groups remaining, albeit at the economic cost of losing considerable human capital; as for those expelled, they are likely to find themselves even more foreign in identity at their destination.

The expulsion of one sort of people by another is a harsh way of building a national identity, but it must be remembered that even in modern times genocide has been perpetrated in the name of that goal. Additionally, but I suspect rarely, a change of identity may be offered as an option, as when in the late 1950s Indonesia's Chinese were allowed to remain if they adopted exclusive Indonesian citizenship (in the 1960s, however, they were bloodily persecuted), or, in one of history's grandest examples, when Spain's Jews were offered in 1492 the choice of conversion, emigration, or the stake.

Forcible expulsion and genocide cannot be treated as variants of migration and mortality that would normally fit within the purview of academic disciplines such as economics, demography, or epidemiology. The difference is not just in the ethics of getting rid of people, whether practiced by Germans upon Gypsies and Jews, by Pygmies upon Watusis, by Turks upon Armenians, or by the Spanish Inquisition upon Jews (with the added option of conversion). These events are different from natural deaths and migrations because they reverberate through history, in social memory and myth, defining affinities and hatreds even as they rigidify the categories and the assignation of identities.

In this, human populations are quite different from the animal populations of ecological models. What animal but man would retain for generations the animus from which Armenians conduct a worldwide terrorist campaign against Turks? What animal but man could have fallen into the spiraling complexity and violence in the Middle East which engulfs Israel and its neighbors and threatens to engulf the world? One root of this situation, it must be remembered, was the creation of a nation-state identity for Jews; another is that variants of Islamic identity are spilling over the boundaries of the nation-states of the region.

The problem with the legacy from the European empires to the third world does not lie in the particular arbitrary boundaries drawn for the new nations, for no set of boundaries would have been without flaw. The problem lies inherently in the conflict between the imperially drawn territorial dimension for the new nation-states and the different dimensions of the historic identities of the ex-colonial peoples. In our interconnected world, there probably was no viable alternative to the nation-state, for the principle of organizational symmetry was and is at work. The functional need for reciprocity between interacting institutions leads new and old countries to shape their structures one to another, and to become organizationally similar. And so, for better or for worse, the problematic nation-state has become the principal vehicle for the modern organization of populations, and rich and poor countries will have to work out the contradictions within and among countries.

Population Interactions in the American Empire

Terms such as "American empire," "colonies," and "client states" might sound accusatory; I mean them to be descriptive. No one can disagree that in the nineteenth and early twentieth centuries the United States acted imperialistically, establishing sovereignty over peoples and territory beyond its national boundary. Many then spoke proudly of a new American empire. But empires have fallen into disrepute, and it has become difficult to use such words in a neutral way in talking of America's current actions as a world power. Critics brand American actions as imperialistic with all the negative implications, while those who take a kinder view speak of leadership of the Free World, defense of legitimate interests, geopolitical realism, American sphere of influence, and so forth.

After some agonizing I have decided to retain "empire" and the related terms for two reasons. The first derives from the structure of my argument, which attempts to contrast identities and population interactions in empires before and after World War II. The second reason is that the terms seem to me reasonably descriptive and the more polite alternatives unnecessarily awkward. By the modern American empire I do not mean, of course, the traditional image of military conquest and subsequent subjugation of alien lands and peoples — altogether too simple a version of how the great empires in history were formed and maintained. I do mean, however, the exercise by the United States of extraordinary military, economic, and political power to influence or control the affairs of other countries for its own purposes and interests, in contrast to the Wilsonian ideals of nonintervention and self-determination for sovereign nations. One may reasonably disagree as to the wisdom, justice, or efficacy of such American interventions, but not about their reality.

The American empire: continental expansion. The fundamental premise of the American Revolution, quite openly perceived at the time, was that the identity of the inhabitants of the colonies was different from that of the population of Britain, that the crown could not command their loyalty, and that this justified severing the ties to the British Empire. The Tory loyalists who disagreed for the most part fled to Canada or to the mother country. European observers were surprised at the purported basis of the new American national identity, said to be predicated on political principles — on a social contract — rather than on the commonality of language, religion, history, and ancestry which were supposed to be the foundation of the European nation-states. The simplicities that would define nationhood either as social contract or as folk are no longer tenable, but to this day the nature of American national identity remains elusive although perceivable, and continues to play a role.

"Westward the course of empire," wrote Bishop Berkeley early in the eighteenth century, prophesying in outline the first hundred years of the nation to come. The early United States, in fulfilling what came to be called its Manifest Destiny, expanded by purchases and by military force from the Atlantic to the Pacific. In this period of continental expansion the factor of identity played some curious turns. It was widely expected that democracy, by contrast to European absolutism, would naturally spread throughout the hemisphere, and many believed that as each new land converted to democracy it would join the union, so that eventually the United States of America would naturally spread from the Arctic Circle to Patagonia. But a pride in Anglo-Saxon virtues and achievements existed in the young republic which sometimes translated into racism and exclusion. Could Mexico become a true democracy, or was it fated to fail because of its Catholicism and *mestizaje*? The American identity might be based on democracy based on social contract, but the notion of hemispheric expansion ran into the notion that perhaps the Mexicans were just too different to become Americans.

Similar issues of identity have influenced immigration policy at various times. The story of the National Origins Act (1924) is well known, but even in the nineteenth century, when the rapidly expanding nation needed people and recruited them actively not only in Europe but also in the Far East, racial considerations led to a barring of further Chinese immigration through the Chinese Exclusion Act of 1880, and to such delicate convolutions as the Supreme Court's ruling in 1898 that a child of Chinese parents born in this country was an American citizen and had the right of reentry.

From continental to regional expansion: Puerto Rico and Cuba. In 1898 the United States leaped from continental to transoceanic expansion. Engaging the tottering Spanish empire in the Spanish-American War, the United States emerged with custody of Cuba, Puerto Rico, the Philippines, and the Hawaiian Islands, as well as lesser possessions, and in the decades following the United States was involved in several wars and occupations in Mexico, Central America, and the Caribbean. It is illuminating to contrast the subsequent interactions with two of these acquisitions, Puerto Rico and Cuba.

Puerto Rico was retained as an American colony and its governor was appointed by the U.S. president until 1947. Its status changed in 1952 to the purposefully ambiguous one of "Commonwealth" (the Spanish equivalent is "Free Associated State"). Its people had been granted U.S. citizenship in 1917 and thus had acquired a position comparable to that of the colonial subjects of the British Empire, with the right of emigration to the mainland. In the 1930s Rexford Tugwell, the American governor, was already worried about the rapid rate of population increase in the island and the likelihood that it would spill onto the mainland.

The first elected governor, Luis Muñoz Marín, launched in 1953 a vigorous and widely acclaimed program of industrial promotion (Operation Bootstrap) using tax, operational, and infrastructure inducements to attract mainland firms. The principal attraction, of course, was the prospect of cheap labor within the tariff boundaries of the United States, and the purpose of Operation Bootstrap was to attract labor-intensive industries which would help soak up the vast pool of Puerto Rican surplus labor. But Muñoz Marín's program to deal with the problem of overpopulation had two other less well-known components, one meant for the short range and the other for the long range. The long-range strategy was to reduce population growth by encouraging birth control. Muñoz Marín had long been an advocate of birth control for Puerto Rico, and upon entering office proceeded to encourage public and private programs aimed at reducing the birth rate. This involved, of course, complex negotiations and accommodations with the strong Catholic hierarchy, but it also involved dealing with the reactions and resentments against the manipulative birth control programs of the prior two decades, programs which had been engineered in the Anglo mainland and which had sometimes treated Puerto Ricans as subjects in a laboratory. For the shorter range, Muñoz Marín's strategy consisted of encouraging surplus labor to migrate to the mainland (mostly to New York) by such means as subsidized airfares, and indeed in the 1950–1960 decade Puerto Rico's population remained nearly constant.

Today Puerto Ricans number a bit over 3 million on the island, and slightly over 2 million on the mainland, with a brisk cross-migration. The high expectations held for Operation Bootstrap, hailed at the time as an exemplar for developing nations, have not been fulfilled, and today Puerto Rico remains an island of poverty and unemployment, highly dependent on transfer payments from the U.S. government to feed and house its people. Puerto Ricans on the mainland are also badly off, scoring lower than blacks on most statistical indicators. Fertility in both locations is still high, but lower than before, and life expectancy is higher than before, but lower than that of other groups.

This capsule history of the relations between Puerto Rico and the United States is not meant as a comment on Puerto Rican development policy, but as an illustration of several features of the population interactions between rich and poor countries in a modern empire, although the example has its own particularities. First, with the imperial relation goes a partial common identity, extending in this case to citizenship in and freedom to migrate to the imperial country. Obviously the commonality of identity is far less than total, since Puerto Ricans retain a sense of their peoplehood and Americans often forget that Puerto Ricans are not foreigners; a tell-tale sign of the separateness is that the figure commonly cited for the American population does not include the population of Puerto Rico. Second, sharply lower mortality and sustained high fertility resulted in rapid growth of Puerto Rico's population, much as happened in nearly all of the poor countries of the world. In response, efforts were made to reduce fertility, initiated by the rich country but increasingly supported by local elites. Third, the relation produced a complex pattern of exchanges of population and labor, of technology, of industrial capital, and of transfer payments.

The case of Cuba and the United States is interesting both for its differences and similarities with Puerto Rico. Also won in the war of 1898, Cuba was granted its independence in 1902, but only after guaranteeing special rights to the United States. In pursuit of its interests, the United States intervened militarily in 1906–1909 and in 1917, and again in the attempted Bay of Pigs invasion of 1961, after the establishment of Fidel Castro's government. Cuba's economy and society had grown differently from Puerto Rico's, although they were also thoroughly intertwined with and dependent on the American economy. The economy relied mostly on sugar, tourism, and tobacco for income, and imported foodstuffs, chemicals, and industrial products. Cuba had developed a large professional and business middle class which had become partly Americanized in a number of ways. After the 1959 revolution, Cuba in effect traded its client status to the United States for a roughly comparable one with the Soviet Union. A diaspora of some one million Cubans followed, mostly of this professional and business class. These were the people with which the United States had forged a partially shared identity, and the States took them in — this, we shall see later, is part of a larger pattern of America's relations with its clients.

The refugees concentrated in Miami, the largest American city near Cuba, which already had a small Cuban colony. Fearing a permanent foreign enclave, the government for a time tried a policy of encouraging Cubans to resettle in other parts of the country, but this failed and most Cubans returned to Miami. At the time of the diaspora, Miami was a shabby resort which had twice ridden a boom-bust cycle. The Cuban influx transfigured it. The foreigners who flooded in were for the most part destitute in material goods, but not in capacity, education, or enterprise, and as they began to rise economically and politically, so did the city. Miami became a combined London, Switzerland, and Casbah for Latin America and the Caribbean, and for some aspects of American society. The city became a haven for well-to-do Latin refugees, a hub of international intrigue, a shopping emporium, a banking and business center, a rumor mill and cultural metropolis, and, it must be said, a capital of drug-smuggling, gun-running, and organized crime that shades into paramilitary adventures and the politics of international terrorism. The Cuban diaspora was the catalyst that made Miami into an international metropolis, a manifold in the field of forces of the Western hemisphere, a powerful player in the shaping of their current and future history.

The tangled population interactions between the United States and Cuba took a further and ironic twist in 1980. The Carter administration had emphasized a policy of "human rights" across the world, which included the demand that Cuba allow dissidents to emigrate. Castro's response had the cunning of low farce: he allowed an impromptu flotilla organized by Americans and exiled Cubans to carry off from the port of Mariel over one hundred thousand Cubans to the United States. Most were political dissidents and relatives of Cubans living in the United States, but the Cuban government used the moment to send to the United States between ten and twenty thousand violent criminals, homosexuals, and mentally disturbed individuals. These new arrivals were not the educated political dissidents and freedom lovers that the United States had bargained for.

The upward-striving Cuban community in Miami was also in shock: these were not people like themselves, but lower in class, darker in color, and many of them deviant (color was particularly important because of the three-way tensions among Anglos, blacks, and Cubans in Miami). Should these rejects from Cuba's brave new world be embraced or rejected? Whose people were they? Castro's sardonic move cast into sharp relief many existing contradictions of class, race, and national identity. The way in which Miami's Cubans responded to this dilemma is particularly interesting: they drew an explicit parallel and decided to follow the example of the American German Jews when faced with the later wave of immigration of Eastern European Jews; that is, they decided to embrace them and help them rather than disown them. This, however, did not resolve a fundamental question of identity: whether, after nearly a generation of exile, Miami's established Cubans were part of the United States or merely in the United States.

The shift in geopolitical orientation has also had population repercussions in Cuba, quite aside from the great emigration. The notable improvement in health care since the revolution has reduced the death rate to a very low level, comparable to that of far richer countries. As to fertility, the euphoria of the revolution at first resulted in a rise in the birth rate, but soon the emphasis on female labor participation, on alternatives to the bourgeois family, and on the preeminence of the social over the familial responsibility for the nurture of infants have had the expected effect: a sharp reduction in fertility, which now stands at replacement. Consequently, Cuba does not face a long-term problem of rapid population growth, which is most unusual for a poor country.

The shift in foreign patrons and the 1959–60 diaspora have had interesting consequences for Cuba's population distribution. Havana had been a typical primate city, very large in relation to the national population and the cynosure of intellectual and commercial life. Castro's policy from the beginning sought territorial deconcentration, but Cuba's regional planners were aware of the concentrating tendency inherent in centralized socialist planning, especially in societies with a rudimentary information technology. Because most of those leaving were from Havana, the city was partially depopulated and this, Cuban planners realized, gave them time and elbow-room to avoid the conflict between policies of population decentralization and of centralized control of the economy for at least a generation.

The contrasts and similarities between the Puerto Rican and the Cuban experiences are suggestive. Puerto Rico, whose people enjoy American citizenship, remains a semicolony utterly dependent economically on transfer payments from the United States. Cuba has retained formal national independence, and in the exchange of patrons has become dependent on massive subsidies from the Soviet Union. But in spite of their different trajectories, each of these two colonial experiments has contributed to the U.S. population distinct and self-aware minorities of expatriates (in the range of one to two million each).

The American empire: geopolitics and shared identities. The sphere of power of the United States grew after World War II from a regional to a global scale, but power was not displayed in the old way. Instead of sending a viceroy or a governor to rule a colony, in most cases the United States has dealt with the third world countries as national states through treaties, economic, technical, and military aid, and the like. Of course it has also dealt with them at times in all manner of intrigue, bribing individuals, planting "disinformation," fomenting coups, landing military forces, attempting assassinations, and other arcanae; but formally it has dealt with them as sovereign nations. Indeed, soon after World War II the United States moved to regularize the status of most of its possessions, granting independence to the Philippines, converting Puerto Rico into a Commonwealth or Free Associated State, and conferring statehood on Hawaii and Alaska.

This format of relations among nation-states is not just an American eccentricity, but a pattern that emerged after World War II from the ruins of empires when over a hundred new nations were created. National identities may match poorly with other identities, as noted earlier, but state-to-state is the formal way in which various populations now relate, even in the exercise of imperial power, be it American or Soviet. In 1979, for instance, several Afghani puppet

governments were propped up and knocked down in order to preserve a charade legitimizing the Soviet invasion as a response to a
call for help from a neighboring country. Only under the most extreme circumstances is imperial power shown nakedly.

If one looks at the experience of the American empire in the last
few decades, one is struck by a demographic difference from the
earlier experience of the European empires: the very large immigration from client states into the United States. To be sure, many
European nations have found themselves permanent hosts to substantial numbers of their erstwhile colonials, but the large influx
occurred primarily after the final collapse of their empires, and it is
my impression that even now the relative numbers for Europe are
smaller than for the United States, if we except the difficult case of
Britain and Ireland.

The United States continues to absorb from time to time large
numbers of people from client states. Looking to the recent past, one
thinks immediately of Cuba, Puerto Rico, and Indochina. Other cases
are smaller and less noticed, but still important. Upon the fall of the
Shah, an unknown number (but over one hundred thousand) of
Iranians remained in the United States, and when Ethiopia shifted
its patronage from the United States to the USSR, over ten thousand
Ethiopians were granted residency. (Technically they were granted
"extended voluntary departure.") It is clear that every time there is
a crack in some portion of the American empire, the probability is
high that the United States will receive substantial immigration; in
years to come there is every likelihood that waves of refugees will
arrive from Taiwan, the Philippines, and half a dozen other countries
around the world.

Why should this be? Three reasons come to mind. The first is that
the United States is the only imperial nation, past or present, which
itself developed through immigration, and perhaps this tradition
makes it more inclined to accept such immigrants. The second is
that, in these more technological times, the schooling of colonial
elites in the imperial country is greatly expanded, for it is now
commonly thought that such schooling, beyond imprinting the
shared identity, may improve technical competence. Thus, whenever
some client country is "lost," it is a virtual certainty that a substantial
number of its students and their families will be in the United States.
The third reason, I think, is the most important, although I must
admit that it is speculation. This is that the United States, because it
engages in the formal fiction of equal dealings among sovereign

nations, must deepen the informal commitments of shared identity. It therefore grants to the client populations (usually ruling elites) not merely the well-specified — almost contractual — duties and entitlements common under older overt colonial rule; what it offers is an open-ended, generic relation not based narrowly on specified shared interests and objectives but more broadly on a form of kinship or shared identity: these are our friends, our allies. The formal conventions of national identity seem to require the use of less formal relationships with client groups, reversing the sequence normally postulated in social theories of a shift from community to contract. The effective consequence is that these groups, when threatened by upheaval in their own society, have effective access to residence in the United States, whether they are a few dozen members of a deposed dictator's close circle, some few thousand of an expropriated elite, or some hundreds of thousands of a broader class displaced by structural change in their society.

These reflections have quite concrete expressions in demographic reality, and they in turn influence American foreign policy. Consider, for instance, the current embroilment in Central America, where the United States opposes and tries to subvert the Marxist government of Nicaragua by aiding the counter-revolutionary guerrillas, while at the same time trying to shore up the governments of El Salvador, Honduras, and Guatemala. It is not my purpose to sort out the rights or wrongs of American policy in this region, but only to note some of its demographic dimensions. The Reagan administration has maintained consistently through the years that a principal aim of American policy has been to prevent flows of refugees from this region into this country. Thus, Secretary of State Alexander Haig warned that unless the "radicalization" of Central America were halted, there would be a massive flow of refugees which "will make the Cuban influx look like child's play" (*Boston Globe*, Feb. 23, 1982). President Reagan has stated that "we cannot permit the Soviet-Cuban-Nicaraguan axis to take over Central America . . . The result could be a tidal wave of refugees — and this time they'll be 'feet people' and not 'boat people' — swarming into our country seeking safe haven from communist repression from the south" (*Boston Globe*, June 21, 1983). William Casey, director of the Central Intelligence Agency, held that "the communists would next be looking to Mexico . . . If we have another Cuba in Central America, Mexico will have a big problem and we're going to have a massive wave of immigration. The effort to prevent this happening is not going to excite Americans as much as the threat they would face if things go wrong" (*Boston Globe*, May 16, 1984).

A closer look at Nicaragua's history will show the bearing it has on the issue of identities. In the early decades of its independence from Spain Nicaragua was racked by fierce internal struggles, and the United States, Britain, and (briefly) Mexico competed for its domination. The nation was so institutionally weak that William Walker, an American adventurer, was able to invade it with a small force in 1856 and make himself president. He was deposed the next year, but from then until recently Nicaragua has been totally dominated by the United States. At first the American interest was in a possible Atlantic-Pacific canal; in the event, the canal was built through Panama, but by then American interests had shifted to banana and coffee production for export, making Nicaragua the prototypical banana republic. The Marines occupied and ran the country from 1912 to 1933, and from that time until the 1979 Marxist Sandinista revolution the country was the personal fief of Anastasio Somoza and his sons under American patronage. Nicaraguan society polarized into a small privileged elite, which considered condominiums and vacations in Miami among life's little pleasures, and a very broad base of very poor Indians — the plantation workers and share-croppers.

The problem of national and group identity comes to the fore in the words of the Nicaraguan secretary of agrarian reform: "What guides Sandinism is the conviction that our country, Nicaragua, has never been a country with real sovereignty or national independence. Nicaragua has been an appendage of the United States. We have been abused and humiliated. Nicaragua was kept dependent and backward, a country of illiterate farm laborers. Our function was to grow sugar, cocoa, coffee for the United States; we served the dessert at the imperialist dinner table." Before the Sandinista revolution, "Nicaragua was a fiction — in truth, we did not exist." He identifies the outsiders: "In an act of infinite generosity, we invited the bourgeoisie to join our government. But they had always been against true revolution, and they immediately sought ways to dilute our program. Their aim was to retain a close relationship with the United States and support its imperial designs . . . These people have no business in Nicaragua. They are not Nicaraguans. They belong in Miami" (Kinzer, 1983). The issues of identity, of who we are and who they are, could not be clearer, and the Nicaraguan officials, like their Washington counterparts, view the client group's migration to the United States as a natural phenomenon.

Identity plays various and sometimes odd roles in the population interactions of the American empire. Four additional examples may convey some of the range.

1. For a brief period in 1983 it seemed that negotiations among the United States, Cuba, the governments of the Central American nations, and various rebel groups might stabilize the Central American situation. The United States indicated in this moment of guarded optimism, through a high but unnamed official, that to help achieve a settlement it was willing to consider absorbing as immigrants the counter-revolutionary guerrillas ("contras") it had been supporting as insurgents against the Sandinista government of Nicaragua. Compare this to the warnings of officials on the need to stand tough in Central America to prevent a great flow of refugees into the United States.

2. American military involvement in Korea and Southeast Asia has produced over the past three decades, *inter alia*, some tens of thousands of illegitimate children fathered by American soldiers, many of them black. By all reports these Amerasian children are ostracized and discriminated against in their Asian homelands. Over the years some of these children have come to the United States through adoption, paternal acknowledgment, or under the auspices of charitable organizations, but it was not until the early 1980s that their existence and their plight were publicized. Legislation now exists to ease their migration to this country, but the actual results have been small and the issue seems to have died down. What more searing issue of identity can there be than that of nobody's children?

3. The most bizarre suggestion, to my knowledge, of the uses of identity in the American empire is that recently made by the foreign editor of the *Wall Street Journal*. He proposed in a major editorial that the United States resolve the principal problem in the Middle East by inviting as immigrants 250,000 Palestinians each year for a decade (Lipsky, 1983). The strategy of removing the Palestinians from the conflicted Middle East and converting them into Americans is breathtaking in its daring and simplicity.

4. The sweep and daring of this last proposal is unmatched, except perhaps by another on an issue of less worldwide proportions. For the last several years the United States has experienced a steady influx of illegal immigrants from Haiti, and has been hard put to handle it. In 1982 consideration was given to relocating these Haitians in Belize, a tiny country wedged between Mexico and Guatemala. Belize, it seems, wants to attract immigrants of African descent "to

insure racial and ethnic balance," according to its financial secretary. The present population of Belize is described as half a mix of Hispanic and Amerindian, and half of black ex-slaves imported by the British. The creole French which the Haitians speak is not anticipated to be a problem, because the current population of Belize speaks either Spanish or English (*New York Times*, March 28, 1982).

Such craziness would be funny, except for its tragic aspects.

Ethnic and Family Identities in the Immigration Policies of Rich Countries

In addition to what may be termed political migrations, two other forms of migration can be recognized, although not always unambiguously differentiated; these are economic and familial migration, and the functioning of each of these is also deeply rooted in matters of identity.

Virtually every country, in its immigration practices, gives preference to relatives of its residents. In the United States, for instance, currently the spouses, dependent children, and parents of U.S. citizens are admitted without restriction; other relatives are accepted on the basis of an ordered set of "preferences": first, unmarried children of U.S. citizens; second, spouses and unmarried children of resident aliens; third, married children of U.S. citizens; fourth, siblings of U.S. citizens. (Certain scarce technical workers are given a preference intermediate between spouses and married children of U.S. citizens.)

Here we see at work an operational definition of the aura of identity which emanates from American residents, and bathes their foreign relatives with varying degrees of strength for immigration preference. Spouses, parents, and young children of citizens are awarded full identity, while grown children get somewhat less, especially if married to foreigners, and brothers and sisters less yet. Note that legal resident aliens are awarded a lesser aura, extending only and more faintly to their spouses and unmarried children. Such a classification of degrees of shared identity is, of course, a practical necessity in a country which more people want to enter than it wishes to allow in. Most legal immigrants now enter the United States under this system of familial preferences.

Before the present immigration policy, the United States had another, established in the 1920s, of quotas based on ethnicity or national origins. Its explicit purpose was to preserve the racial and ethnic composition of America's white population, and to discourage those called "the new immigrants." Accordingly, preferential treatment was extended to northern Europeans, with whom this nation presumed a greater shared identity; far less preference was extended to eastern and southern Europeans, and almost none to third world people, except for those from the Americas. The social and political evolution of American immigration policy is richly fascinating, but too complex to summarize here; one may note, however, that throughout its history every effort has been made to adjust it to the construction and preservation of national identity.

Economic Exchanges and Identity

Familial and ethnic identity also plays a role in the type of immigration policy that is more clearly based on economic motives, and it is interesting to contrast the strategies and experience of Northern Europe, Japan, and the United States in this respect.

During the 1960s and until the oil shock of 1973, the economies of most of the developed countries grew rapidly and began to experience varying degrees of labor shortage, some of it absolute and some resulting from the fact that the general prosperity and higher education had made many menial and low-paying jobs unattractive to the nationals of these countries. The rich countries responded by shifts in the composition of their output and, more relevant to our subject, with diverse trade strategies ranging from importing labor to channeling production beyond their borders by exporting capital and technology.

Northern Europe, on the whole, chose to import labor, primarily from countries around the Mediterranean: Portugal, Spain, southern Italy, Yugoslavia, Greece, Turkey, and North Africa. This alien labor force was to be a revolving one and individual workers, of course, were not meant to become permanent residents. This policy might also be characterized as an attempt to export cyclical unemployment from the rich countries to the poor ones. In boom times workers were to be recruited from the periphery, and during downturns these workers were to go home, so that the domestic labor force might be maintained at full employment, good times and bad. At the same time it was expected that these labor exchanges would accelerate development in the sending countries by helping their balance of payments and capital formation through remittances, by reducing their surplus labor, and by giving the guestworkers technical experience and "modern" attitudes that would prove useful upon their repatriation. Thus, it was argued, the exchange would benefit countries both at the center and in the periphery.

Things have not worked out as planned at all. From the point of view of the sending countries there has been precious little increase in modernity or industrial culture from returning workers, who seem to have preferred to become *petit rentiers* rather than entrepreneurs upon returning, and most savings and remittances seem to have been spent on imports of consumer durables rather than on production goods. Neither have things worked out as expected in the labor-importing countries. Many of the foreign workers have gained legal rights as national residents and as union members and have proved difficult to repatriate, even when offered inducements. Far from serving as a cyclical balance-wheel, during the economic slowdown of recent years the unemployment rates among foreign workers in northern European countries have often been lower than those of native women or young people. The net outcome of the policy of importing "temporary" labor has been that the northern European countries, which had been fairly homogeneous societies, have now acquired a substantial minority, apparently permanent, of people quite unlike the native population. The social and political consequences of this economic immigration have been as many, as varied, and as complex as they were in the European countries that had to absorb some of the client populations from their crumbled empires — although, curiously, the leading countries in the guestworker experiment, Germany, Switzerland, and Sweden, happen to have been among the European countries least involved in earlier empires, France being an exception.

The situation poses a wide range of difficulties. First, even when an active policy (including financial inducements) is adopted to encourage guestworker repatriation, as West Germany has done, net immigration may be positive because the residence rights gained by the foreign workers also give them some rights of family completion.

Second, difficult choices are faced in educational policy: if the children of these immigrants are to be permanent residents of Germany or Sweden, they must be taught and acculturated to be like other German or Swedish children; but educating them in their own language and culture, which makes it likelier that they might choose to repatriate, maintains their foreign identity while they remain.

Third, economic democracy, popular in Scandinavian countries, involves workers' participation in economic decisions, a practice based partly on the conception that a common national identity provides a degree of shared identity among the various economic classes and interests. But what happens when upward of 20 percent of the labor force in certain categories is composed of foreign nationals?

Fourth, foreign workers and their families encounter prejudice and discrimination which seems directly proportional to their foreignness or lack of shared identity. Thus in West Germany, East Germans (who are technically refugees, but whose motives in many cases include the economic) are granted citizenship, while the Turks (being the most foreign) are the most disliked and discriminated against by the Germans. Although the higher unemployment rates of recent years have exacerbated the antiforeign animus, polls and statements by members of all of the political parties reveal that the fundamental problem is not economic competition for jobs (which is questionable), but that the foreigners "are not like us." For instance, according to Chancellor Helmut Schmidt, whose position had been on the whole moderate, only those who can "truly fit into our society should be immigrating here" (*Boston Globe*, May 1, 1982). Farther to the right, a large group of intellectuals have signed the Heidelberg Manifesto, to the effect that the protection of the Federal Republic's constitution extends only to the German folk and not to other residents of the national territory.

On the whole, it is a virtual certainty that Northern Europe will not repeat the guestworker experiment. This is not because there may not be labor shortages again in the future, and possible economic advantages in importing a labor force complementary to the domestic one, but because of the dissonance of identities; not because of the harm which discrimination and racism may do to the foreigners, but because the presence of the foreigners generates these evils in the host society. One is reminded of Lewis Thomas's observation that in many diseases, including the great plagues, the problem lies in a perverse overreaction by the host, and "the defense mechanism becomes itself the disease and the cause of death, while the bacteria play the role of bystanders, innocent from their viewpoint" (Thomas, 1979, p. 97).

Japan adopted a strategy diametric to Northern Europe's. When extraordinary economic growth presented Japan with labor shortages, it resorted to exporting capital and technology, dispersing physical production to Taiwan, Korea, Singapore, Latin America, and even to Europe and the United States. It has been absolutely firm about rejecting immigration of any sort, and explicitly devoted to maintaining its racial and cultural homogeneity. Indeed, a high Japanese official was recently quoted as saying that the Japanese have triumphed economically over the Americans because they are not a mongrel society. On the other hand, one problem with this strategy is that the technicians and managers Japan must send abroad, and especially their children, tend to lose some of their cultural identity and to acquire Western values and attitudes which make difficult their reintegration into Japanese society.

It is worth noting that the policy of excluding foreigners extends to political migrants as well. From Japan's imperial past, the only demographic detritus within its national territory consists of some half-million ethnic Koreans, who constitute a low caste within Japanese society and who are segregated in certain areas in Tokyo. In the 1970s, when the United States was pressing Asian countries to accept refugees from Indochina, Japan was quite willing to contribute money for their relief, but not to accept people.

The experience of the United States in the exchanges of labor, capital, and technology is extraordinarily complex and beyond a ready summary, although I touched earlier on some aspects when discussing Puerto Rico. A few aspects of the American demographic relationship with Mexico may serve to highlight the complexity. Illegal immigration from that country is opposed for many reasons, including racism, competition with domestic labor, worries about cultural and linguistic identity, ecological concerns, and a sense that a nation should be able to control who comes across its borders. Whatever the correctness or justness of America's effort to control this population movement, I will only call attention to some facts and dilemmas.

A large but unknown number of Mexicans reside illegally in the United States, including many who migrate temporarily and then return to Mexico. For many years the United States has been trying to formulate an immigration policy to deal with this situation, thus far without success. With respect to the illegals already in this country, it is impracticable to find and expel this vast number of people, and unthinkable that millions should live indefinitely in a country yet outside its law. There is thus general agreement in principle that they must somehow be granted legal residence and eventual citizenship, but no agreement on how to do this. Many Americans fear that if American identity is extended to these illegal immigrants, they will make use of the family preferences in the immigration law to bring in their relatives, and that the present millions will thus multiply several fold. Granting legal residence without rights of family completion would create a second-class citizenship unacceptable to the American legal system. No useful solution has been proposed to this dilemma.

The presence of illegal aliens presents difficult problems. For instance, under present law it is not a crime in the United States to employ an illegal alien, even if it is done knowingly. This is the result of successful lobbying by certain industries, including Texan agriculture, which rely on this source of cheap labor and which, in effect, recruit it clandestinely. Changes in the law now under consideration would make this a felony, but they are being opposed by an unlikely combination of civil rights groups (concerned that it would lead to a national identity card system), of industries which rely on this cheap labor, and of the Chicano leadership, which fears that it will lead to greater discrimination against Mexican-Americans and Hispanics in general. It is this last position which is of interest for the theme of this essay, for it amounts to a fear that rather than being an accepted part of the American polity, Mexican-Americans will have to operate against a presumption of foreignness. This concern is also interesting because there are many illegal immigrants from different countries of Latin America in the United States. They see themselves as very different from one another, but under the pressure of issues such as this begin to see common interests and to forge a common identity within the American plurality under the recently invented social category of "Hispanics."

Mexico's ostensible position has been that its citizens are free to emigrate, even if the migrants may be illegal from an American point of view, but the fact is that the migration has served as a welcome safety valve to Mexico's crushing unemployment problem. The relation of this migration to broader issues has manifested itself in several ways. For years the United States and its allied agencies, such as the World Bank, saw the rapid growth of the Mexican population as the fundamental problem and used both persuasion and threats of withholding development aid to get Mexico to adopt birth control policies. On the other hand, during that brief period of the late 1970s when Mexico felt powerful because of its oil and gas while the United States was experiencing an energy crisis, Mexico sought to link the negotiations for its resources to an accommodation on the migration issue. One cooperative result of the population pressure has been the large development of the Mexican *maquiladora* (piece work) cities along the United States border, where American manufacturers send components for assembly and reimport the finished goods without paying tariffs in either direction, thus taking advantage of cheap Mexican labor while it remains in Mexico.

These few examples from Europe, Japan, and the United States serve to illustrate the diverse roles that identity can assume in the exchange of production factors, including economic migrants. Economic calculation certainly plays a part, but it is not a total determinant. Above a certain number (near zero for the Japanese) the question turns not so much on some economically optimal number of foreign workers but on their foreignness, on the clash of identities, and on the allergic reaction to the foreign presence, with its corrupting pathology of prejudice, discrimination, and racism.

Conclusion

Identities shape and are shaped by the interactions among human populations. This happens in subtle and complex ways, and sometimes dialectically, yet the effects are easy to see. Why then has identity been so neglected in the formal study of populations and their interactions? The answer lies, I think, in the very strengths of the demographic approach, which has the firmest metrics among the social disciplines: demography can *count* births, deaths, migrants, and populations. It can make use of the cardinality of these numbers to perform calculations of great technical virtuosity. But counting is matching the elements of a *well-defined* set to the set of real integers, and the ambiguities of identity fuzz the boundaries of the sets and make it difficult to count and to perform unambiguous operations. This complication does not negate quantitative approaches, but it adds more qualitative dimensions. The projections of well-defined populations by country, region, or social group we see so frequently are useful and necessary, but they give us only a partial understanding. Identities have played a fundamental role throughout human history, and we ignore them at our peril in the consideration of the future of population interactions among the rich and the poor countries of the world.

11

Economics, Politics, and Community

FIVE

International Migration and the International Division of Labor

Juergen B. Donges

IN THE POSTWAR decades until the seventies the economies of the world had been integrating steadily, as world trade grew faster than production and income. The stimulus was the considerable opening of national markets made possible by successive rounds of multilateral trade policy negotiations. Concomitant with the expansion of world trade, capital moved to countries yielding the greatest return, technological advances spread among a rising number of economies, and international migration of labor, at all levels of skills, grew enormously.

Since the seventies, however, the pace of integration has slowed down. Governments around the world, and in particular those of advanced countries, have returned to sectoralism and bilateralism in international trade, thereby increasing protectionism and inviting retaliation by other countries. Large-scale investment flows, in particular those from industrial to developing countries, have become controversial and are frequently obstructed by the implementation (or intensification) of foreign exchange controls and policies of nationalization of private enterprises. Technological nationalism has become more widespread, pitting governments against each other by providing generous aid to domestic high-technology firms and discouraging foreign competitors. Finally, discriminatory treatment of foreign labor, including severe restrictions on further immigration and outright expulsion, is spreading in many developed and developing countries.

Against this background, the purpose of this essay is to trace the roots of the present frictions in the world economy, and thereby to place labor migration in a broader context, one defined by the development of the national economies, the shifts in comparative advantage, and the functioning of the international trading system.

The International Trade Context

As mainstream economics shows, a country's comparative advantage changes in the process of (industry-led) economic development, in which the supply of productive factors grows at different rates. Typically, the accumulation of physical capital outpaces the growth of the labor force, and the supply of skilled labor expands faster than that of workers with low or no qualifications. If price mechanisms are functioning properly, the technological progress is labor-saving and the production pattern will continuously shift toward new and higher-value-added activities, with concomitant moves of the productive factors in the same direction. There is a continuous obsolescence of jobs, skills, installed capacities and locations on the one hand, and a sequence of product and locational innovations with a concomitant absorption of labor and capital on the other. International trade commonly reflects these structural adjustments and transmits them to the various countries, so that the international division of labor among industrial, as well as between developed and developing countries, is in constant flux.

The pattern of international trade in the postwar period fitted this description. Trade barriers were progressively removed in the fifties and sixties following the General Agreement on Tariffs and Trade (GATT) of 1948, especially for manufactured goods, leading to rapid industrial specialization among countries. From 1955 to 1973 world manufacturing production grew by 6.6 percent yearly in real terms, but world trade in manufactures grew by 9.2 percent yearly, raising its share of the total from 50 percent to 65 percent (calculated from United Nations, *Monthly Bulletin of Statistics*, various years). At the same time the composition of this trade shifted toward capital and skill-intensive goods, mainly chemicals, machinery, and transport equipment. These trends are consistent with an industry-led world economic development, and with rising scarcity and cost of labor relative to physical and human capital in the industrial countries.

The industrial countries accounted for the lion's share of this expansion. The similarity of their factor endowments and of levels of development has resulted in a largely intra-industry type of specialization. By contrast, the developing countries have integrated more slowly into the international industrial division of labor and, in spite of the increasing diversification of manufactured exports from the newly industrializing countries (NICs), North-South trade has been characterized by inter-industry specialization, as one would expect from the prevailing differences in relative factor prices and levels of per capita income characterizing both groups of countries.

As long as trade expands in a more or less balanced fashion, shifts in comparative advantage will not necessarily exert pressure for major structural adjustments at an aggregate level. Employment displacement from increased imports is compensated by additional jobs in the export sector and in the sector producing nontradable goods, the net effect depending on the labor intensity of import-competing industries as compared to the other activities. In any case, much stronger overall adjustment pressures can be expected to result from continuing technological innovation, which generally increases labor productivity, and from changes in domestic demand as rising real incomes shift consumption toward capital and skill-intensive goods. A dynamic market economy will almost always have enough labor turnover, process and product innovations, and relocation of activities abroad to respond successfully to external and domestic adjustment pressures. Thus in an increasingly interdependent world, these pressures are a potent and necessary source of sustained economic development with growing employment.

Various government policies can help the adjustment process, by strengthening competition, increasing the mobility of the factors of production (especially labor), and encouraging productive investment. But other policies can retard structural adjustment, as occurs almost inevitably when the government pursues far-reaching social aims (welfare state), when it subsidizes declining domestic industries and protects them against imports, or when it subjects investment to bureaucratic control. Examples abound, both in industrial and developing countries, of government interventions which have reduced cumulatively the capacity of national economies to adjust efficiently to changing circumstances. Many rigidities formed already in the sixties, but these went largely unnoticed because with rapid economic growth structural changes generally produced only a relative decline in the industries adversely affected rather than an absolute one; there really was no challenge to adjust. Since the early seventies the slowing down of economic growth and the ever-increasing unemployment have revealed, especially for Western Europe, that much desirable structural adjustment had been suppressed in the past, resulting in arteriosclerosis of the market process.

When deep adjustments were called for by the oil price shock, new technological breakthroughs, and the aggressive export performance of Japan and a number of NICs, the loss of economic flexibility became manifest, leading to sectoral pressures for public assistance almost everywhere. One government after another, in an attempt to avoid popular discontent and to stay in power, has given way to such demands, either by extending subsidies and trade protection to new branches (as in most industrial countries) or by resorting to import-substitution policies (as in many developing countries). The benefits of making a necessary adjustment are diffuse while the costs are typically concentrated, so that in practice there is no effective counter-pressure in favor of open, competitive markets.

Thus the current trend is toward trying to shift the adjustment burden onto other countries through competing government aids (Tumlir, 1982). It appears that by now more than one-fifth of world trade in manufactures is subject to nontariff restrictions, in some cases covering entire industrial branches (textiles and clothing, iron and steel, automobiles, for instance). Not surprisingly, the rate of growth of world manufacturing exports has been declining since 1976 in real terms, became negative (1 percent down) in 1982, and averaged yearly only 4.1 percent in the period 1973–1982. Sectoral intervention has reduced the structural adaptability of the developed economies, prolonging stagnation with high unemployment, hampering the catching-up of developing countries, and inducing a worldwide misallocation of resources, which includes certain international migrations among its adverse side effects.

Interactions of Trade Policies with Labor Migration

The relations among shifting comparative advantage, trade policy, and international labor mobility are different for industrialized and developing countries. The more developed countries are typically countries of labor immigration; the less developed ones, of emigration. In the industrial countries trade policies are shaped in a response to adverse shifts in comparative advantage; in the developing countries, trade policies are a pillar of the overall industrialization strategy.

The rigidity of the economies of the industrial countries, particularly in Western Europe, originates for the most part in the least liberalized and the most distorted of internal markets: the labor market (Donges and Spinanger, 1983). In the course of creating the modern welfare state politicians and trade union leaders came to believe that the terms and conditions of employment had to be continuously improved to the benefit of the active population (and its families), and that this objective could be achieved at little or no cost. An ever increasing number of laws and regulations, in addition to various social components introduced in collective wage bargaining, led to sticky minimum wages (which are by definition too high), unduly narrowed the wage structure (in spite of existing differences of skills in the labor force), and made it unattractive for many employees to change jobs between firms and regions (they risked losing the accumulated benefits, such as employment security or pensions on retirement).

Under such circumstances the labor market does not react with sufficient flexibility to adverse shifts in comparative advantage. By restricting the imports of labor-intensive products, the governments of the industrial countries can satisfy the interests of domestic workers and entrepreneurs threatened by competition from developing countries, at the expense of the consumers and the nonprotected sectors. As a result, real wages will be higher than under free-trade conditions (as stated by the Stolper-Samuelson theorem), the protected output will increase relatively or absolutely rather than be displaced by imports, and the rate of return to capital in the affected sector will be restored (other things being equal).

Accordingly, the Western governments have at all times been more reluctant to open their markets to labor-intensive products from developing countries than to other manufactures. For instance, the GATT rounds on trade liberalization, including the 1973–1979 Tokyo Round, left higher barriers on the industrial products of greatest export interest to developing countries, most notably textiles and clothing. Another conspicuous example is the Multi-Fibre Arrangement, which first came into force in 1974 (replacing other regulating arrangements going back to 1961) and covers over four-fifths of world trade in textiles and clothing. It has permitted the industrial countries to tailor outsiders' access to their markets by setting global limits on the annual growth of imports and by bilaterally forcing developing country producers to restrain ("voluntarily") their exports accordingly. Even when the industrial countries have granted tariff concessions for manufactures from the developing countries, as under the Generalized System of Preferences established in the early seventies, labor-intensive imports (such as textiles, clothing, and shoes and leather manufactures) are regarded as "sensitive" and are therefore treated in a less preferential manner.

As an alternative response to the loss of comparative advantage, the government may allow a greater, if not completely free, inflow of foreign workers. Immigration increases the total supply of labor, contributes to wage moderation, and thereby slows down the adverse shifts in comparative advantage. This alternative is particularly attractive for labor-intensive industries subject to increased foreign competition precisely because labor has become so expensive at home. Entrepreneurs in these industries might welcome immigration of foreign labor on the grounds that it would allow for a restoration of output and an improvement of the earnings-to-wage ratio (although, as Rivera-Batiz wrote in 1983, the factorial income distribution may remain unchanged under certain conditions).

A policy of labor immigration might appear to be superior to a policy of import protection from an economic welfare point of view. While tariffs and other import-restrictive measures normally reduce the level of welfare in the country applying them, a liberal labor immigration policy tends to increase welfare as Bhagwati (1982) and Sapir (1983) have shown for various conditions of intersectoral mobility of labor and capital. This is because a policy which increases the inflow of foreign workers does not involve a consumption-distortion cost (a loss of consumer surplus), whereas trade protectionism does. In the real world, however, governments generally do not choose between the import-protection and the labor-immigration options. On the contrary, they tend to restrict "sensitive" imports and to allow at the same time for a greater though regulated entry of foreigners, or to restrict severely the importation of both goods and labor.

The first option is likely to be chosen when the economy grows fast, the degree of capacity utilization is high, and the supply of native labor is inelastic. While such conditions prevailed, most governments of the advanced countries maintained moderate immigration systems, up to the limits of their prevailing tolerance (Kubat et al., 1979). As long as the consequences are concentrated in certain industries and regions, the corresponding interest groups (entrepreneurial associations, labor unions, municipal officials) will lobby for trade protection. This protection makes other sectors worse off, but if log-rolling in the political market works, those sectors can be compensated by increasing the total labor supply through immigration, in accordance with the needs of various segments of the domestic labor market. The lower the elasticity of substitution between foreign and domestic workers, the less labor unions will oppose such an immigration policy, and they may even consider it helpful in facilitating the progress of domestic workers up the income ladder. This view assumes that the aliens are willing to take low-paying jobs however unpleasant they may be, in view of their typically poor skills. It follows therefore that under a favorable macroeconomic environment, trade protection will be joined with a policy of immigration to be determined largely by the labor demand of individual industries, as has been shown empirically for West Germany (Bhagwati et al., 1983).

By contrast, in a stagnating economy with soaring unemployment, the political forces do not work in favor of a government-brokered compromise among sectoral interests. Not only will firms regard imported labor-intensive manufactures as close substitutes for their products, but workers across industries (including the first-generation immigrants) will see immigration as a threat to their jobs. The overall pressure will therefore be toward restricting both the importation of labor-intensive manufactures and the inflow of foreign workers; this has in fact happened almost everywhere during the last ten years (UN, 1982). Growing trade protectionism and immigration restrictions in the advanced countries have the same root: the widespread refusal to adjust to shifting comparative advantage.

For the sending (typically developing) countries, the interaction of trade policy and international labor movements is of a different nature. Suppose that a country industrializes according to its comparative advantage, and that this is determined by a highly elastic supply of labor. Its emerging activities will have a relatively high labor-capital ratio (within the limits of efficient factor substitutability), and its overall output mix will favor labor-intensive products. The growth of its industrial production will expand employment opportunities, all the more so as it is oriented to world markets where an open international trading system exists. If for demographic reasons the domestic labor force is growing very fast, the emerging local industry may not create enough job opportunities, so that emigration becomes an alternative to unemployment or underemployment at home. But in general, "pull" rather than "push" factors will determine the degree of emigration; noneconomic motives apart, migrants will be moved most prominently by the expectation of higher earnings, of gaining skills, and of benefiting from a wide range of public services abroad.

The situation changes when a government's industrialization policy leads to an allocation of resources which does not suit the country's comparative advantage. The basic reason for policy makers to neglect, quite deliberately, comparative-costs criteria is their belief that a rapid and sustained rate of industrial (and overall economic) production is possible only if industrialization, which typically and easily starts with the production of nondurable consumer goods, moves onto "modern" durable consumer, intermediate, and investment goods. Static allocative efficiency is sacrificed for the expectation of dynamic external economies and of international competitiveness in a wide range of new activities in the future. Consequently, the industrialization policy is built around import substitution across the board. The cost disadvantages between the new domestic producers and the original foreign suppliers are neutralized by tariff and quantitative restrictions on imports, which in general are kept longer than would be justified on infant-industry grounds. The widening and premature deepening of the productive structure makes for a capital intensity in the manufacturing industry higher than would be the case if price mechanism were allowed to operate more effectively. Moreover, the import-substituting firms (both domestic and foreign ones) have little incentive to adjust technology to existing labor abundance, since the exchange rate overvalues domestic currency and thereby keeps the price of imported capital relatively low (apart from other distortions of the factor-price relationship, such as interest subsidies and minimum wages).

A great number of empirical studies (surveyed in my 1983 article) show that import-substitution strategies, as applied in most developing countries including Southern Europe during most of the postwar era, not only failed to realize the economic growth which would otherwise have been possible, but also dampened considerably the capacity of the economy, particularly in the newly established manufacturing industries, to absorb the available indigenous labor. Under such conditions, unemployment becomes chronic and the lack of jobs in their country induces workers to emigrate, the direction of the migration depending on the location of economic growth poles and the ease of crossing the borders of the potential countries. Contrary to the case discussed earlier, push factors now dominate pull factors. One may view in this light the migration of workers from North

Africa and Southern Europe to Central and Northern Europe, from the Commonwealth countries to Great Britain, from Mexico and the Caribbean Islands to the United States, from Sub-Saharan Africa to the Republic of South Africa, or from India and Thailand to Singapore. One may even think of the possibility that the earlier open-door policies of immigration countries have generated a "moral hazard" in the sense of taking the pressure off the governments of developing countries to pursue policies which aim not only at rapid economic growth but also at creating employment opportunities in line with job demand, let alone taking the pressure off the need for population control policies.

This analysis can be taken further by including the interactions with international capital movements. In theory, capital flows between countries depend on differences in the real rates of return (defined in the broadest sense), which obviously are influenced, among other things, by shifts in comparative advantage. Once Western governments restrict labor-intensive imports, they raise the profitability of investment in the protected industries, retarding locational innovations in the form of investment in the country where the competing imports come from. In the developing countries, on the other hand, the many distortions created by their governments' own protectionist import-substitution policies, particularly the overvaluation of local currency, discourage many potential foreign investors and induce those who nevertheless come to internalize (just as domestic firms do) the protection-related economic rents rather than to develop jobs.

It thus appears that the considerable international labor migration from developing to developed countries that took place up to the early seventies can be interpreted as an increasing integration of national labor markets concomitant with an insufficient integration of national commodity markets and national capital markets (Hiemenz and Schatz, 1979). Both the developed and the developing countries experimented with wrong patterns of specialization rather than with efficient ones. Shifts in comparative advantage, which in a framework of competitive and open markets would have given rise to new patterns of world trade, in the context of protection-ridden economies had to be expressed in a greater international labor mobility. In relation to one another, the developed countries maintained an undervalued currency, the developing countries an overvalued one. Consequently, gains from trade between the two groups were lost, whereas the welfare and growth effects of increased international labor migration were, and are, uncertain for reasons that will be discussed in the following section.

Economic Gains and Costs of Migration

Generally speaking, international labor migration has long been considered to have net positive effects for both sending and receiving countries. The sending countries benefit from: less unemployment at home (thereby raising the overall productivity and avoiding social unrest); remittances of foreign exchange by the emigrants (thereby increasing the capacity to import and helping to overcome typical balance-of-payments constraints on economic development); reduced demand for scarce food and other basic goods and services (thereby freeing domestic savings for growth-oriented investments); and workers' learning or improving their skills while abroad (thereby ameliorating the development bottlenecks arising from a lack of human capital). In the receiving countries the benefits of inflow are: keeping wage pressures in check (thereby making for a greater price stability at high levels of employment); increasing the flexibility of the labor market, as the foreign workers revealed a considerable intra- and interregional mobility (thereby improving the responsiveness of the economy to structural changes); settling regions with a low density of population (including the border areas); and widening the availability of human capital without incurring costs of education (when highly skilled persons immigrated).

Positive effects of this sort are easy to identify, though they certainly vary from country to country. We may also hypothesize, however, that international labor migration, which is induced by protectionist trade policies, is a somewhat mixed blessing. It may be profitable privately, but not necessarily socially.

In the receiving countries, for example, the greater elasticity of labor can delay structural changes in the economy, lead to an over-agglomeration of activities, contribute to an excessive expansion of the conventional tertiary sector (in particular the public sector), and slow down the increase of per capita income, as in West Germany during the sixties when the number of foreign workers increased so rapidly (Schatz, 1974, pp. 202–217). Moreover, additional investments in infrastructure are required to meet specific needs of the immigrants (in particular housing and school education for their children), which increase public expenditure. Public budgets must also cope with the additional social benefits paid to foreign employees, such as the allowances for their dependent children — and they are likely to have more children than native workers do.

Even worse, in a situation of widespread unemployment the presence of alien workers could be regarded by many as destructive, even if the immigrants are noncompeting or not numerous. The anxiety of unemployment breeds xenophobic or racial sentiments among the indigenous population and gives rise to discriminatory treatment of the aliens, which is bound to cause strong political reactions from concerned sending countries. The present-day frictions between West Germany and Turkey are a case in point. Illegal immigration (Mexicans into the United States) or rapidly increasing numbers of people seeking asylum on debatable political grounds (Africans in West Germany) compound defensive actions in the receiving countries, as do fears within the native population about cultural conflicts and violations of law and order. In this kind of environment, the governments of the receiving countries (right-wing as well as left-wing) will push immigrants to agree to repatriate (using financial incentives), severely restrict attempts of aliens to launch any private enterprises, and rigorously oppose any new entry of foreign workers at all. The industrial countries will exert political pressure on the governments of the sending countries or bribe them with financial aid to discourage further emigration of their citizens, just as they frequently do in manufactures trade to reduce import competition (via the so-called voluntary export restraint agreements).

From the point of view of the sending countries, one can conceive of at least four factors that may cause the expected benefits from emigration to fade away. First, the immigrants may return, voluntarily or under compulsion, at a time when employment opportunities in their homelands are scarce at given real wage levels, so that the level of unemployment increases further, as is occurring currently.

Second, the remittances of foreign exchange may fall short of expectations. The emigrated workers will not transfer the savings when the domestic currency in the home country is overvalued and under foreign exchange controls. Sometimes remittances are affected by restrictions of capital exports in the country of settlement, as applied in the United States, Great Britain, and France from time to time. Another reason is that many emigrants and their families become permanent residents or nationals of their country of settlement, losing the sentimental and moral bonds to their country of origin.

Third, the expected improvement in the level of skills may not accrue to the home country because many of the emigrated workers (and their children) either do not acquire higher skills at all or learn skills that do not fit the requirements in the domestic economy; and many emigrants who have upgraded their skills do not return unless forced to do so. Those who do return are frequently less efficient at home than they were abroad owing to differences in the social environments.

Fourth, the returning emigrants can trigger unanticipated negative consequences: by maintaining a semblance of the modern lifestyles they have learnt (houses, automobiles, consumer electronics, clothes) they make those who never emigrated feel discriminated against; they may also press for unsustainable wage increases or abandon their village to become unemployed elsewhere.

Other problems arise in connection with the international migration of skilled manpower or human capital. Qualified people (not only workers but also businessmen, engineers, scientists, doctors, nurses, teachers, and other specialists) have always had a high degree of international mobility. While the numbers of such migrants are small by comparison with those of the unskilled, the economic implications and the direction of this migration are important. When qualified people move from the advanced into developing countries, the weaker economies benefit. Additional human capital, together with the inflowing foreign capital and technology, has a positive impact on the rate of economic development. The best-known examples are the migration (and investment flows) from Europe to North and South America and to Australia during the nineteenth and much of the twentieth century. The more recent migration of Chinese and Indian businessmen to Southeast Asia and East Africa also fits this model.

The situation is reversed when highly qualified people emigrate from developing into industrial countries (mainly to North America, Great Britain, and France), including international organizations such as the UN, World Bank, IMF, and GATT. This trend, apparently accelerating since the 1950s, reflects the rapidly increasing creation of human capital in some developing countries (most notably in India) and more liberal immigration regimes for qualified people than for unskilled labor in a number of advanced countries, most notably the United States, Canada, and Great Britain. From a cosmopolitan point of view, this migration may be regarded as the rational behavior of citizens who choose in freedom where to work. Yet it is widely held that thereby the developing countries suffer a "brain drain," losing a production factor which is still scarce there, whereas the addition to the useful stock of human capital in the receiving countries is small, particularly if these migrants do not use their specialized skills — for example, teachers working in construction or as taxi drivers. Furthermore, it is argued that the out-migration of skilled labor constitutes a "reverse transfer of technology" toward the industrial world. This view implies adverse allocative, growth, and distributive effects for the sending countries.

In theory, the effects of the brain drain are not straightforward. One can conceive of (strong neoclassical) conditions under which the emigration of skilled labor has no ill effects on the population staying at home (Grubel and Scott, 1966). The most important assumptions are that markets are competitive, that the skilled individuals earn the social marginal product of their work, and that the size of the public sector in the economy is small. Then, as long as the human capital per emigrant equals the average physical and human capital per worker, the emigration will not lead to a reduction of the total capital productivity and will not affect the salaries of the skilled and unskilled workers remaining behind; the migrants just take their marginal product along and do not claim any remuneration out of the national income.

However, once the strong neoclassical assumptions are removed and market imperfections, externalities, structural rigidities in the labor market, and distributive aspects are taken into account, the emigration of skilled people can lead to a reduction of the per capita income of those left behind in the country of origin, contribute to unemployment among the professionals (because the expectation to emigrate into higher-salary countries will induce more people to learn the skills than the domestic economy can absorb), and perpetuate wage differentials between rich and poor countries (Bhagwati, 1976). In such a situation, corrective measures would seem to be justified, but care must be taken not to create additional problems. For example, government restrictions or prohibition of emigration would violate fundamental civil rights and probably demoralize domestic labor. The same holds true if citizens are allowed to emigrate only after they repaid the costs of government-financed education and training; such a requirement taxes the international movement of human capital and can be misused for political purposes (as the Soviet Union did, in 1972, against her Jewish citizens who wanted to emigrate to Israel, and as Rumania practiced until 1983 against her citizens of German origin in Transylvania who wished to emigrate to West Germany). Even the well-known Bhagwati proposal to levy an additional tax on the income of the skilled foreign nationals in the receiving country, the revenue to be used for development projects in the poor countries, seems to lack a compelling rationale; it would be hard to implement both politically and technically.

Whether or not the emigration of skilled people adversely affects the country of origin is an empirical question. Policy makers, led by their own intuitions and by casual empiricism, are often tempted to take the adverse effects for granted, particularly in the developing countries. But much more in-depth case studies are needed to get a better understanding of this complex effect. A particular country may be turning out an excess supply of skilled labor (academic proletariat); or the skilled people may behave in destructive ways (when they engage in revolutionary activities or terrorism, for instance). Possibly the home country has neither a congenial intellectual climate nor an adequate research infrastructure to allow scientific talents to prosper; or the emigration may be a consequence of domestic political upheaval, not to mention repression and persecution for ideological, religious, or racial reasons. It should also be noted that the professionals who emigrate may nevertheless work to the benefit of their countries of origin; in frequent instances they choose an area of endeavor that suits the basic needs of their homelands (tropical medicine or high-yielding seeds under the "green revolution" in agriculture, for instance) or they become consultants in development projects (mainly through international organizations). And finally, the brain drain that does occur might be marginal, considering that the observed annual flows amount to less than 1 percent of the stock of skilled labor (and of human capital) in most countries of emigration.

Bringing the Capital to the Workers

Under today's policies of protectionism and immigration restriction international migration flows are economically suboptimal, so a strong case can be made for moving capital rather than people across national frontiers. Although this would not put a stop to migration driven by the push factor of poverty, it would have some positive effects. Increased foreign investment in the developing countries by the industrial and the capital-surplus OPEC countries could accelerate the structural changes under way in the world economy.

The industrialization of developing countries will maintain the momentum of change in the international division of labor. The first generation of NICs, which specialized in labor-intensive manufactures for export, has already found imitators in recent years, assuring increasing competition for those products in the United States and Western Europe. Though export growth might promote more trade among the developing countries themselves, the greatest absorption capacity is still within the advanced countries of the West. Consequently Western industries must adjust if they want to survive. The redeployment of production to developing countries, where labor costs are lower, is one possible choice for such adjustment; product and process innovations are alternatives. It might be more advantageous for the developing countries to have industries from the advanced countries move in and create new jobs on the spot than to speculate on the possibility that labor will emigrate to find employment abroad — all the more since the advanced countries have tightened immigration controls, including those over illegal immigration, and some countries have established discriminatory official or de facto national or racial quotas.

New technological developments such as microelectronics, industrial robots, and biotechnology, together with the continuing shift toward the modern service sector in the advanced countries, carry important implications for the structure of their labor demand. First, they imply that the main effort is directed toward new lines of skill- and brain-intensive activities. Second, increased automation of the production process will be at the expense both of conventional machines and of craftsmen's muscles and dexterity. Routine jobs hitherto filled by unskilled or semiskilled labor will become redundant, whereas employment opportunities will widen for people who adapt to the new technologies. Under these conditions jobs for unskilled foreign workers will be scarce in the industrial countries, particularly if technology reduces overall employment, thus strengthening the case for creating more employment in the countries of emigration with the help of foreign investment.

Economic theory suggests, and many empirical studies support, that foreign investment has the potential to convey net benefits to host countries in the form of foreign exchange earnings, tax revenues, technological and managerial know-how, output growth, and employment opportunity including on-the-job training (Frank, 1980). However, the topic of foreign investment in developing countries has become a highly sensitive, two-edged issue. On the one hand, many developing countries are keen to bring in as much foreign capital as possible and frequently compete with each other for it by offering far-reaching incentives even at the risk of bidding away some of the potential gains. On the other hand, various spokesmen for the developing countries persistently demand the implementation of restrictive "codes of conduct" for foreign investors, multinational enterprises in particular, and they threaten expropriation of their investments according to national rather than international law, possibly with only token compensation. If potential foreign investors become fearful, capital flows from industrial to developing countries will fall short of what is necessary for accelerated economic development at high levels of employment, and for obtaining needed technology. The pressure to emigrate would not abate in that case.

Many people take for granted the benefits of private foreign investment and deplore, with often merely anecdotal evidence, its negative economic and noneconomic effects. While some concerns are quite legitimate, the critics unfortunately give little consideration to the possibility that the harmful effects might result from ill-advised economic policies of the host governments. Many criticisms follow the "nirvana approach" of comparing a real situation with an ideal or a utopian one. A nationalistic and xenophobic approach to cost assessment often prevails, as in the case of foreign workers in the advanced countries, whom some politicians and intellectuals blame for economic and sometimes even political difficulties.

When the issue is the transfer of technology, the critics resent that knowledge is not treated as a "public good" and cannot be had free of charge by the developing countries; they also complain that the foreign technology is not appropriate to conditions of abundant unskilled labor and small markets. Even admitting the existence of imperfections in the technology market, these allegations suffer from basic flaws. They fail to take into account that the production of knowledge, which is an important engine of growth for the world economy, depends among others on the ability of private firms to appropriate rents for their past investment in research and development. Equally, if they could obtain technical know-how from abroad at little or no cost, the developing countries would probably not be stimulated to intensify their own research and development activities. Their technological dependence would be perpetuated and the temptation to use only the most modern technology, which typically is labor-saving, would be reinforced, thereby fueling the push factors for emigration. In actuality substantial possibilities for labor and capital substitution exist in manufacturing as well as in agriculture. Often this potential is not used owing, to a considerable extent, to constraints on the demand and the supply side in the developing countries themselves (Ranis, 1979). Distorted factor prices and the lack of competition, among other things, restrain the demand for appropriate technology. The main indigenous supply constraints are lack of information about technologies and the bias of science and technology institutes for large-scale advanced technology. Under such circumstances the responsibility for improving the suitability of imported technology rests with the governments of the developing countries themselves.

All these aspects have been discussed in detail in the literature, but they are crucial nowadays because huge amounts of risk capital are needed everywhere, not only to carry out the normal amount of structural adjustment in the national economies, but also to cover the requirements stemming from the prolonged recession and the ongoing deep changes of the international division of labor. It is still a matter of controversy whether or not the worldwide supply of risk capital will be much scarcer in the eighties and nineties than in past decades. But it is a fact that the competition among countries for capital has already become stiffer. Many developing countries may find it difficult to obtain as much foreign private capital as they want even if their marginal productivity of investment is relatively high. In particular the burden of debt accumulated in the recent past, especially if due to inefficient domestic economic policies, will limit future private capital inflows from abroad. However, the more efficiency-oriented and forward-looking its economic policies are, the more attractive for foreign capital a developing country should be. In this case the emigrants may be encouraged to make their savings available for productive investment in their country of origin, although experience shows how difficult it has proved to do this (Körner and Werth, 1981).

An additional problem is the protest by organized interest groups in the industrial countries against growing private investment abroad, particularly when governments favor such outflows. As long as the national economy grows rapidly, the level of overall employment is high, and the balance of payments is in equilibrium, the public shows little concern about domestic firms investing in other industrial countries or in the third world. But in periods of high unemployment labor unions and others argue that this capital outflow replaces domestic investment and export production while strengthening competition, especially from developing countries. The outward flow of capital "exports" jobs and adds to domestic unemployment. Moreover, as already mentioned, some governments are inclined to restrict capital outflows when their countries suffer persistent balance of payments deficits, despite the floating exchange rate system prevailing since 1971.

Although the scarcity of empirical research hampers effective discussion, the statement that investment abroad creates employment there and not in the home country is merely trivial. In a world of continuous shifts in comparative advantage, the "exporting jobs" hypothesis is not as conclusive in practice as it appears at first sight. First, outward foreign and domestic investment are not necessarily substitutes, but can be complementary to each other, in such a way that capital outflow can improve rather than reduce employment opportunities in the home country. Second, exporting firms may find that to maintain or increase their shares in international competitive markets they must establish plants in the importing countries and come closer to the user. Among other things, this can reduce transportation costs, enable them to adjust quickly to the changing preferences of buyers, improve their chances for government purchasing contracts, and reduce their vulnerability to tariff and other barriers. Investment abroad may also lead to the development of new markets for exports of intermediate products and capital goods used as inputs by the newly established plants. This would contribute to employment in the home country, though not necessarily only within the parent company, assuming the needed regional and sectoral labor mobility. Investors would not be limited to investment at home for export or investment abroad, but would have the broader choice between investment and noninvestment.

Finally, the decision to invest abroad, particularly in a developing country, may constitute an appropriate response to greater import competition based on an adverse shift in comparative advantages. In this case, the outward foreign investment would not destroy domestic jobs because these are already economically obsolete; jobs of this sort could only temporarily be protected through import restrictions, though at the expense of employment opportunities in the more viable national industries.

All in all, government policies in advanced countries that aim to discourage capital outflows for reasons of job preservation run the risk of counterproductive results. It makes more sense, given the state of knowledge about the domestic impact of outward foreign investment, to construct a policy framework in which government incentives are basically neutral as between investment in the local market and investment abroad.

Conclusion

This essay delineates in brief some aspects of the interaction of international trade and the movements of labor and capital. To be sure, further conceptual and empirical research remains to be done. But it should already be clear that international labor migration is not a panacea for relieving poverty and solving the problems of underdevelopment in the third world. Neither would the present economic stagnation and chronic unemployment in the developed countries be overcome just by cutting off immigration.

The thrust of my argument leans heavily on factual observation. The unprecedented levels of prosperity throughout the industrialized world in the fifties and sixties were based on worldwide exchanges of goods and services, capital and manpower, promoting specialization, and overcoming the narrowness of domestic markets. This orientation also permitted other countries to progress up the scale of economic development, most spectacularly Japan and the Asian and Latin American NICs. And it made an important contribution to peaceful coexistence between societies.

It cannot be remarked too often how much the nature of global framework for trade and factor movements has deteriorated since the early seventies, to the point of serious danger of disintegration of the world economy. If nothing is done to reverse the downward slide, economic recovery in the industrialized world and sustained economic development in the third world will become improbable, and economic warfare and political disputes among governments most probable. It is worth recalling the twenties and thirties to realize where this route can lead. Because the world economy is more integrated now, the potential for disaster is much greater. Such grim prospects ought to be a challenge for governments to rebuild a system of liberalized international trade and factor mobility based on the principle of nondiscrimination, transparency, and stability of rules. Given their strength in the world economy, the advanced countries — especially the United States, the European Community, and Japan — should take the lead.

Equally important, and complementary to concerted international action, governments in both industrial and developing countries must strive vigorously for greater efficiency in their pursuit of economic and social objectives. Some countries have introduced or are introducing the policy changes needed; more countries have to follow. Only thus is there a good chance that competitiveness in trade will be enhanced, that the worldwide allocation and use of capital will be improved, and that the intercountry migration of labor will be stabilized — with a view to a widely shared global recovery and sustained world economic growth of benefit to all.

SIX

Social Integration and Cultural Pluralism: Structural and Cultural Problems of Immigration in European Industrial Countries

Hans-Joachim Hoffmann-Nowotny

MIGRATION from the Mediterranean basin and from third world countries brought to central and northern European countries a heavy influx of ethnic groups socially and culturally different from the native population. This immigration, based exclusively on economic considerations (as far as the immigration countries are concerned), has had many unforeseen and unintended consequences (Rist, 1980). "We called for labor, and human beings came" (Frisch, 1967, p. 100) sums them up in one sentence. The so-called rotation principle (a foreign worker would come for a few years, return home, and be replaced by another immigrant) has not stood the test of reality. Instead of going back the foreigners stayed; for the return they substituted a "Heimkehrillusion" (illusion of return) (Braun, 1970, ch. 5). The share of foreigners staying for good has increased greatly since the beginning of the seventies, when free immigration came to a halt in all host countries. European immigration countries thus face the prospect of having to live with large ethnic minorities and with the resulting social tensions.

Most of the receiving countries still deny the permanence of the immigration, with only a few exceptions, such as Sweden and the Netherlands. Instead of "immigrants," the newcomers are called "foreign workers," "guestworkers," "foreign employees," or "migrant workers." Consequently immigration policies are not well defined, and a situation that has lasted for about thirty years remains "provisional."

The outline of Europe's immigration that follows will set the stage for a discussion of its structural and cultural problems. The social, cultural, and political consequences of immigration will be interpreted in terms of a sociological theory that will account for *the interdependence of social integration and the cultural heterogeneity of ethnic minorities.* The theory is, I believe, a general one, related to fundamental sociological issues and applicable to situations outside Europe.

Immigration to Europe after World War II

Migration must be viewed along two basic theoretical dimensions: structure and culture. World society, the context of international migration, is a stratified structure, and modern migrations usually occur across the development gaps between its levels (Hoffmann-Nowotny, 1970, 1978, 1981). A development gap is a necessary but not a sufficient condition for migration: several other prerequisites must be met.

A certain degree of cultural homogeneity or integration is necessary for would-be migrants to perceive development gaps, compare their actual situation with a potential one, and decide to migrate. This cultural integration includes shared modern acquisitive values like "development" or "standard of living." At the same time that migrants learn to look beyond their societies of origin, however, the problems of underprivileged groups and regions become problems for the larger system, which has to deal with the claims of the underprivileged for their share of goods according to common values.

To improve their situation the underprivileged face two possibilities: collective action and individual mobility. The high level of emigration from the less developed parts of Europe, Turkey, and North Africa to highly developed European countries suggests that millions of people are no longer willing to wait for the success of collective efforts in their home countries and that they prefer to act individually by migrating. Migrations create ethnic, racial, and class problems as soon as the newcomers penetrate ethnically different and more highly developed groups (Campfens, 1980; Crum Ewing, 1975; Esser, 1980, 1982; Hoffmann-Nowotny, 1974; Nauck, 1983; Korte, 1982; Waltner, 1982; Schmidt, 1981). On the other hand, their arrival is advantageous to the stronger economies. Because of their developmental lead and capital accumulation, the highly developed countries are able to recruit foreign workers, who are seen as a kind of industrial reserve army by the political authorities, by entrepreneurs, and by a broad segment of the native work forces.

A self-evident prerequisite for migration is that the potential immigration countries be accessible, both legally and geographically. The European countries fulfilled this condition when they began to open their borders for immigrants in the 1950s, even recruiting actively in emigration countries. As these immigration policies continued into the early 1970s, the number of migrants increased rapidly (Hoffmann-Nowotny, 1978).

While the general flow of migration follows development gaps, the distribution of emigrants from different countries among immigration countries is uneven. Migration spurts vary considerably in duration and size between particular sending and receiving countries (Hoffmann-Nowotny, 1978). Geographic distance and historic factors are, of course, important determinants. In the postwar years, for instance, Italy, the classic emigration country, accounted for the largest share of migrants to the major immigration countries (Germany, France, Belgium, and Switzerland), but Italian immigrants have lost this leading position except in Switzerland and Belgium. Yugoslav immigrants made up the largest share for a while in Germany, but they have now been replaced by the Turks. In France, the share and the absolute number of Italians has decreased; today the Portuguese make up the largest share, closely followed by the Algerians. In Belgium, the share of Italian immigrants has decreased but they are still the largest group. This is also the case in Switzerland, where the Yugoslav and the Turkish shares are increasing.

The number of migrants and their share of the population in European industrial countries increased greatly from 1960 to 1980, and in most cases even from 1970 to 1980 (see Table 6.1). Except for Liechtenstein and Luxembourg, Switzerland had the largest share of foreigners (15 percent), and the absolute number of its immigrants tripled from 1950 to 1960 and doubled again from 1960 to 1974. In 1980 Belgium's share of foreigners in its population was 9.2 percent, France's 7.7 percent, and the German Federal Republic's 7.2 percent, or 4.5 million.

From 1951 to 1961 the number of immigrants in Germany was almost stationary, but it increased by 600 percent between 1961 and 1974. This does not mean, however, that until 1961 Germany had no need for immigrants. Rather, in that decade Germany (or the three zones occupied by the Western powers) took in about 10 million people expelled from the former German East, and later on took in about 3.5 million refugees from the German Democratic Republic; these people were not officially considered foreign immigrants. After the construction of the Berlin Wall in 1961 the large flow of refugees

Table 6.1. Agricultural and industrial annual growth rates, 1960–1980 (percentages averaged by decade)

Country	Agricultural		Industrial	
	1960–1970	1970–1980	1960–1970	1970–1980
Algeria	0.1	3.1	11.6	7.9
Colombia	3.5	4.9	6.0	4.9
Greece	3.5	1.7	9.4	5.3
Mexico	3.8	2.3	9.1	6.6
Morocco	4.7	0.8	4.2	6.6
Tunisia	2.0	4.9	8.2	9.0
Turkey	2.5	3.4	9.6	6.6
Yemen A.R.	NA	3.7	NA	14.7
Yugoslavia	3.3	2.8	6.2	7.1

Source: World Bank, 1984

suddenly stopped and the expanding German economy was forced to recruit foreign immigrants (see Table 6.2). If the mass influx from the East did count as immigrants, the Federal Republic of Germany would have absorbed the largest number of immigrants since the war, both absolutely and relatively.

The thesis that migrants move across development gaps applies to Spain and Italy as immigration as well as emigration countries. Both have received immigrants from still less developed countries. Besides Portuguese immigrants in Spain, both countries have a considerable number of immigrants from North Africa. These are statistically nonexistent, however, because they enter the country illegally. The same situation occurs in Greece.

As a consequence of economic recession and restrictive immigration policies, legal labor migration came more or less to a halt in the early 1970s. Since then some workers have returned, but legal immigration has continued mainly on grounds of family reunification. Illegal immigration has increased, and the number of persons asking for a refugee status has risen dramatically. Thus, although accessibility has been curtailed, the brake this put on migration has been imperfect given the existence of the other two prerequisites. The situation is parallel to that of migration from Mexico to the United States.

Table 6.2.   Workers abroad as percentage of total national labor force of exporting countries, 1973–1974

Exporting country	Migrants (percentage of active population)
Algeria	19.5
Greece	6.8
Italy	6.0
Morocco	12.3
Portugal	15.8
Spain	4.3
Tunisia	10.6
Turkey	5.2
Yugoslavia	8.8

Source: Sassen-Koob, 1978, p. 525 (derived from OECD data).

Structural, Cultural, and Political Consequences of Immigration

One of the most obvious structural consequences of immigration is a change in the class structure of the receiving countries, which can be seen as a reproduction of the international stratification system, with immigrants entering the social and occupational structure at the very bottom (Hoffmann-Nowotny, 1973, p. 37 ff). They form a new social stratum below the original stratification of the receiving society. Not only is this new stratum socially as well as culturally more distant from the middle classes than the native lower stratum, but it adds distances within the lower strata, which after immigration consist of ethnically different groups. The reproduction of the global system of stratification in the immigration country extends, moreover, also to the stratification of immigrants according to the level of development of their home countries.

The new bottom layer of immigrants pushes large sectors of the native population upward, although not in a uniform and equilibrated way. The native workers who are unable to take advantage of immigration to leave the lowest positions find themselves together with the immigrants at the lowest level, thus experiencing downward mobility in a psychological as well as in a structural sense.

These processes exacerbate the familiar tensions characterizing stratified societies where privileged and underprivileged groups com-

pete for scarce goods. However, because the underprivileged belong
to ethnically or racially different groups, these tensions may then be
projected upon them as a powerless minority, and their legitimate
demands may be refused (Hoffmann-Nowotny, 1973; Crum Ewing,
1975; Possony, 1976; Yinger, 1975; Yletinin, 1982; Zubrzycki, 1976).

Not only structural but also cultural distance separates immigrants
and natives. The extent of cultural distance may vary between guests
and hosts, and may be larger between North Africans and French or
between Turks and Germans than between Italians and Swiss, and
may also exist between guests, such as Turks and Spaniards for
example. These cultural distances do exist all over the world and
they cannot be neglected (Bass, 1976; Beer, 1976; de la Garza, 1976;
Glazer and Moynihan, 1970; Makielski, 1976). Although migration
would not occur if the immigrants were completely alien to the host's
system of values and norms, the social tensions will magnify existing
cultural differences. Mass immigration leads to a negative stereotyping of migrants, accompanied by a general tendency to strengthen
ascribed criteria to the detriment of achievement criteria. On the other
side of the scale, the native population places more value on its
national identity. The cultural distance is thus increased at both ends.

On their side the immigrants also heighten their cultural identity,
often far beyond what it was and meant to them in their country of
origin. It may even be said that in the absence of specific cultural
elements (because they never existed or were lost) such elements are
invented or reinvented. It seems that cultural identity is heightened
most among those immigrants who have experienced some upward
mobility that was later blocked. Immigrants who have remained at
the bottom of the status pyramid tend to see their own identity
negatively and as inferior to the culture of the immigration country.

The indigenous population's heightened cultural awareness together with the foreigners' negative evaluation of their own culture
introduces a traditional feudal element into a modern society. This
expresses itself for instance in the openly stated demand of natives
that access to higher positions be based on the precondition of nationality (only inferior positions should be open to immigrants), and
the partial acceptance of this notion by the aliens. Politically such
demands are paralleled by strong nationalist or even chauvinist currents. This process harks back to a neofeudal cultural and social order
by replacing achievement with ascribed criteria of status distribution.
And it is the strength of these sentiments, much more than the

economic recession, that have caused the European governments to call a halt to immigration.

In the light of the structural and cultural consequences of immigration, political consequences were inevitable. We shall deal here with two of them: reactions against further immigration, and reactions related to the question of integration and assimilation of immigrants. Although these political consequences are by no means restricted to Switzerland, they are most visible in that country, and I shall therefore report on its political reactions in more detail.

By the end of the sixties a growing resistance against further immigration arose in several European immigration countries. In Switzerland free immigration came to a halt in 1970, when the share of resident foreigners in the population had reached 16 percent. Beginning in 1968, several constitutional initiatives demanded that the population of foreigners be limited by an amendment to the federal constitution, and the government was forced to take strict measures to limit immigration. While the other European countries blocked immigration in reaction to the recession caused by the oil prices, Switzerland did it at a time when its economy was still booming.

A grassroots movement opposed to "over-foreignization" came to public attention in Switzerland around 1965. The Democratic Party of the canton of Zurich launched the first constitutional popular initiative demanding an amendment to the federal constitution limiting the total number of foreign residents to no more than 10 percent of the *total* population of Switzerland. This initiative was withdrawn in 1968 before coming to a vote, its initiators declaring themselves satisfied with the measures already taken by the authorities.

When it later became obvious that the number of foreigners continued to increase despite these measures, a second initiative was launched by the National Action against the Over-foreignization of the People and the Fatherland (*Nationale Aktion gegen die Überfremdung von Volk und Heimat*). James Schwarzenbach was the campaign leader. This initiative went much further than the first one: it demanded that foreigners not be allowed to exceed 10 percent of the *Swiss* population in any canton, with the exception of Geneva. The plebiscite took place in June 1970 and the initiative was defeated by a narrow majority (54 percent opposed versus 46 percent in favor). If this initiative had been accepted by the voters it would have been necessary, at that time, to reduce the number of foreigners by 44 percent.

This threat made such an impression that vigorous and effective political action became imperative, and the so-called global ceiling was introduced. Without mentioning any numbers, the legislators proposed that a balanced relationship be sought between the size of the Swiss and the foreign population. As a first step the foreign population would be stabilized; a gradual reduction in its size would come afterward. The introduction of the global ceiling, together with the reduction in the foreign population brought about by the recession, proved sufficient to take the edge off the grassroots movement for the moment.

But the National Action did not give in. In 1972 it launched another initiative, more drastic than its previous one, demanding that the number of foreigners in Switzerland not be allowed to exceed 550,000 and that the necessary reductions to achieve this figure be completed before January 1, 1978. A split occurred in the National Action, and James Schwarzenbach left to found the Swiss Republican Movement (*Schweizerische Republikanische Bewegung*). The vote on this initiative took place in 1974 and received 34 percent of the votes.

In the same year, but before this plebiscite took place, two more antiforeigner initiatives were launched, one by the Republican Movement and another by the National Action. The Republican Movement's more moderate initiative demanded that the number of foreigners in Switzerland not be allowed to exceed 12.5 percent of the Swiss population. The National Action's initiative demanded a limit of 4,000 naturalizations per year as long as the total population of Switzerland exceeded 5.5 million (the actual population at that time was close to 6.4 million). The plebiscite on these two initiatives was held in 1977 and both suffered considerable defeats. The Republican Movement's initiative was turned down by 71 percent of the voters and the National Action's initiative by 65 percent.

On the same date another initiative, also launched by the National Action, was presented to the voters. It did not directly refer to the foreigners; instead, it demanded first, that international treaties be made subject to the referendum and second, that this provision apply even to existing international treaties if at least 30,000 Swiss citizens demanded it. The initiative was clearly aimed at the 1964 treaty between Switzerland and Italy, which established regulations concerning immigration between the two countries. It was rejected by 76 percent of the voters. Though none of the xenophobic constitutional initiatives ever passed, the narrow margin of defeat for the 1970 initiative, the very fact that series of initiatives were successfully launched, and several further votes on matters related to foreigners made it quite clear that the Swiss government had to hold strictly to the policy of the global ceiling.

And antiforeign sentiment persists; a constitutional initiative demanding improved conditions for foreigners (especially seasonal workers) was rejected in 1981 by 84 percent. In 1982 a new law (AuG-Ausländergesetz), which was meant to replace the 1931 law on the stay and residence of foreigners, was submitted to referendum; again it was the National Action that had demanded this referendum and had collected the necessary 50,000 signatures. The AuG would have brought with it some minor improvements of the situation of the foreigners in Switzerland, but it was voted down.

In 1983 an amendment to the federal constitution to make naturalization procedures easier for second-generation immigrants was turned down by 55 percent of the voters. And in that same year the National Action launched a new constitutional initiative to reduce the number of foreigners in Switzerland by 200,000 to 300,000 within fifteen years, and to reduce as well the number of seasonal workers and border commuters.

The mechanisms of plebiscitary democracy make evident that for the past fifteen years immigration policy in Switzerland has been primarily a compromise with the grassroots movement. Other European countries lack these voting procedures, but public opinion data show similar reactions to immigrants influencing the policies of the respective governments. France has paid considerable amounts of money to foreigners as inducement to return home, and a similar policy was introduced in the Federal Republic of Germany in 1983.

Various additional political reactions to the presence of foreign ethnic minorities are mentioned below:

1. The German government coined the term "two-fold integration" for its immigrant policy, meaning that foreigners should become partially integrated in the receiving society, but at the same time should maintain their links to their home country and cultivate their ethnic identity (or acquire it in the case of the second-generation immigrants) to leave open the possibility of return migration. One means of achieving this is a kind of two-fold education using teachers from the home countries.

2. The clear-cut notion that an immigrant who wants to become permanent has to assimilate himself completely to the host culture predominates in Switzerland. A report to the Swiss federal government postulates that an applicant for citizenship "should already be

assimilated to the degree that he thinks and feels in a Swiss way and that our customs and habits should have become natural for him" (Bundesamt, 1964, p. 167). The policy of complete assimilation, however, is not being actively pursued and requires only that children of foreigners attend regular Swiss schools leaving any "ethnic studies" to the private initiative of the parents.

3. Recently the notion of cultural pluralism or cultural diversity has gained some importance, especially in France and in the Netherlands. In support of French government reports (Giordan, 1982; Ministère, 1982), social scientists participating in a conference on "Diversité culturelle, societé industrielle, état national" launched "an appeal to the leaders of the State and the mass-media to encourage all cultural communities to consider their diversity as a historic opportunity which must not be missed" (Colloque, 1983, p. 2). In this view ethnic identity of immigrants and the consequent cultural diversity of society is not a source of conflicts, but on the contrary contributes to national unity and helps to overcome many social problems.

In summary, the European countries which experienced this immigration are confronted with structural and cultural changes which have created serious unforeseen social problems. In reaction, immigration has been brought to a halt and attempts are made to repatriate migrants. For the immigrants who remain, the solutions attempted or suggested range in their aims from complete integration and assimilation, to a two-fold integration and assimilation, to the creation of a multicultural society.

A Theoretical Framework for the Interpretation of the Consequences of Immigration

A theoretical framework will allow us to explain and interpret immigration and the political reactions to it, and to consider possible futures. It is based on a general systems theory and uses as its fundamental dimensions the concepts of *structure* and *culture*, which are basic sociological categories in ordering social reality. Structure is defined as a set of interrelated social positions (or units), and culture is defined as a set of interrelated symbols (values and norms). These dimensions are interdependent: structural factors and structural change influence cultural factors and cultural change, and vice versa. Interdependence does not exclude the possibility that the relationship between structure and culture might also be asymmetric: under certain conditions culture might be determined by structure to a stronger extent than structure is determined by culture. In addition, structure and culture carry their own dynamics.

This conceptual and pretheoretical scheme is applicable to all levels of societal systems. It is represented graphically in Figure 6.1. The behavior of groups and individuals is partially determined by collective interests at different system levels, and these are determined by different configurations of structure and culture, finding expression in the processes shown in the graph (Hoffmann-Nowotny and Hondrich, 1982, p. 602 ff).

The relevant collective interests in modern industrialized societies, such as the European immigration countries, can be categorized into three types: political interest (participation in a group that takes binding decisions free from outside pressure and asserts itself vis-à-vis other groups); economic interest (one that is derived from the production and marketing of goods produced by the group); community interest (participation in social relationships based on the commonality of values, standards of behavior, and feelings).

The arrival of foreign ethnic groups may present the native population with opportunities or problems in terms of these three types of interest. For instance, hiring foreign workers may advance the economic interests of the host society; but if the foreign workers stay indefinitely and develop their own power base, the native population may perceive a threat to their cultural identity and political interest, and — if the economic situation deteriorates — to their economic interests. Three approaches to this problem come to mind: after a short stay, the foreigners can be expelled (rotation system) and a limit set to the number allowed into the country; the foreigners become (or remain) structurally and culturally segregated; or the immigration country absorbs the foreign workers, becoming in the process a new kind of society — a society that has a place for people with a different physical appearance, culture, and behavior, a society that must re-identify and formulate the mutuality of its collective interests on a higher, more abstract level.

In this theoretical framework we associate each of the interests with a specific subsystem and look for the mechanisms that are set in motion and the results they produce. Thus we associate the political interests with the subsystem "state"; the economic interests with the subsystem "economy"; and the identity or community interests with the subsystem "communities" (*Gemeinschaften*). The mechanisms

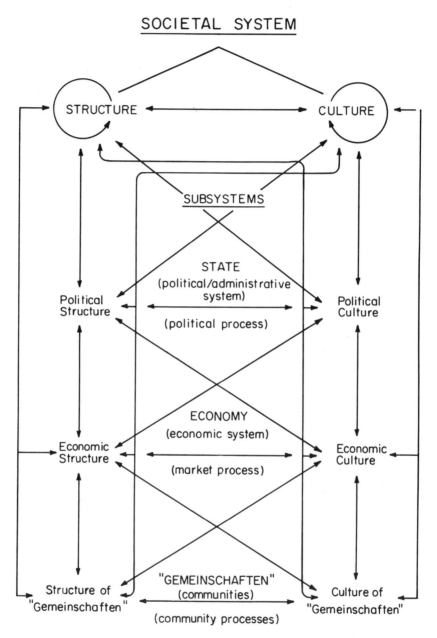

Figure 6.1. Societal system and its structural and cultural dimensions.

inherent in these subsystems are the following: legal and administrative regulation as the political mechanism; exchange as the economic mechanism; and consensus as the sociocultural mechanism.

The different experiences of the European immigration countries result from different impacts and degrees of interdependence of the mechanisms of the three subsystems. It was the economic interests in all cases that invited the foreign workers into the host country. Neither community interests (such as sense of solidarity and social responsibility for people in poor countries) nor political interests (such as the desire to dominate the immigrants or their countries of origin) played a role. By the same token, neither considerations of cultural identity nor political interests were obstacles to the recruitment of foreign workers.

There is a remarkable degree of consensus on the economic arguments for employing foreigners — a consensus that transcends class lines. Even though the employers were the main recruiters and principal beneficiaries of immigrant labor, while the labor unions watched with some degree of concern, the institutions representing their interests achieved a broad measure of agreement. The potential threat of competition from the migrants for domestic jobs was defused by a policy of letting the foreign workers go first in a period of recession, and through other devices designed to accommodate the interests of organized labor.

Against this background it is interesting that the employment of foreigners gave rise to intense political conflict in Switzerland, while in the Federal Republic and in other European immigration countries, where social and political disputes are commonplace in many areas, migrant worker issues have not produced open clashes of interest. This seeming contradiction can be easily explained: in practically all European immigration countries (including Switzerland) a consensus on the foreign workers had been worked out among the key economic interest groups — labor unions, employers, government, and the political parties. But the sectors that remained outside this consensus had a chance to speak out only in Switzerland, owing to the unique mechanism of its plebiscitary democracy. And their efforts set off a period of intense political conflict.

In the first stages of immigration the collective political interests of the host countries did not seem to be affected, as foreign workers were not seen to enter the country with any claim on political participation or activity. Only when the proportion of foreigners in the host country rises does the consensus begin to get shaky: is it possible to have 10 percent or more adults who are precluded from sharing in the country's political processes? Such a situation would be at odds with the image that many people, particularly the younger and middle-class voters, have of a just and democratic society. This image is an integral part of their sense of identity, but it has not yet made an impact on the collective interests as defined by their governments.

More than political interests, large-scale immigration has engaged cultural interests — interests related to the national sense of identity, which expresses itself in an accentuation of national feelings and symbols, in a commonality of external appearances and language. Many European countries have feared being "overwhelmed" by foreign influences. And in these highly industrialized societies, conflicts and problems are nowadays sparked not so much by economic issues, as Marxist theoreticians believe, but by concerns of ethnic and national identity, although it cannot be denied that something like an economic recession tends to reinforce interethnic conflicts.

One may conclude, then, that neither political-administrative regulation nor the market mechanism can be expected to yield a satisfactory and comprehensive policy for the management of issues relating to the immigrant workers, least of all when it comes to the collective interests of the community. Therefore, it remains to be determined what role the community plays in the context of various tension management mechanisms.

There is no social context and thus no society in which there does not exist a minimum of agreement, consensus, or similarity among those who constitute the group. This is the basic insight to which sociology owes its origin and which distinguishes it from older social sciences, such as political science and economics. Political science is based on the premise of differences among people in relation to power; and economics deals with the somewhat less profound differences among people that find expression in exchanges on the market — exchanges in which people seek to meet each other's needs. Sociology, on the other hand, emphasizes the noncontractual elements of the relationship, as Emile Durkheim put it, which means that it deals with elements of consensus that transcend differences in power or economic interest. Sociology becomes critically important at a time when these components of social consensus tend to get lost in the face of growing differences in political and economic interests, and when therefore there is a need to raise consciousness and reaffirm them through explicit and systematic analysis.

Social regulation or control through the mechanism of consensus requires that similarities be emphasized and a sense of identity or community be strengthened among the different people in the nation. This applies to the case of foreign workers in Europe, for without their developing similarities of attitude with the local population, attempts at integration based only on political and economic factors appear doomed. Developing and strengthening a sense of community is a prerequisite for effective policy decisions and actually helps to smooth their implementation.

The state, as the source of policy decisions, looks for evidence of adaptation before it acts. In Switzerland it is officially stated that "only foreigners who are suitable and worthy of it can acquire citizenship. The foreigner must have adapted himself fully to Swiss conditions, to the point where he has actually become integrated into the national community. His manner, his character, his entire personality must warrant the assumption that he will become a good and dependable citizen of Switzerland" (BBL. 1951, II:680).

Integration and Assimilation of Immigrants in Switzerland and Germany

A comparative study of the immigrant population in the Federal Republic of Germany and Switzerland (Hoffmann-Nowotny and Hondrich, 1982) yields some interesting empirical and theoretical insights into the mechanisms that promote or hamper integration and assimilation of ethnic minorities. The principal finding was that in comparison with German foreigners, Swiss foreigners appear to be better integrated and assimilated on the basis of virtually all indices used in the study. How can one explain the differences between Switzerland and Germany?

It is conceivable that the three mechanisms of control (regulation, exchange, and consensus) are operating more effectively in Switzerland. Its economic advantages are particularly attractive to foreigners and motivate them to stay in the country, and Switzerland's relatively liberal policies permit foreign workers to stay longer, so that they become more effectively integrated and more reluctant to return to their home countries. On the other hand, it is also conceivable that social management or regulation works more effectively in Switzerland than in the Federal Republic, that is, that the sense of community has become weaker in Germany, and that one could actually speak of a "community failure" there. Such a supposition could be supported as follows.

The sociological effect of higher efficiency and technology in the economies of modern societies is a restructuring of social groups in several ways. Large organizational contexts are breaking up into smaller units characterized by a means-to-end relationship. People are increasingly compelled to shape their relationships to others in terms of specific purposes or activities, and to distinguish them from other relationships, often with the same individuals. These functional differentiations are accompanied by a hierarchic structure, which reflects different segments of activity and levels of relationship. The hierarchical levels in turn carry different values and corresponding rewards in terms of salaries or wages. The classical sociologists have described this as the transition from community to society (Ferdinand Tonnies), or as the replacement of mechanical (static) solidarity based on similar types of activity by organic solidarity, based on complementary activities (Emile Durkheim).

It appears that Germany has suffered a greater loss of community, in all three dimensions, than has Switzerland, where the small scale at the level of the nation and of local communities provides a more intimate context which strengthens people's sense of belonging to a place and thus operates as a community-building factor. Moreover, the Swiss have a strong and historically unbroken consensus in their political culture, characterized by libertarian components and even more so by the processes of direct democracy. This tradition has proven stronger as a community-reinforcing element than the language culture, which has a potentially divisive effect.

If the explanation about the role of the community in general and the Swiss in particular is sufficiently persuasive, the question arises how this factor manifests itself in the integration and assimilation of foreigners. For it is by no means self-evident that strong local and national community structures facilitate the involvement of foreigners in these communities. On the contrary, communities that have a strong sense of identity and of "us" against "them" can be particularly rejecting. And the various initiatives to shut off immigration through plebiscite show that such feelings are still strong in Switzerland. Yet the Swiss system has produced a comparatively higher degree of assimilation and integration of foreigners than that of the Federal Republic. How can this phenomenon be further explained?

1. Communities generally find it difficult to tolerate different values, standards, life-styles, and external appearance. They can deal

with the problem through physical segregation, or through pressure on the foreigners to adapt themselves to the indigenous community. Because Switzerland is a small country whose people have a deep personal relationship with their home community, and since there is very little evidence of local people moving away from areas where foreigners are settling, there is only one way for the Swiss community to manage the problem: put strong social pressure on foreigners to mold them more in the Swiss image.

There is little reluctance in Switzerland to let foreigners know how things are done in daily life and to reward or penalize them accordingly. This kind of social control can operate successfully as long as the number of foreigners remains limited. Once the share of foreigners becomes large, local pressure for adaptation begins to fall short, and there is demand for support by the central political-administrative apparatus — the initiatives for plebiscites against "over-foreignization."

2. Our second hypothesis is that pressure for assimilation at the community level is more successful when a country has had experience in dealing with foreigners. Switzerland has a long tradition of such interaction, on both economic and political levels, with foreigners who come as tourists, workers, businessmen, refugees, and employees of international organizations.

3. That Switzerland is a multilingual society might seem an obstacle to the development of a strong sense of community, but in fact it helps speed the integration of some foreigners such as Italians whose mother tongue is one of the major Swiss languages, and of other speakers of Romance languages, such as Spaniards. In terms of language and "southerness," their differences from the majority of the Swiss are less pronounced than the corresponding differences in the Federal Republic. Clearly, the fewer the dissimilarities between indigenous and foreign residents, the easier the process of integration.

This background reinforces my point about the capacity (at all times limited, to be sure) to manage the assimilation of culturally alien minorities at the community level: it is most effective when the minority group is small; when there is ample time for the community to become accustomed to the new group; and when the minority culture is not too glaringly different from the local system of values and standards. Otherwise minorities can be integrated into the society only via the market mechanism and by political-administrative means. Integration via these means carries the risk of a negative reaction by the indigenous community, expressed in xenophobia and segregation. At best we may expect only a partial (political or economic) integration.

We return to the conclusion that when the community level has become weaker and less effective as a result of structural changes in the wake of large-scale industrialization (as in the German Federal Republic when compared to Switzerland), or when community-based mechanisms can no longer meet issues raised by minorities which are very different and have grown too fast or too big, then purely economic interests become the basis of collective and individual interaction (which Marx has described as one main feature of capitalist society) and special interests are pursued mainly by use of economic or political power. But it is unrealistic to expect any one mechanism — the community, the market, or the political apparatus — to solve social problems single-handedly. Communal structures can deal with issues only selectively and up to a certain scale, depending on their strength.

Even when economic factors become dominant and erode the effectiveness of community-level management, this does not mean that the community has faded away. It remains a significant factor in informal settings, in specialized institutions outside the economic and political systems, and in personal and family relationships. And it remains essential to a sense of identity attached to the traditional structures of the nation-state, the sense of peoplehood with a common language, physical features, and feelings. Strangers just do not fit into these groupings.

The essential problem of modern communities, whose economy and political system cover a wide range of products, labor markets, and federal systems, is that traditional economic structures are being replaced by new organizational forms, which in turn lead to social settings that transcend existing communal ties. The result is a more impersonal kind of thinking about the community, even as people continue to cling to their accustomed ways of communal behavior. To broaden a community and make it more inclusive is much more difficult than, for instance, extending the frontiers of a country, and this in turn is more complicated than broadening the reach of economic systems.

In short, cultural change lags behind structural change. Thus in the Federal Republic, when the community has to perform social control, it cannot do the job. Social control operates more effectively in Switzerland, both within the indigenous population and toward foreigners. The analysis of the community mechanism shows that on one level there can be too much community reaction (antiforeign attitudes), and on the other there may be too little community-generated activity (social control).

Assimilation, Integration, and Cultural Pluralism

Considerable resentment against foreigners has built up in the European countries with large minorities, even in Switzerland. The economic recession has deepened this resentment, and has forced European governments to take action against further immigration, and even to try to reduce the number of foreigners. But there can be no doubt that the large majority of immigrants will remain where they are and will become permanent members of the receiving societies.

The idea has been gaining favor in several European immigration countries that immigrants (including the second or third generation) should be integrated, not discriminated against, and at the same time encouraged to preserve their culture and their linkages with their home countries. The native population should be taught not only to accept and to tolerate cultural pluralism but to value it as an enrichment of the country's global culture and as a solution to all interethnic conflicts (Colloque, 1983; Giordan, 1982; Ministère, 1982). In short, this strategy is seen as a kind of philosopher's stone for integration without assimilation. The same notion is also being supported by several associations of foreigners.

It remains to determine whether this strategy is feasible and, more broadly, what strategies might secure for immigrants a position in the immigration societies that would be in accordance with collective interests and with the principles of social justice. This goal will be reached when foreigners enjoy the same access to the goods and values of the societies in which they live as do the members of the native population, and discrimination based on ethnic origin has disappeared.

Assimilation and integration, two of the central concepts that will be used in the following discussion, are related to the societal dimensions culture and structure. Assimilation is the degree of participation in the culture, and integration is the degree of participation in the structure of society. When considering the assimilation and integration of immigrants a sociological truism should be kept in

mind, namely, that not all native members of the immigration societies can be said to be fully assimilated or integrated.

Immigrants come mainly either from underdeveloped countries
such as Turkey, Algeria, or Portugal, or from the underdeveloped
regions of more developed countries like Italy or Spain. They bring
with them achieved characteristics which distinguish them from the
population of the highly developed immigration countries. They
often lack educational, vocational, and social skills which are normal
for all native members of the immigration societies. A considerable
social distance separates most immigrants from the native population, and it is no wonder that immigrants form a kind of underclass
below the stratification systems of the receiving society.

The interdependence of structural and cultural aspects implies that
first-generation immigrants are unlikely to become assimilated, particularly because their contacts at work and in the neighborhood will
be mostly with each other and only minimally with the native population, and these mainly with the native lower class, which is itself
marginal to the dominant culture. Only as the immigrants' structural
positions and structural heritage change can their assimilation make
any significant progress.

In addition to the structural distance there is a cultural distance
between the immigrants and their host society, and the two differ
from each other in important respects. Structural distance lends itself
to ratio measurement (level of income, years of schooling, degree of
urbanization, and so on) and all agree that it should be diminished.
As to measurement, cultures can be compared on a large number of
dimensions (complexity, differentiation, stability, change, and so on),
but it is indeed problematic to speak of them as more or less developed as we do not hesitate to do in structural comparisons. Culture
is now regarded as a societal element which has to be valued im-
manently and must not be compared evaluatively with other cultures,
as was done, for example, when certain cultures were labeled "primitive."

There is on the other hand no doubt, at least since Weber's essay
on "The Protestant Ethic and the Spirit of Capitalism," that cultural
elements are decisive for structural developments (and vice versa).
This implies that it is not possible to combine just any culture with
any structural setting. The question arises therefore about whether

certain cultural traits of immigrant groups are compatible with the structure as well as the culture of the immigration country, and with the collective and individual interests of the immigrants.

It is quite evident that there is no one single answer to this question. We shall nevertheless try to arrive at some hypotheses starting from the fact that migrants left because they wanted to improve their economic and social standard of living. Any behavior that is an obstacle to this goal would be regarded as dysfunctional, and their assimilation to the dominant culture would be regarded as functional.

In European immigration countries migrants from very different cultural backgrounds have proved able to fulfill their economic functions, although on the lowest ranks of the system. But they have not acquired the characteristics that would grant them significant upward mobility, except in Switzerland (whose unique traits we have noted) and in countries with few immigrants such as Sweden and Norway. The reasons for this gap seem clear. The structural and cultural origins of immigrants put them into structural positions in the immigration country in which their chances for integration and assimilation are low, and this turns into a vicious circle. This circle is reinforced by the neofeudal attitudes of the native population, which tend to increase the cultural distance by making cultural differences more conscious and more pronounced, even (re)constructing them, thus legitimizing the behavior and attitudes of the natives toward the immigrants.

Cultural distance, which is so often regarded as the main obstacle to assimilation, is only one of the factors relevant to the problem and one created, at least in part, in the course of social processes resulting from the immigration. The issue is not so much whether immigrants can or want to assimilate to reach the goals for which they emigrated, but the existence of structural and cultural mechanisms which function as severe barriers against assimilation.

Integration without assimilation, economic integration of minorities which remain culturally distant from the majority: these notions we would call ideological because they obviously neglect the sociological determinants and regularities that operate in reality.

From a cultural point of view integration without assimilation would require that the indigenous population identify with people who look different, have different traditions, customs, values, norms, life-styles, and family patterns — with Muslims, with people who speak Turkish, and with people who empty the garbage cans. This calls for either a redefinition of their identity as Germans, Swiss, or French that would make it natural for Turkish or Algerian Muslims to become part of the German, Swiss, or French national communities; or it requires a definition of the community on a highly abstract level, one that views Germans, Swiss, or French and Turks, Muslims, Christians, laborers, and intellectuals in terms of their shared characteristics as human beings, and as interdependent individuals whose opportunities in life are enhanced by the pluralism of the society.

These are morally utopian demands on the community as well as on the political and economic system. But if one pleads for a true culturally pluralistic society, one has to realize that these are the sociological requirements which would have to be fulfilled.

In the context of the political system, to what extent would the indigenous population be willing (or could be influenced) to tolerate a deviating political culture, especially if it is expressed by foreigners? From the German experience with Turkish immigrants one would conclude that the range of tolerance in the political field is rather narrow. And the same is true for other immigration countries, where it goes without saying that the foreigners are expected to adapt themselves completely to the political culture of the host society. Or could and would European countries tolerate two legal systems regarding, say, the position of women in society, one granting equal rights to them and another setting migrant women apart as demanded by a conservative Muslim group to preserve its culture?

More tolerance extends to the economic sector, but only for ethnic restaurants, ethnic shops, and the like. There would be very little tolerance if immigrants claimed for themselves a deviating work culture. As for the community, by its very nature it is based on similarities of its members and cannot tolerate large deviations. It is an open question about the extent to which such similarities could be made more abstract, making it possible to reconcile hitherto irreconcilable characteristics.

In any case, the issue is not so much whether individuals or systems of different levels can and will tolerate culturally different groups, but the extent to which cultural differences are compatible with a given societal structure on any one of its levels: the political, the economic, or the communal (Krausz, 1976; Korte, 1982; Lebon, 1983).

Open versus Closed Societies: Structural versus Cultural Policy

From a global point of view the existence of cultural pluralism by necessity implies structural segregation, and vice versa. If structure and culture are in discord, collective or individual anomie will be the consequence. This is a general and fundamental characteristic of all human societies and nothing peculiar. Extreme structural and cultural segregation are institutionalized in caste and feudal systems, which are therefore called "closed societies"; but segregation is also a reality, although to a much lesser extent, in modern Western societies which, because they are ideally regulated by universalistic norms, are called "open societies."

Closed societies can and do tolerate cultural heterogeneity as an interclass or intercaste phenomenon, but not intraclass heterogeneity. The tolerance of heterogeneity in caste and feudal systems is thus nothing but a necessity for the maintenance of their structural design. It follows that if a society wants to enforce cultural pluralism or heterogeneity it will also have more structural segregation. And a certain degree of cultural homogeneity in tandem with structural segregation (as seems to be the case for large numbers of black Americans) produces anomie. If the European immigration countries are to avoid anomie, they should anticipate that their relatively open societies will become more closed, refeudalized, ethnically layered. This would be at the cost of the immigrants, who have left their home countries to escape from the strains of a closed society.

A *cultural policy* drawn up by the immigration countries or by the immigrants themselves, which aims at conserving or even enforcing cultural heterogeneity (in a fundamental sense of this term), will thus cement social inequality and structural segregation. A *structural policy* would instead seek to provide equal chances of participation in the goods and values of the immigration countries for all its members. It would not aim, however, at preserving the cultural identity of foreign ethnic groups if this were meant in the sense of folklore.

The result of a structural policy will not be a harmonious society free of tensions and social problems, like the one the advocates of a cultural policy expect from their strategy, when they see "the presence of different cultural communities . . . as a way of reinforcing national unity and of helping society out of the crisis in which it finds itself" (Colloque, 1983). If it is historically true that closed societies generate and experience less social tension than open societies, they may even be right.

Conclusion

What can one say responsibly about the future of European migration? Migration pressure will no doubt continue but so will the resistance to immigration. The large majority of immigrants will remain where they are, but will they establish themselves as more or less permanent ethnic minorities? There is, of course, no uniform and single answer to this question. The answer would have to be given country by country; for brevity we refer only to three: Switzerland, Germany, and France.

In Switzerland the immigrants seem to be fairly well integrated with assimilation lagging somewhat behind. This is mainly true for the first generation of immigrants, and the second generation is also fairly well assimilated (Gurny, 1978, 1983; Koschitzky, 1983; Nolli, 1982; Christliche Arbeiter-Jugend, 1980). My impression is that developments in Switzerland will parallel the experience of the United States with its European immigrants.

In France integration seems to lag behind assimilation, and assimilation has not gone very far either, especially if we look at the second generation of North African immigrants (Marangé and Lebon, 1982). It thus seems that the situation in France is also comparable to what has happened and is still happening in the United States, but more specifically to that country's and its black population's painful experience (Rose and Rose, 1972; Glazer and Moynihan, 1970, 1975; Yinger, 1975; Wilson, 1976; Makielski, 1976).

Germany has to be placed somewhere between the extremes of Switzerland and France. In dealing with its Italian or Spanish immigrants it is somewhat closer to Switzerland; regarding its Turkish immigrant population, it is more like France, again especially with respect to the second generation (Gerstenmaier, 1974; Untersuchung, 1980; Wilpert, 1980; Yletinin, 1982; Nauck, 1983).

Migration is not and cannot be an alternative to development. But this is true only on the system level, whether in a single country or in world society. For many millions of individuals migration has been an alternative to the development of their home country, and one should not overlook and forget this. When immigration to European countries was brought to a halt, this meant also the destruction of the hopes of millions for a better life.

SEVEN

International Emigration and the Third World

Myron Weiner

INTERNATIONAL migration creates anxieties in both sending and receiving countries. The issues are only partly economic — do migrants take jobs away from natives, does emigration mean the loss of needed manpower? The movement of people from one country to another also raises social and political concerns over the place of the foreign element in the receiving country, or, for the sending country, issues of national humiliation and dependence. International migration like international trade is asymmetrical; receiving countries ordinarily exercise more control than the sending countries. Indeed, it is a mark of a country's sovereignty that it can control who may enter, and a mark of a country's freedom that it permits its citizens to leave.

In Western Europe and the United States there have been public debates over how many and what kind of immigrants and foreign workers should be admitted; what place they should have in the economy; whether and how much displacement of local employment takes place; whether and how migrants should be incorporated into the economy, culture, and polity; whether indeed they should be helped to stay or pressed to return to their native land; and, above all, what should be done about their children, especially the children of migrant workers born in Western Europe.

Overshadowing these questions for many is the fear that the population explosion in the third world, the vast disparity in incomes and opportunities between the advanced industrial countries and developing countries, and the violence, instability, and repressiveness of many regimes in the third world will result in a still greater flow of populations from the poor to the rich countries. Already Europeans are unwilling to extend to Turkey the right of free labor migration that accompanies associate status in the Common Market.

President Reagan has warned that political chaos in Central America will result in another large flow of refugees across U.S. borders. The oil-producing Persian Gulf states continue to admit foreign workers, but have become fearful that they may stay on or that too many people from a single country might prove to be politically disruptive. Consequently their governments have sought to diversify the sources of imported labor and to restrict permanent residence.

Anxieties in the recipient countries have risen because of the growth in illegal migration. These anxieties are not relieved when critics of proposed legislation to restrict employment of illegals in the United States argue that legislation will not work, that illegal border entries cannot be controlled, and that the employment of illegals cannot be regulated effectively. The French are concerned that black migrants to Britain will enter France under the EEC freedom of movement rules, adding to the illegals trickling across the eastern Pyrenees. And in the United States, where the influx of boat people from Vietnam, Laos, Cambodia, Haiti, and Cuba led to an initial outpouring of sympathy for the plight of refugees, there is now a concern that the openness to refugees could increase their numbers.

Finally, the labor-importing countries of Western Europe recognize with anxiety that temporary workers do not readily return home even during a recession. There was a modest decline in the number of migrant workers in Western Europe from 1970, a peak year, to 1978. In Germany the numbers declined from 2.4 to 2 million, in France from 2 million to 1.6 million, in Switzerland from 710,000 to 489,000. But at the same time the number of dependents increased by 200,000. In 1970 there were 11,120,000 foreigners in Western Europe, of whom 6,074,000 were workers and 5,046,000 were dependents; the comparable figures in 1978 were 10,290,000 foreign residents, consisting of 5,046,000 workers and 5,244,000 dependents.

While for the countries of emigration, as we shall see, these are small numbers, for the countries of immigration they often appear large. In France foreign workers form 9 percent of the labor force, in Austria and Belgium 7 percent each, and in Switzerland it has been as high as 24 percent. The flow of Latin Americans into the United States continues, and it is expected that by the end of the century Latin Americans will supplant blacks as the largest ethnic minority. But nowhere has the proportion of migrants been as large as in the oil-producing states in the Persian Gulf, where foreign workers have become a majority of the work force: in the United Arab Emirates foreigners make up 85 percent of the labor force, in Qatar 81 percent, in Kuwait 71 percent, in Oman 45 percent, and in Bahrain 39 percent.

In some regions and urban centers the migrants loom particularly large. The racial composition of many cities in the United Kingdom has been transformed by the presence of Indians, Pakistanis, Bangladeshis, and by blacks from the Caribbean. France has an estimated 4.3 million foreigners, 40 percent of whom live in and around Paris. In some neighborhoods Portuguese (680,000) and North Africans (1.5 million) outnumber the French. There are similar concentrations in West Germany, where there are 4.6 million foreigners, including 1.7 million Turks.

For a few sending countries emigration has made a noticeable demographic difference. As much as a third of the population of Surinam and Puerto Rico has emigrated. The exodus from other small Caribbean states has also been proportionately large. In the case of the North African countries the proportion of emigrants to the total national labor force in the mid-seventies was considerable: 19.5 percent for Algeria, 12.3 percent for Morocco, and 10.6 percent for Tunisia. For the countries of Southern Europe the proportions were 8.8 percent for Yugoslavia, 6.8 percent for Greece, 5.2 percent for Turkey, and 6 percent for Italy (Sassen-Koob, 1978, p. 525).

For most of the third world, however, emigration is of minor demographic importance. The population of the low-income economies is expected to increase from 2,160 million in 1980 to 2,607 million by 1990, and that of the middle-income economies from 1,139 million to 1,441 million. The population increase in the third world thus averages from 70 to 80 million per year. The United States is the largest single recipient of migrants from the third world; in the early eighties it is estimated that perhaps a million persons entered the United States each year, some legally, many illegally. The annual influx into the countries of Western Europe is substantially lower than in the sixties and for some countries there may now be a net outflow. The Middle East continues to attract migrants, but the annual increments are modest.

The total annual emigration from the third world to the developed countries and to the oil-producing countries may, at most, constitute 2 to 3 percent of the annual population growth in the third world. No conceivable increase in emigration could provide significant relief from the burden of high population growth.

In this respect the experience of the contemporary third world is different from that of the countries of Western Europe during their periods of high population growth. Demographically significant numbers of people left the United Kingdom, Scandinavia, Italy, and Central and Eastern Europe in the nineteenth and early twentieth centuries, mostly to North and South America, but with some migration to Australia, New Zealand, and South and East Africa. Some forty million European migrants settled in the United States alone — a far higher proportion of the European population than is the case for all but a handful of contemporary developing countries. The very size and population growth rates of the third world preclude the same kind of demographic impact that emigration had on the smaller and slower-growing countries of Europe.

Although some people in the advanced industrial countries express a concern that the high rate of population growth in the third world will lead to large-scale emigrations — a kind of "population dumping" policy on the part of overcrowded countries — there is no evidence that emigration rates and population growth rates are related. Algeria (2.5 percent), Morocco (2.8 percent), and Mexico (3.2 percent) have had above average population growth rates among middle-income countries, but Greece and Portugal have had population growth rates under 1 percent per annum since 1960, Tunisia's growth rate is 2 percent, and Turkey's is 2.5 percent, average for a developing country. The population growth rate of Colombia has been high (3 percent in the 1960s, 2.3 percent in the 1970s), but its emigrants move to Venezuela, a country with a population growth rate of 3.3 percent.

Nor is there evidence that low economic growth rates in developing countries induce emigration. The per capita average annual growth rates of many countries of high emigration is no less and in several instances is higher than that of the countries to which migrants go. Mexico's per capita growth rate between 1960 and 1980 was actually higher than that of the United States; Colombia's economy grew faster than Venezuela's; Turkey, Greece, and Yugoslavia did better than Germany. Puerto Rico was the source of the largest single emigration from the Caribbean to the U.S. mainland at the same time as it experienced very rapid industrial growth and a rapid expansion in the demand for labor. The evidence is overwhelmingly persuasive: economic migration to the United States, Western Europe, and the oil-producing states is primarily demand-induced, not supply-induced.

The ebb and flow of international labor migration into the United

States, Western Europe, and the oil-producing countries of the Persian Gulf, Nigeria, and Venezuela reflect the changing demands for labor within these regions, and the immigration policies that shape the source, numbers, and composition. Neither population growth rates in the sending countries nor, for that matter, changes in the unemployment rate in the sending countries seem to be related to changes in emigration rates.

On the other hand, both internal upheavals within developing countries and expulsions have led to large-scale emigrations. Indeed, there may be as many refugees in the world as there are people who migrated in response to employment opportunities. A million or more fled Indochina after the Communist victories, and another half million left Cuba. The largest single exodus in recent years has been the movement of some three million or more Afghans into Pakistan and Iran, the consequence of a Communist coup and Soviet invasion. In the late forties there was a large-scale exodus of Arabs from Israel and in the early fifties a similar exodus of Jews from North Africa and West Asia into Israel, all related to the emergence of Israel as a Jewish state. There have also been large-scale refugee movements within Africa, especially between Ethiopia and Somalia. And there have been government-sponsored expulsions from Burma, Uganda, Indonesia, Sri Lanka, and Vietnam. Demand-side migration inducements are largely economic, but supply-side inducements are largely political.

Political Factors

For governments of sending countries emigration may serve a variety of political objectives. Emigration can be a solution to the problems of cultural heterogeneity; it can be a device for dealing with political dissidents, including class enemies; and it can be a mechanism for affecting the domestic and foreign policies of other states.

Emigration as a solution to the problems of cultural heterogeneity and ethnic rivalry. At least since the fifteenth century European states have ejected religious groups that did not subscribe to the established religion, and ethnic minorities that did not belong to the dominant ethnic group. The Spanish crown expelled the Jews, the French expelled the Huguenots, and the British crown induced Protestant dissenters to settle in the colonies.

In the past several decades many third world countries have expelled their own ethnic minorities, particularly when these minorities constitute an industrious class in competition with a middle class belonging to the ethnic majority. In some instances the minorities are of migrant origin, but often their settlement is as old as of those who claim to be indigenous. Many Chinese settled in Malaysia before the Malays came from Sumatra, and the Tamil of northern Sri Lanka are no less indigenous than the Sinhalese. But a government facing unemployment in the ranks of the educated, and conflicts among its ethnic groups over language and educational opportunities, often sees the expulsion of a prosperous, well-placed minority as a politically popular policy. Many governments have expelled their minorities or deliberately created conditions which induced the minority to leave, and forced other countries, on moral and humanitarian grounds, to accept their refugees.

Emigration as a means of dealing with political dissidents and class enemies. The ancient Greeks were among the earliest to strip a dissident of his citizenship and cast him into exile. Socrates himself was offered the option of going into exile rather than be executed. In recent years authoritarian governments have expelled their dissidents (Solzhenitsyn from the Soviet Union) or allowed their dissidents to go into exile (the late Aquino from the Philippines). In the United States the image of the exile as a European political refugee has long since been replaced by the image of the exile as someone from the third world — a Chilean, Ethiopian, Iranian, Cuban, South Korean, South African, Nicaraguan, or Vietnamese.

Governments may expel not only a handful of their critics but large portions of the population. Revolutionary regimes may even see large-scale emigration of a social class as a way of transforming the country's social structure. The Vietnamese government justified the expulsion of the Chinese on the grounds of eliminating a bourgeois social class opposed to the regime; similarly, the exodus of some 400,000 middle-class Cubans was seen by the Castro government as a way of disposing of a class hostile to socialism. The Cambodian government killed or forced into exile vast numbers of people tainted with French or other Western cultural influences in an effort to reduce its dependence, cultural as well as economic, upon the West. In 1971 the Pakistani government hoped to weaken the insurgency in East Pakistan by forcing large numbers of Bengali Hindus out of the country. And most recently, Soviet military forces in Afghanistan have forced populations hostile to the regime to flee across the borders to Pakistan and Iran.

Forced emigration as an instrument for affecting the policies of other states.
Apart from reducing the number of dissidents, governments may
also see forced emigration as a way of putting pressure on neighboring states. Governments will, of course, deny this, but neighbors
often understand that a halt to forced emigration is not likely to take
place unless they yield on a demand made by the country from which
the refugees come. The Haitian government, it was believed in Washington, encouraged or at least would not prevent their citizens from
fleeing by boat to Florida unless the U.S. government substantially
increased its flow of aid to that country. In 1971 New Delhi was
persuaded that the government of Pakistan forced East Pakistan
Bengalis to flee to India in order to pressure the Indian government
to withdraw its support for the insurgents. Similarly, many officials
in Islamabad now believe that Soviet pressure on Afghans to flee to
Pakistan is intended to force the Pakistanis to seek a settlement with
the Afghan government and to withdraw their military aid to the
insurgents. And the Thai and Malaysian governments fear that the
Vietnamese government seeks to destabilize them by forcing them
to accept Chinese refugees.

The presence of one country's citizens in another country can also
provide the home government with an opportunity for extending its
political and cultural influences. In the nineteenth century the German economist Frederick List advocated emigration as a form of
colonization of the Turkish empire by Germans. Many German leaders and nationalist intellectuals also saw emigration as a way of
extending Germany's political and cultural influence. Some advocated emigration to Greece, for example, to provide support for the
Bavarian king of Greece, and migration to the United States as a way
of ensuring connections to Germany. However, German intellectuals
became critical of migration to the United States when it became
apparent that there was a high rate of assimilation. Instead, they
advocated emigration to Latin America where migrants might retain
German culture (Walker, 1964, p. 118). Seven million Europeans
emigrated to Argentina between 1857 and 1940, and five million to
Brazil between 1821 and 1945. Another five million Europeans settled
in Africa. Gross migration to the United States from 1801 to 1935 has
been estimated at 38.5 million (Erickson, 1976).

The contemporary governments of a number of developing countries — Turkey, Greece, India, Algeria, and Yugoslavia — actively
promote the language and culture of their country among the emigrants and their children. Koranic schools have been organized in

Germany by the Islamic Cultural Center, a private Turkish group in Cologne. The Bharatiya Vidya Bhavan, an Indian government-supported organization, promotes Indian culture among both Indians and non-Indians in the United States. Hundreds of such institutions can be found throughout the United States and Western Europe. How effective these groups are in promoting the foreign policy interests of the country of emigration, in addition to promoting language and culture, is a matter that bears study. It is well known that Greek migrants to the United States have played an influential role in U.S.-Greek and U.S.-Turkish relations and that Jews, Poles, Cubans, and other groups of migrant origin play an influential role in shaping our foreign policy. There is good reason to believe that as Algerians, Turks, Greeks, and other migrant groups acquire citizenship and voting rights within European countries they may play a similar role.

Emigration was thought to be useful in other ways. In the nineteenth century German authorities believed that "a large body of indigent subjects constitute a social danger and a serious burden on meager public funds; better let them go" (Walker, 1964, p. 16). Reacting to this policy, the American Richard Mayo-Smith wrote that "there is something almost revolting in the anxiety of certain countries to get rid of their surplus population and to escape the burden of supporting the poor, the helpless and the depraved" (1890, pp. 197–198). The British also had a policy of "shoveling out" prisoners. The crowding of jails in Britain in the 1770s and 1780s induced the crown to send convicts to Australia (Jonston, 1972). Cuba followed a similar policy when it sent some of its prison population on boats to the United States.

Today some receiving countries view immigration from a neighboring country as a form of colonization, with its implication of political control. In northeastern India, for example, the native Assamese hold this view about the Bangladeshi migrants, many of whom entered illegally; the West Bank Arabs think the same thing about Jewish settlements, as do the Lebanese about the Palestinian camps.

A retrospective look at many contemporary population movements reveals that countries of emigration have more control over international population flows than is widely believed. Among the postwar migrations that can be viewed from this perspective are the flows from East Pakistan, Ethiopia, Cambodia, Vietnam, Uganda, Burma,

Sri Lanka, Haiti, Cuba, and Afghanistan. What often appears to be uncontrolled illegal migrations and refugee movements may in fact represent deliberate emigration policies on the part of sending countries. To view refugee flows simply as the *unintended* consequences of internal upheavals or the response of certain classes and ethnic groups to government policies is to ignore the very real desire of some governments to reduce or eliminate from within their own borders selected social classes and ethnic groups and to affect the politics and policies of their neighbors.

Emigration from the third world is the result then of three factors: the demand for labor by recipient countries; political upheavals within developing countries that generate large numbers of refugees; and actions by third world governments to force some part of their populations to emigrate. To these three factors we should add the familiar ones — that substantial income and employment differences among countries make international migration attractive, that the improvement in international communications makes potential migrants more aware of opportunities to move, and that the lower costs and better transportation make migration easier.

Economic Effects

Few subjects in the field of either development or migration have stirred as much controversy as the assessment of the economic effects of labor migration for the sending countries. Those who view labor migration as economically beneficial see international migration as an equilibrating mechanism for shifting workers from labor-surplus, low-wage areas to labor-short, high-wage areas, a shift which pushes wages up in one and brings wages down in the other and serves to stimulate investment and increase productivity in both. A variety of gains have been adduced for the poorer sending countries: relief for the unemployed, an improvement in wages for those who remain behind, a stimulant for technological investment and innovation as the labor supply declines, a source of remittances that benefit a country's foreign exchange, an increase of resources for investment, a source of income to families improving their (and the country's) human capital, a stimulant to exports as overseas migrants buy from the home market, and an opportunity for migrants to acquire useful new skills and attitudes.

To each of these presumed benefits critics have their reply: remittances are used for wasteful consumer expenditures, not investment in productive activities; migrants create a hunger for foreign-made goods whose import reduces the foreign exchange benefits that accrue from remittances; the young, the innovative, the energetic tend to emigrate, draining a country's human resources; the loss of the rural unskilled reduces the manpower supply to the detriment of agriculture; the loss of the skilled decreases the quality of labor available to the industrial sector; investment by the home society in the education of its migrants benefits the receiving country which has borne none of the costs; the departure of workers does not lead to an increased investment in technology since sending countries have little capital to invest; when labor-saving technologies are introduced, they only worsen the employment plight of returned migrants.

Remittances are also said to induce inflation by pushing up the price of land, housing, and consumer goods. The return of migrants, it is argued, adds little to the productivity of their society since many of the returnees are failed migrants who were unable to adjust to migration, while the skills they may have acquired are rarely of use to the home country.

Finally, say the critics, the gains of emigration for the sending society are short-term. If migrants remain abroad or are joined by their families, then the remittance flows cease. Return migration increases when employment opportunities have declined in the receiving country and when the economy of the sending country is likely to have declined as well; thus, receiving countries transfer their unemployment back to the sending country at a time when the sending country is least able to provide employment to those who return.

Even if many of the assertions, both critical and supportive of emigration, can be proved or disproved by empirical evidence, the arguments rest on larger theoretical perspectives and values. For some scholars the issue is not only the balance of gains and losses within the emigrant society, but how these gains and losses are compared with those of the receiving society. W. R. Bohning, an economist with the ILO, writes that "the migrants actively contribute to the process of income generation and wealth creation in the richer country and thereby make it still richer as well as stronger relative to the country of origin." Bohning sees this as the moral basis for a system of compensating the sending countries, apart from the loss-of-human-capital justification. He calls this the "widening-gap rationale" (1979, p. 13).

Other scholars are critical of emigration because they value independence and view emigration as a mark of the opposite: dependence upon remittances to satisfy a deficit in the balance of payments; creating a situation whereby the home country needs to adjust its labor market and educational system to the demands for labor by advanced industrial countries; and the growing demand by migrants and their families for (and hence dependence on) Western-made and Western-type consumer goods. For the critics, "unequal exchange" and "dependence" are created by the migration process; these notions are embedded in a larger view about the structural relationship between developing and developed countries and about the nature of capitalist relationships.

Supporters of international migration chart up the economic benefits and losses of emigration with a view toward formulating policies that will increase the gains and reduce the losses for the sending societies. Thus, if there are losses in skilled manpower that might affect productivity, then manpower training policies should be developed which will anticipate manpower needs both at home and abroad; and if remittances are not being used productively, then the task of policy makers is to create incentives for their productive use. But to many critics of the international migration process these policy proposals merely tinker with a system that is inherently unjust.

This "structuralist" school of thought includes such scholars as W. R. Bohning, Ivo Baucic, Stephen Castles, Godula Kosack, Manuel Castells, Saskia Sassen-Koob, Joshua Reichert, Richard Mines, Alejandro Portes, Nermin Abadan-Unat, and Demetrios Papademetriou. Many of these critics are Marxists with an anticapitalist perspective. If they had their druthers, they would end international migration between developing and developed countries, but they believe that since it is an inherent feature of the world capitalist system, which benefits the center and impoverishes the periphery, little can be done until there is a new international economic order. Still others among the critics are nationalists who resent what they see as the unequal benefits from migration, the psychological sense of dependence, and the cultural losses that they perceive accompany the migration process. Alejandro Portes, for example, characterizes the illegal flow of immigrants from Mexico to the United States as inevitable, the product of a particular pattern of capitalist development in both countries and an expression of their interrelationship and dependence (1979, p. 434).

Labor Supply and Productivity

"Labour exports," writes Saskia Sassen-Koob, "cut into the labour supply of sending countries" (1978, p. 517). After surveying the work of other scholars she concludes:

> Decrease in the rural labour surplus through workers' emigration has not promoted the economic development of the pertinent regions . . . Thus, labour surplus countries such as Greece, Turkey, Yugoslavia have regular labour shortages during their peak agricultural seasons . . . Decrease in land utilization has been found in all the rural areas with high incidence of workers' out-migration . . . In North Africa, Turkey, Greece and Yugoslavia emigration did not shrink the labour surplus and hence unemployment; it increased unemployment by shrinking the economic base of the areas . . . The general effects of emigration from the rural areas have included decreased land utilization and hence decreased agricultural production and, in view of this, a potentially higher unemployment upon the return of migrants.   (pp. 533–535)

The result of migration from poor to rich countries is the emergence of a "new type of dependence in addition to the existing ones: dependence on the labor-importing countries for the employment of a segment of their labor force and for a share of national income" (p. 541).

A number of recent empirical studies in communities in Mexico emphasize the negative economic effects. Joshua Reichert, in a study of the town of Guadalupe and the surrounding regions, notes that the number of hectares under cultivation has decreased by as much as 50 percent since 1960, due, he says, to the growing number of migrant landlords and the shortage of townspeople willing to work as sharecroppers. He concludes on the pessimistic note that seasonal migration from Guadalupe to the United States "actually serves to maintain (if not increase) the very conditions of underdevelopment, underemployment and unequal distribution of capital resources that make migration necessary in the first place" (1981, p. 64).

Another critic of emigration, Richard Mines, reports that the rural Mexican community he studied also suffered a decline in the amount of cultivated land and in the demand for unskilled sharecroppers.

He reports no significant improvement in agricultural technology or new investments. Returns on investment in agriculture are low: in 1978 earnings to landowners from the corn and beans harvest netted a 4 percent return, and land rental only 5 percent at a time when Mexican banks were paying 16 percent on long-term deposits (1981, p. 134). But rather than ask why the return on agricultural investment was low and why the growth rate in Mexican agriculture was only 2.3 percent per annum in the 1970s as compared with 3.6 percent in the 1960s, Mines concludes that the rural economy "has been distorted by migration flows." As a result of emigration, he concludes, "the village economy remains frozen in its traditional low-productivity system" (p. 155). He asserts but does not demonstrate that emigration is the causal factor in the decline in agricultural productivity, although his data show a low investment in agriculture even among cultivating farmers, not simply among absentee landlords.

In their study of a Mexican village, James Stuart and Michael Kearney report heavy investment in housing rather than in "productive investment" and conclude that migration has "not significantly contributed to long term economic development. Instead, it is a palliative for unemployment, land shortage, lack of credit and all the other typical conditions of rural stagnation. Many of the presumed benefits of migration such as introduction of new skills, technological innovations, equalization of income, and decreased land rent have not resulted" (1981, p. 37).

The most positive report on the effects of emigration in rural Mexico comes from a study by Wayne Cornelius. His survey of nine communities, all with high emigration rates, indicates that severe labor shortages have not developed in the rural communities so that, "contrary to the fear of some Mexican government officials, emigration to the United States does not seem to depress agricultural production" (1976, p. 32). Again, in contrast to other community studies in Mexico, he finds that considerable productive investment took place in the communities he surveyed, not in agriculture but in small, hand-operated cloth-weaving machine shops. He also finds that many who were landless have been able to acquire land and that "more generally migration to the U.S. has improved possibilities for social and economic mobility in small towns and villages where most wealth (especially in the form of land) had formerly been acquired through inheritance. Thus social stratification is less rigid and the local distribution of wealth is more equitable than would otherwise be the case" (p. 47).

Has the loss of labor in the agricultural sector led to the withdrawal of land from cultivation, increased absentee landlordism, and a failure to invest in new agricultural technologies? Has emigration from developing countries resulted in a decline in agricultural productivity? If the community studies give mixed results, so do the national data provided by the World Bank (1982).

Compared with other middle-income economies, the countries of emigration were about average in agricultural growth rate. In 1960–1970 the average agricultural growth rate was 3.5 percent, equaled or exceeded by four of the eight countries with available data, and in 1970–1980 the average agricultural growth rate was 2.9 percent, exceeded by five of the nine.

Many scholars cite Yemen as the extreme case of a country whose agricultural production has declined as a result of the emigration of 1.23 million Yemenis, 19 percent of the total population of the country. Yemen, writes Jon Swanson, depends upon hand labor for its irrigation and terrace farming. Available farming cannot replace labor lost through migration. The result has been a rise of wages, the abandonment of marginal lands, a decline in production, and increased dependence upon others for food (1979). According to World Bank data, however, agricultural production has increased in Yemen by 3.7 percent annually in the 1970s, but the farmers apparently shifted from food production to the more profitable production of *qat*, a widely used drug. "It is true," replies Kindleberger, "that population can be depleted below some optimal level and leave villages, regions, and even countries suffering from the diseconomies of too small scale," but he doubts that this has occurred in Portugal, Spain, southern Italy, Greece, and Turkey, where rates of economic growth were high during the period of high emigration. As for the argument that because emigrants are the younger, more skilled, healthy, intelligent, and so on and their loss pulls down production more than their consumption saves, "this is the familiar complaint of the agricultural partisans who bewail rural exodus" (Kindleberger, 1967, p. 97; see also Lipton, 1980, pp. 1–24).

Human Capital and Emigration

The emigration of educated or skilled workers is criticized from two perspectives. The first is that the country of emigration has borne the costs of educating individuals while the receiving country reaps the gains. Bohning, a leading exponent of this viewpoint, sees this skill drain as a form of return aid from developing to developed countries, one not matched by remittances. "Migrants have accumulated human capital at the taxpayers' expense in the country of origin," writes Bohning (p. 10).

It is this perspective that leads Bohning, Bhagwati, and others to argue that compensation should be paid, either by the migrant himself or by the country of employment. The justification is not merely economic but, writes Bohning, is "rooted in morality and ethics. It questions the morality of obtaining one's education or training at society's expense and then leaving that society in the lurch. It further questions the fairness of the existing international economic order which as a rule puts a price tag on international resource transfers, such as the movements of financial capital or of capital embodied in machinery, but does not do so in the case of the largely one-way traffic of human resources from low income to high income countries" (p. 10).

The reply of neoclassical economists is that one should view what the state has invested in a young person's education as a "sunk cost" and the question is not the real cost but opportunity cost. "What is the most effective use to make of existing labor, to employ it abroad or leave it unemployed at home; or, if there are job opportunities at home, to employ it at home with a small amount of capital or abroad with more?" (Kindleberger, 1967, p. 99).

Neither the critics nor supporters of emigration who see the migrant as human capital deal explicitly with the question of whether education should be viewed as a *right* or as an *investment* by the state. The investment concept (which both critics and supporters share) assumes that the state or society (as distinct from the individual) is entitled to a return on that investment. In contrast, the conception of education as a *right* assumes that how (and where) citizens utilize the skills and knowledge they acquire through education is their own private concern.

For some years the government of Rumania used the migrant-as-human-capital justification in its policy toward citizens who wished to emigrate. The government permitted Jews to leave, but only if they compensated the government for the cost of their education; if they were unable to do so, then Jews abroad (or the Israeli government) were required to pay the Rumanian government to release those who wished to emigrate. This policy — defined as compensation for educational expenditures by the Rumanian government and as selling Jews for hard currency by its critics — was ended when the U.S. government threatened to cancel its favored-nation tariff policy toward Rumania unless the policy were ended.

A curious feature of the compensation position is that it implies that individuals who received an education at state expense should reimburse it if they go abroad, while those who paid for their education should be free from such a requirement. Thus both the degree of freedom and cost to the individual is greater in a society where advanced education is private than where it is public; and where both are present the policy is more beneficial to those who are rich and can afford to pay for their education than those who are poor and must depend upon state support. It is not always clear whether the returns on the investment in human capital are to be made to *society* or to the *state*. The advocates of compensation often speak of a return to *society* for the costs of education, but invariably call for compensation to the *state*. Bohning is the most explicit in this view, arguing that the *public* costs of education and training should be repaid (1979, p. 11). In contrast, neoclassical economists are concerned with returns on educational investment to the *society* from which the migrant comes.

The critics of emigration have also pointed to the shortage of skilled manpower as a serious consequence of emigration. Some sectors of the economy may suffer attendant losses in productivity. Internal migration and occupational mobility could remedy manpower shortages, but there can be lags, particularly in jobs where substantial skills and experience are necessary. Replacement costs may be very low in the case of comparatively unskilled workers, or very high if there are training costs. In some instances investments in technologies will reduce the need for labor. Some critics of migration have also suggested that manpower shortages may push labor costs up with the result that an industry may lose its competitive edge if it is producing for export. It is possible therefore, suggests Charles Stahl, that emigration "could generate unemployment from the supply side as well as from the demand side . . . emigration may lead to an output loss and unemployment in those industries which cannot find workers to replace migrants" (1982).

Reports abound from Egypt, Jordan, Turkey, and Yugoslavia of labor shortages in particular industries and occupations, but how detrimental these have been for those industries is not clear. Reports on the impact of emigration on industrial growth in Puerto Rico suggest that these concerns may be exaggerated.

Puerto Rico has had the highest rate of emigration of any country in the third world. In the 1950s the average out-migration was over 40,000 persons per year, reaching 70,000 in 1973. By 1970 there were 1.4 million Puerto Ricans living on the U.S. mainland, while Puerto Rico itself had a population of 2.7 million. Thirty-five percent of the total population of Puerto Ricans lived on the mainland and another third of a million were returned migrants. In all over 42 percent of all Puerto Ricans had lived or were living on the mainland (Levine, 1982; see also Johnson, 1982). This massive exodus to the mainland took place at a time when Puerto Rico experienced a major infusion of new investment, rapid industrial growth, and an impressive increase in per capita income. Per capita income rose from $110 in 1940 to $889 in 1965 and by 1977 it was $2,472 (Levine, 1982, p. 169). Industrial growth rates were among the highest in the third world.

Throughout the sixties and early seventies *emigration* and *industrialization* took place simultaneously. The development plan known as Operation Bootstrap offered tax exemptions, aid in the construction of manufacturing plants, inclusion within U.S. tariff walls, and a variety of incentives to entice private investment. The result was investment not only from mainland capitalists but from returned migrants as well. There was considerable upward mobility on the part of returned migrants, and a new successful middle class came into being, "who having taken advantage of opportunities which became available as a result of modernization resumed their lives in Puerto Rico under favorable circumstances — as professionals, white collar workers, and highly skilled technicians. Many started life in rural areas but ultimately settled in San Juan, thus experiencing a fair degree of social mobility" (Levine, 1982, p. 262). The rapid growth of factories in Puerto Rico — new factories were opening at an average of five per week in the early sixties — was apparently not hampered by high emigration. The factories drew their labor from the countryside. From 1940 to 1970 Puerto Rico's rural population declined from 70 percent to 41 percent and its urban centers grew from 30 percent to 58 percent. At the same time a large part of the Puerto Rican rural (as well as urban) population emigrated to the mainland.

The *compatibility* of emigration and rapid industrialization is demonstrated by data from other countries of high emigration. Italy, with 1,172,000 of its workers employed in Western Europe in 1973, experienced a 6.2 percent annual growth rate in industry from 1960 to 1970. Turkey (850,000 workers in Western Europe) grew at 9.6 percent per annum; Algeria (500,000 workers, or 19.5 percent of its work force, among the highest in the countries of emigration) grew at 11.6 percent; Greece (246,000 workers) grew at 9.4 percent per annum. Mexico (reliable emigration data not available) had an industrial growth rate of 9.1 percent and Colombia 6.0 percent.

Five of the eight labor-exporting countries for which data were available grew at above industrial growth rates from 1960 to 1970 (middle-income economies averaged 7.4 percent per annum growth rates) and seven of the nine equaled or exceeded the average industrial growth rates from 1970 to 1980 (6.6 percent). In virtually every instance, it should also be noted, both the agricultural and industrial growth rates of the labor-exporting countries exceeded that of the countries of Western Europe and the United States which imported labor.

Remittances

In 1978 remittances to the third world from migrants totaled $23 billion, a tenth of the earnings that came from exports. By 1982 remittances reportedly rose to $40 billion. For some countries — Yugoslavia, Greece, Turkey, Italy, Portugal, Jordan, Morocco, Pakistan, India, Egypt, and Yemen — remittances were equal to a third or more of earnings from exports. For several countries remittances from emigration made up the total deficit in the balance of payments.

Critics of emigration have, however, suggested that how the remittances are used by the migrants and their families is at least as important a determinant of the costs and benefits of emigration. W. R. Bohning explains that emigration means a loss of effective manpower for a developing country. Hence "to obtain positive effects, the contribution of migrants to the home country's economy would have to be larger than before migration. For instance, remittances must overcompensate output losses without counter-productive inflation effects; or return migrants must make good in the long term the negative effects arising in the short term; or emigration must free resources for a more rational and efficient organization of the economy" (1975, p. 261).

After surveying a number of studies on the use of remittances, Bohning concludes that remittances as currently used represent a loss. The money is not productively spent. "Observers are generally agreed that returning migrants engage in conspicuous consumption of durables, non-durables and housing . . . The adoption of modern consumer patterns is . . . of questionable benefit." Moreover, "an equivocal effect of the return of rural migrants to their place of origin is the widespread construction of new houses in areas of doubtful viability and lacking in infrastructures. Apart from providing employment in construction, this saddles the administration with the task of providing roads, electricity, water and sewage systems that might be more cost-effectively allocated to viable areas" (1975, p. 262).

The "wasteful" use of remittances is also lamented by Demetriou Papademetriou, former editor of the journal *International Migration Review*. "Why are the obvious benefits from remittances so controversial?" he asks in his report on emigration from Greece. "The answer . . . is found in some of the economic consequences of such remitted earnings and in the uneconomical, unproductive, and often wasteful manner in which they are expended. As much as two-thirds of repatriated savings are spent on housing. The remaining funds are spent primarily on land purchases, home appliances, clothing and debt repayment, with only insignificant amounts going toward the purchase of industrial or agricultural equipment" (1979).

In the same vein Sassen-Koob writes: "There is little doubt that the individual migrants and their families benefit from the increase in their incomes. But some serious doubts are being raised as to, among others, the inflationary effects of an increase in national income which is not related to an increase in real productive capacity and which, given the kind of consumption it creates, does not have an economic growth function" (1978, p. 517).

Critics also point to the possible maldistribution of income that may result from remittances. Writing about Turkey, Suzanne Paine says that in assessing the income distribution effects of migration,

> it is necessary to take into account not only the change in the circumstances of migrants and their families but also the effect that this has on the income of others. For instance, although a poor peasant may return, buy land and set himself up as a farmer using mechanized techniques, this may force existing tenants and sharecroppers not only to join the ranks of the landless rural proletariat but also to become unemployed if only some are subsequently hired . . . Within industry, migration will affect workers' income distribution if, for instance, by creating skilled labour shortages it increases skill differentials — or leads to the introduction of more capital intensive machinery so that workers are made unemployed. (1974, p. 51)

Paine also reports that "since the poorest among the Turkish population have not been recruited for work abroad, and have shared in little, if any, of the rewards from the operation of the migration system . . . the adoption of a labour export strategy has probably not improved and may have actually worsened the distribution of income in Turkey" (p. 148).

Ecevit and Zachariah in their study for the World Bank suggest that the impact of remittances is positive only if these are channeled into productive investments and if the increased demand for domestic consumer goods is satisfied "through existing productivity capacity," and not through imports that cannot be paid for through increased domestic productivity (1980, p. 36). Indications are clear that some proportion of remittances is used to bring in imported consumer goods, exemplifying the nonproductive, wasteful effects of remittances.

Finally, "remittances symbolize dependence," writes Bohning (1981). Another study describes the effect of remittances in a Caribbean isle: "It [a St. Lucian fishing village] has the appearance of prosperity . . . but the impression is illusory, for the new houses and bright paint are not the result of economic growth in the area, but of remittances from London-based villages" (Brana-Shute and Brana-Shute, 1982, p. 281). The Turkish social scientist Nermin Abadan-Unat makes a more explicit statement of the dependence inherent in the relationship between remittances and emigration: "The strong increase of remittances, secured by the migrant workers, is in reality connected to a subordinate pattern of industrialization and does not permit to break the spiral of development" (1976, p. 3). And again: "To sum up, the asymmetric interaction of Turkey as a manpower exporting country with a number of European industrial countries indicates the existence of an undeniable degree of economic dependency" (p. 44).

To summarize the charges: remittances are wastefully spent on consumer goods rather than productively invested, nurture a consumer mentality, worsen imports, are inflationary, result in a maldistribution of income, and increase dependence.

It is curious that the assessment of how productive is the use of remittances by migrants and their families has become such a central criterion in deciding the costs and benefits of emigration. At first it would appear to be a reasonable criterion: clearly a country gains more if migrants use some of their remittances to improve the technology and productivity of agriculture, start businesses, or invest their savings in new or expanding industries. The propensity of migrants to save and to transmit part of their savings to family at home, and for returning migrants to bring substantial savings with them, makes the question of whether these savings contribute to economic growth reasonable.

On the other hand, the same criterion is not normally applied to others in the society who have experienced substantial increases in income. What is the propensity to save and to invest in productive activities, for example, on the part of doctors, lawyers, engineers, and other professionals with high and expanding incomes? Or workers in the industrial sector who have received large salary increases? Or the vast numbers of government civil servants in most developing countries?

Moreover, the failure to make productive investments is rarely linked to the question of the opportunities for such investments. In many instances (Yugoslavia is one) opportunities for private investment are severely restricted. The failure of agricultural families to use remittances in agriculture suggests that the lack of availability of credit is not necessarily the barrier to productive investment. The system of land tenure, the profitability of agriculture, the availability of marketing opportunities, and a variety of other factors may determine whether remittances are used for investment.

Oberai and Singh, writing on the impact of remittances on a village in the Indian Punjab, the center of India's green revolution, find that a significant portion of households receiving remittances do use them productively. They report that investments in implements, fertilizers, high yielding variety seeds, and land improvements were high. In contrast, those with smaller holdings were more likely to spend remittances on debt repayment and on consumption (1980; see also Stark, 1979). Other studies — Gilani on Pakistan (1982), Cornelius on Mexico (1978) — reveal that in numerous instances remittances are used productively in the agricultural sector. The problem is not how to persuade migrants and their families to invest in agriculture, but more broadly how to make investment in agriculture attractive.

The question of whether remittances are used productively *by migrants* may in any event be recast as the question of whether savings are productively invested by *banks* and *borrowers*. Migrants do have a propensity to save and much of their savings is used for building or expanding their homes. The central question is whether savings entering the official banking system increase the availability of credit, and then whether the credit is productively employed — not whether the migrants themselves start businesses, purchase agricultural equipment, or invest in the stock market.

Moreover, the charge that migrants are engaged in wasteful consumer expenditures rests on two normative judgments. One is that only investments in agriculture and industry are productive. From this point of view investment in housing for rental purposes — a common practice in Turkey, for example — is not productive though it yields a high return to the investor. Nor are expenditures on education and health classified as productive, though they may contribute to a growth in human capital. Finally, the purchase of land — often the largest single expenditure — is considered nonproductive, though how the sellers of land spend their earnings (the second order effects) has not been studied.

The second value judgment is that consumerism, especially as practiced by low-income people, is morally undesirable, even though many of the purchases made by migrants and their families are the same as those made by the native middle classes. Portes, for example, decries the "cult of consumption" (1979, p. 434). Nationalist-minded elites are critical of a growing consumer preference for things Western. The diffusion of consumer tastes from developed to developing countries — the preference for jeans and other Western clothes, digital watches, soft drinks, video tapes, hi-fi sets — is bitterly opposed by many nationalists who see this diffusion as destructive of indigenous values and culture. Particularly disturbing is that these consumer goods are valued not only for their utility but for the status they give to their owners, with the implication that things that are not Western in origin are of low value.

The concern that nationalists express over the growth of consumerism is part of a general anxiety about the value system of the migrants themselves and the impact of these values on other members of society. In communities with a high rate of emigration the attitude develops that employment abroad is the key to economic success and social status, while staying at home means only failure and poverty. Emigration can thus lead to the denigration of one's own society — its economy, social order, its polity, what it produces and, above all, what prospect it offers for a better life. The issue of dependence is thus as much a statement about the psychological state of the relationship between the sending and receiving countries as it is about the economic relationship.

Dependence, of course, is in the mind of the beholder. Migrants and their families are more likely to see remittances as a source of independence. Remittances, for example, may permit a young married couple to purchase their own home, freeing them from having to live with their parents. A Thai study reports that the primary goal of migrants is to accumulate enough savings to establish their own independent household. Ordinarily, a low-income Thai couple may take fifteen to twenty years to purchase a permanent home and establish its independence, while only two to three years of working in the Middle East will enable a couple to build a house (Singhanetra-Renard, 1983).

Remittances have sometimes also increased the independence of women in the household. A study of villages in the Indian state of Kerala reports that more women from migrant households have been operating the family bank accounts, acknowledging the need to learn to read and write, and generally becoming more able to manage the family income and property (Gulati, 1983).

Intergenerational conflicts over the use of remittances may flare up as young couples resist the financial claims of their parents and kin. Among the consequences of migration therefore may be a decline in the traditional authority relationships within the extended family, increased nucleation of the family, and a growing egalitarian relationship between wives and husbands (McIntosh, 1981), all of which can be regarded as indications of growing independence by nuclear families and the wives of migrants. That a price is paid for this independence — psychological strains within the extended family, a loss of authority by migrant husbands over their children and wives, and an increase in divorce rates — is also evident, though it should be noted that these costs (if indeed they are costs) may accompany urbanization, education, an increase of women in the labor force, and other social changes that transform the traditional family structures.

However, the consumerism of migrants and their families can be seen as an effort on the part of people who have newly acquired wealth to achieve the comfort and status hitherto enjoyed only by landowners and the more educated urban classes. Acquiring consumer goods is the route of many migrant families to move up the social scale through socially advantageous marriages. (It is reported that male migrants often seek to marry educated women or women from higher-status families.) The purchase of land and investments in education are additional indications of the effort the migrant families make to improve their social and economic status. From this perspective migration can be viewed as a family strategy, not simply the act of an individual migrant. Rather than being merely an attempt to achieve limited economic gain, migration is part of a larger set of goals and a broader set of social processes (Moch, Page, and Tilly, 1979; Stark, 1982).

However much critics of emigration have lamented the dependence by the poor countries on the rich and deplored consumer mentalities, occasional labor shortages, the failure of remittances to provide the expected benefits, and the risks of return migration during a period of economic downturn, the fact remains that the major labor-exporting countries have not sought to slow down the process. To the contrary, even as migration to Western Europe has declined, many third world countries are now competing for opportunities to export their manpower into the oil-rich countries of the Middle East. Emigration is part of the panoply of development policies pursued by many developing countries. The neo-Marxist and nationalist critics of emigration have not persuaded governments to forgo the benefits of remittances, reduced unemployment, and construction contracts that result from exporting labor.

The Unit of Analysis

Both Marxist and neoclassical scholars distinguish between the costs and benefits of migration for the migrants and their families and the costs and benefits for the community or country from which the migrants come. Most scholars agree that the migrants and their families are gainers; their disagreements are over the impact of migration on the natives in the countries into which migrants move and upon those from which they come. But both sides generally assume that the *country* is the appropriate unit of analysis. This view is clearly expounded by Charles Stahl, an economist writing for the ILO:

> Any benefits and costs which accrue specifically to the emigrant while outside his home country do not count in the calculation of social costs and benefits. Only the benefits and costs which the emigration decision confers upon those remaining behind count. However, once the emigrant returns any benefits and costs which continue to accrue to him because of his migration enter into the calculation of social benefits and costs. (1982, p. 187)

Stahl calls this "a domestic perspective," by which he means that "the principal aim of economic development should be that individuals are not forced to leave their socio-cultural-linguistic milieu to realize their economic aspirations." From this perspective the total emigration of the population of one country (say Yemen) to another (say Saudi Arabia) would be a development loss even if the Yemenite population were better off by partaking in the higher rate of development in Saudi Arabia. Given the importance of the nation-state in the contemporary world, this is not an unreasonable position. There are, however, alternative perspectives that are no less valid.

If one's welfare perspective took as its starting point the well-being of an entire national population wherever it lives, then a cost-benefit assessment should not be limited to the country of origin, and the cost-benefit ratios would change. Consider for example what the World Bank's annual World Development Report would look like if populations, not nation-states, were the units of analysis. Assume there were tables on per capita income, per capita growth rates, population growth rates, education, longevity, and so on by nationality rather than by country. Turks, Yugoslavs, Portuguese, Greeks, Algerians, Tunisians, Moroccans, and other emigrating peoples would look better than do the equivalent tables by country.

Politically this is not an absurd position. Indeed, the governments of sending countries often take a nationality rather than nation-state perspective. Governments of sending countries may consider the gains of their emigrants as part of the net national gain. It is not simply that remittances go up, or that employment opportunities for those who remain improve, but that the benefits to the migrants themselves constitute a national gain.

The well-being of the migrant community abroad is generally regarded as an important concern in the foreign policies of states. Do former citizens receive equal treatment? Are they able to improve their education, income, social status, and political influence? Do they have the opportunity to preserve their culture and identity? However much some nationalists may lament the loss of their citizens to another country, governments continue to view the well-being of their expatriates from a national perspective. They are, psychologically at least, incorporated into the fictional mental tables of national well-being. It would be interesting if these fictional mental tables were in fact made by such data gathering and reporting institutions as the World Bank, the Overseas Development Council, and the

Population Council. These institutions might prepare tables with development data, quality-of-life social indicators, and changing fertility and mortality rates by nationality rather than by country.

A cost-benefit calculation takes on still another dimension from the viewpoint of a particular *ethnic group* rather than from the perspective of either a nationality or a country. For example, the emigration of an ethnic minority may represent a significant loss to a developing country if the group has substantially higher education, occupation, and income levels than does the majority of the population. The emigration of Chinese merchants, professionals, and other middle-class elements from Vietnam, of the Indian business and professional community from East Africa, of the Indian trading community from Burma, and of educated Tamils from Sri Lanka represents an economic loss to the countries of emigration. These considerations were obviously not paramount in the policies of those governments, which were more concerned with eliminating a despised ethnic minority and providing new employment opportunities for the middle classes belonging to the majority ethnic group than they were with the economic well-being of the country. Indeed, a government engaged in the expulsion of an ethnic minority may be thinking of its own ethnic group as the unit for its cost-benefit analysis.

Conversely, an emigrating ethnic group may take itself as the unit for assessing effects. Members of an ethnic minority, even though they are better off economically than the average within their own country, may feel that their opportunities are so constricted that they prefer to emigrate. Consider, for example, the position of Jews in the Soviet Union. On the average they are better educated, hold higher-status occupations, and earn higher incomes than most Soviet citizens. Studies conducted of Soviet Jewish emigrés to Israel and to the United States report that their income, educational, and occupational levels are higher outside than when they were in the Soviet Union. From the point of view of world Jewry, the Jewish community is economically better off — let us put aside the question of religious and political gains — if Jews emigrate from the Soviet Union to Israel, Western Europe, or the United States than if they remain in the Soviet Union.

Many other diaspora communities (both those that are a minority and those that are a majority in their native land) share this perspective. The contrast with the perspective of scholars is striking. Many scholars, for example, point to Ireland as a country which has suffered as a consequence of large-scale emigration. Even if the argument is correct (it is by no means clear that there is a causal relationship between emigration and Ireland's low per capita income), it is worth considering whether the Irish as a people are better off for these emigrations. Some 4.5 million people emigrated from Ireland to the United States between 1831 and 1930. The number of Irish living outside Ireland clearly exceeds the 3.4 million living within the country, where the per capita income was $4,880 in 1980 (as against $11,360 in the United States). Are the Irish of the world worse or better off economically as a consequence of large-scale emigration?

A great many Poles, Hungarians, Czechs, Sri Lankan Tamils, Malaysian Chinese, Iraqi and Iranian Kurds, Turkish Armenians, Eritreans, Ethiopians, Haitians, and Cubans living outside their home country believe — probably correctly — that the well-being of their ethnic group is enhanced if large numbers emigrate. For them their people, not their country, is the unit of analysis. This perspective is translated into political action: migrant communities are often active in promoting legislation within their host country which would enable larger numbers of their countrymen to emigrate.

Conclusion

Governments in the third world see control over emigration as both a political and economic policy instrument. Exile or forced migration can be a punishment inflicted upon critics of the regime and upon out-of-favor social classes or ethnic groups. Control over emigration can also be a benefit to be distributed, a form of patronage. And it can be an instrument for forestalling social and political costs by reducing employment. The key centers of power within a government may all see the benefits of emigration. The finance ministry sees the benefits from remittances and an improved balance of payments. The labor ministry (and many politicians) sees the benefits of relieving unemployment, both unskilled and educated. The commerce ministry sees the ties between labor export, construction contracts, and export promotion. The ministry of external affairs may be a less enthusiastic booster of emigration, but it too may see benefits in creating new interdependencies. Forced emigration, as we have seen, may provide a government with a bargaining chip in negotiations, a means of exercising pressure on one's neighbors for the achievement of bilateral assistance or for influencing security policies.

Ideological rhetoric is a poor guide to what elites of the countries of emigration actually think or believe. Marxist critics of emigration notwithstanding, it is many of the Marxist countries that have most encouraged and even forced emigration; and it is third world nationalist critics who are among the most opposed to restrictions on immigration into advanced industrial countries.

As one would expect, a number of third world countries actively promote emigration, oppose restrictions on immigration by advanced industrial and oil-producing countries, and seek within the countries of immigration political allies, including their own nationals or former nationals, to permit migration to continue. The growth of immigration restrictions by the advanced industrial and oil-producing countries — shaped as much by political as by economic conditions within these countries — could well become a source of conflict between sending and receiving countries. Even more sensitive than the question of how many migrants are allowed to enter is the question of whether the nationals of a third world country have the same opportunities for immigration as others; and a second question is whether their nationals are treated at least as well as other migrants and perhaps equal to citizens of the labor-importing country.

Long after migration flows and remittances have diminished, the major effects of international migration will be felt. Western Europe and North America will have significant numbers of people from the third world, and the labor-importing countries of the Persian Gulf will have substantial numbers of Arab and Asian migrants. How these populations are treated by the host society, and what role the migrants and their descendants play in forging economic, cultural, and political links between the host country and their country of origin are questions that have significant long-term consequences.

EIGHT

Refugees and Mass Exoduses: The Search for a Humane, Effective Policy

Francis X. Sutton

THE MOST celebrated of refugees or exiles? Worldwide, one supposes it must be Karl Marx, with Lenin trailing a hyphen behind. Norman Davies, in the course of describing the Great Polish Emigration of 1831, takes a more Western and literary perspective and assumes it must be Dante (Davies, 1981, p. 276). Nominations will differ according to tastes and passions, memories, nationalities, professions. We Americans like to remember the refugees who have come to us — Albert Einstein, Igor Stravinsky, Thomas Mann — perhaps John von Neumann if we revere mathematics; Czeslaw Milosz if we love poetry; Alexander Solzhenitsyn if we relish jeremiads. Italians would surely start with Dante and add Garibaldi, Mazzini, and then maybe someone like Enrico Fermi. (Would any remember the Popes in Avignon?) The Poles would surely list Prince Adam Czartoryski, Mickiewicz, and Kosciuszko; the Hungarians, Kossuth, Béla Bartók. I am not brave enough to guess who would now head the list of educated Chinese or Indians or Africans.

It is a game that ought to be played with people from various walks of life and parts of the world, not simply as a diversion among friends for an evening, but as a kind of spiritual exercise to remember those who have needed to run away and find a place that would take them in, the bitter loss that exiles feel, but also the undefeated resilience which makes it possible for the uprooted to take up new lives and go on with their work.

Not many of us in this hurrying age can remember if Dante was a Guelf or a Ghibelline, or indeed what a White or a Black was in Florence, but we know that he was a political exile, and that throughout history tensions and vulnerabilities erupt from time to time in wars and revolutions, persecutions and expulsions. Many are forced to flee for their lives and when they do, we speak of refugees. Notorious difficulties in defining who precisely is a refugee will have to occupy us through the course of this chapter, but some elementary distinctions can readily be made. Not all exiles are refugees. James Joyce writing in Trieste, Zurich, and Paris was surely an exile but not a refugee. Whatever other criteria may be pertinent, refugees are for some cause, and are commonly, if not always easily, distinguished in law and practice from the large numbers of voluntary migrants the world has had and continues to have. Also, there have obviously been involuntary migrations that were not refugee movements, the Atlantic slave trade being a major, but, unhappily, not an isolated example. And in our own day, Solzhenitsyn and others might better be called expellees than refugees.

These elementary and rough distinctions apart, we need to remember that beside the great and famous there have been and are masses of refugees we can only enumerate uncertainly. Political leaders, scholars, and intellectuals have importance, both real and symbolic, that makes them objects of particular attention when they are forced to be refugees. But it is the mass movements that create the main issues of refugee policy and practice, and the twentieth century has had a plethora of them. We hardly need be reminded of the major ones, but a broad review of the movements of populations since the First World War will help to examine the types of response that have occurred and provide the background to the now-troubling question about possibly chronic refugee problems in the future.

In the first half of this century wars, revolution, and the pressure to uniformity in nation-states produced a great sea of population movements out of which grew much of the law and practice the world now has for dealing with refugees. Eugene Kulischer, who had himself fled from Russia in 1920, from Germany in 1936, and from occupied France in 1941, put together the standard enumerations for the period following the 1914–1918 war (summarized in Tilly, 1978, pp. 61–62). He counted:

- 1.2 million Greeks to Greece from Turkey (1922–1923)

- 1.15 million Russians to Europe outside the Soviet Union (1918–1922)

- 1.1 million repatriated from Russia to Poland (1918–1925)

- 900,000 Poles from former Russian and Austrian Poland to former German Poland (1918–1921)

- 700,000 Germans from Western Poland, Danzig, and Memel to Germany (1918–1925).

World War II brought displacements that make these numbers seem small:

- 6 million Reich Germans from New Poland to Germany (1944–1947)

- 5 million Jews from Germany to extermination camps in Poland and elsewhere (1940–1944)

- 4 million Reich Germans from the Soviet Zone in occupied Germany to the U.S. and British Zones (1945–1946)

- 3 million Poles from Old Poland to New Poland (1945–1946)

- 2.7 million ethnic Germans from Czechoslovakia to Germany and Austria (1945–1946)

- 1 million ethnic Germans from Old Poland to Germany (1944–1945).

Kulischer's summary estimate was that by May 1945 there were 40.5 million uprooted people in Europe, excluding non-German forced laborers and those Germans who fled before the advancing Soviet armies.

An estimated 1.6 million persons displaced from East European countries between 1939 and 1945 refused repatriation after the war, and the appalling fate of those sent back to the Soviet Union makes for regrets that this number was not larger. Subsequent movements from Eastern Europe in the period 1945–1966 amounted to some 1.27 million, according to the records of a U.S. Escapee Program. Some 60,000 refugees from Czechoslovakia in 1948 and 200,000 from Hungary in 1956 made part of this total.

As European movements rather slowly declined after World War II, an array of movements mounted in other parts of the world, continuing into the present.

In Asia

The great process of colonial devolution that followed World War II produced an enormous dislocation in the partition of India. The numbers are estimated between 13 and 15 million, as Muslims went to East and West Pakistan and Hindus and Sikhs fled to India.

In 1971, the breakup of Pakistan brought for a brief time some 10 million Bangladeshis across the border into India.

Following the 1945 Potsdam Conference's division of the country at the 38th parallel, 4 to 5 million Korean repatriates and refugees from North Korea and Japan to South Korea added some 25 percent to the population of South Korea by 1959.

Two million Chinese refugees from the mainland entered Hong Kong and Macao in the period 1948–1966.

From 850,000 to 950,000 Vietnamese moved south of the 17th parallel after the 1954 Geneva Conference.

In the Middle East

An estimated 500,000 Palestinian residents, mostly Arabs, fled the 1948–1949 Arab-Israeli conflict and by 1966 a total of 1,317,000 Palestinian refugees were registered with the United Nations Relief and Works Agency for Palestine Refugees in the Near East (UNRWA).

During the period 1948–1964, 1,209,282 immigrants were admitted to Israel from East and Central Europe, Africa, and the Middle East.

In Africa

About 1 million left Algeria during and after the independence struggle (to 1962).

Other French repatriates from Africa included 138,000 from Tunisia and 172,000 from Morocco after independence (1956), and about 10,000 from Guinea (1958).

About 750,000 Portuguese were repatriated from Angola and Mozambique following independence in 1975.

Within Africa, following the wave of independence in 1960–1961, an estimated 650,000 had fled to neighboring countries by 1966.

Since 1961 a private organization, the U.S. Committee on Refugees, has published an annual world refugee survey assembling statistics from the office of the United Nations High Commissioner for Refugees (UNHCR) and other sources. The survey has usually included in its totals displaced persons within their own countries as well as those fleeing across national boundaries. The 1961 survey counted 15 million refugees and displaced persons, and in subsequent years through 1984 its totals ranged from a low of 8 million in 1964 to a high of 18 million in 1970 with the average at about 14 million (*World Refugee Survey, 1961–1984*). There have been various changes over the years in the way the estimates are made that make trends difficult to discern, and some of the data are very rough and unreliable (for example, the estimate of the number of Iranians internally displaced in the Iran-Iraq War, or the number of Ethiopians displaced since the late 1970s). But the U.S. Committee represents humanitarian and service concerns and thus is not disposed to minimize the numbers it reports (unlike some official sources). These rough enumerations do at least suggest that refugee totals have shown no clear tendency to diminution.

Most of the refugees in the latter half of this century have continued to originate in the third world, with Asia and Africa providing the largest numbers. A Pan-African conference on refugees, held in Arusha in May of 1979, concluded that there were between 3.5 and 4 million refugees in Africa at the time, representing approximately 1 percent of the continent's population. Oppressive regimes in Guinea, Equatorial Guinea, and Uganda have been responsible for hundreds of thousands of refugees. But the greater number have fled wars and civil strife with an ebb and flow depending upon the course of these struggles.

The statistics in the 1984 World Refugee Report show a total of 2,633,000 refugees in various countries of Africa, 700,000 of them in Somalia and 690,000 in Sudan. In Asia, large flows of refugees since 1970 have been generated by the Indo-Pakistan war already noted, war and oppression in Indochina, and the Soviet invasion of Afghanistan. A September 30, 1985, summary by the U.S. Department of State on Indochinese refugee flows since April 1975 counted 1,676,148 arrivals in Southeast Asia. The number of departures has been sadly and substantially larger, with many lost at sea, refused landing, thrust back over the Cambodian border, or left there in uncertain status. By this date in 1985, while most of these refugees had been resettled, 176,265 remained in refugee camps. Refugees from Afghanistan now in Pakistan are estimated at 3 million or more and constitute the largest group of refugees in the world at present. At least a million of these refugees have been in Pakistan since 1980 and only very small numbers have been resettled in other countries. An estimated 750,000 Afghans have also sought refuge in Iran.

In the Middle East the Palestinian refugees are currently enumerated at about 1.9 million and this population is growing through natural increase at about 50,000 per annum. Cyprus and Lebanon contribute further, much smaller numbers. The strife in El Salvador has brought Latin America to significant totals in recent years with an outflow to neighboring countries, Mexico, United States, and Canada totaling perhaps 500,000 at the present time.

In many respects it is difficult to discern broad patterns or trends in these movements. The oscillation in total numbers in the World Refugee Reports and in earlier figures makes it uncertain that there is a general tendency toward greater world totals of refugees, although this seems likely. Lengthy stays in refugee status now cause concern in such cases as the Palestinians, the Afghans in Pakistan, Ethiopians or Somalis in the Horn of Africa, or Indochinese in the camps of Thailand. But recalling the slow decline of displaced persons' camps after World War II and other cases, it is not clear that the plight of refugees is now more protracted nor is there a clear shift in their ultimate location through repatriation, settlement in the country of first asylum, or resettlement elsewhere. Two broad conclusions do, however, seem to emerge from this review: in recent decades the third world has become the principal source of refugee flows; and these flows are sufficiently varied and numerous to suggest that refugees may be a chronic feature of the present world scene. If these conclusions apply to the refugee situation over the next decades, they clearly have basic significance for what national governments, international organizations, and nongovernmental agencies concerned with refugees must expect to face. And if policy and practice are to be built on the expectations that large flows of refugees will be recurring chronically in the third world, there is need for analysis of underlying causes to support the generalizations the statistics suggest. Were the great dislocations in Europe the product of unique historical events? Are the present troubles of the third world a colonial aftermath that will diminish as the successor states take consolidated form? Or are they symptoms of lasting tensions and disabilities that will persist for many decades to come and may be exacerbated by rising populations, slow development, and migrations?

The state of our understanding of these broad and fundamental questions is anything but satisfactory. An enormous amount of attention has been devoted to refugees, but the greatest part of it has been spent in dealing with particular situations, treating them as if they were unique or isolated crises. Even descriptions of what has happened have been neglected when those who have coped with refugees hurried on to other crises or simply turned to other business. The kind of wide-ranging reflection and scholarly analysis that might provide guides to likely futures has been rare. Only one university course on refugees has been taught regularly in the United States in recent years (by Barry Stein at Michigan State), and scholars with the necessary competencies are only now beginning to give serious attention to the causes and characteristics of refugee movements, going beyond the studies of international law and resettlement problems which have hitherto had most attention.

Aristide Zolberg, for one, argues that the process of formation of nation-states has been responsible for a great part of the refugee flows in and around Europe that were described above, and that the third world flows we are now experiencing derive from the same process there (Zolberg, 1983, pp. 24–38). The turbulent instability we now see in the third world is in this analysis no rapidly transitory phenomenon but promises to be rather long-lasting. The multiethnic composition of third world nation-states, their meager economic and organizational resources for development, and the widespread existence of sharp inequalities within these countries make for formidable difficulties in nation-building, with resulting high probabilities of repressions, persecutions, and violent strife. The difficulties of relating such analyses of the problems of third world nations to the likelihood of refugee flows are formidable and it is possible to take optimistic views, as Astri Suhrke has argued in a recent article (1983, pp. 157–173). Linking underlying conditions to the emergence of an Idi Amin or a Macias Nguema or a revolution like the one in Iran involves many uncertain inferences in particular cases and more uncertainties in generalization. We are, in particular, likely to have to settle for very uncertain conclusions about the role of population pressures and disparities in the causation of refugee flows. There are some refugee situations, such as the flight of the Afghans into Pakistan or the persistence of the Palestinians as refugees, in which such population effects would appear to be only remotely relevant if at all. But there are other cases, such as the flight of the Vietnamese since 1979, in which population pressures seem to have had a clearly detectable role (see Woodside, 1979, pp. 381–409).

Analysis of the conditions that produce flights of political and intellectual refugees may be less beset with uncertainties than a probe of the deep disturbances that result in mass exoduses. What political scientists call the "succession problem" has not found orderly and temperate solutions in much of the third world. Changes of government by coups or mass risings are common and ring with proclamations that the old regime was corrupt and unworthy. Being a leader in a third world country is a dangerous occupation that often presents stark choices between flight and imprisonment or worse. With such examples as the fate of Bhutto in Pakistan or Tolbert in Liberia before them, it seems normal for deposed leaders to flee if they can, even if they do not have a well-prepared refuge and an overseas bank account. Likewise, third world intellectuals and professionals are likely candidates for refugees whether or not masses of their countrymen flee with them. The line between voluntary emigration and refugee flight for these people is likely to be a blurred one. The "brain drain" seems to be largely a voluntary migration, but the departing brains are impelled by economic, professional, and political conditions that produce many reluctant exiles or even refugees. Whether or not intellectuals and professionals were politically active in their home countries, they would be especially likely to suffer under the constraints on freedom of expression and personal life that many third world countries impose, and as a group to be a fertile source of refugee flows.

A general prospect of continuing refugee flows from and within the third world — sometimes as mass flights, and more continuously in smaller numbers of political and intellectual figures — can be traced with some melancholy confidence to conditions in the third world. But where and when and in what magnitude such flights may occur are questions that have made the search for preventive action or "early warning" — subjects to which we will return in a later section of this essay — thus far ill-rewarded.

We are thus likely to face great uncertainties about future world refugee flows, and have to depend on cautious extrapolations from the current scene to judge what must be done. The likelihood that the third world will be the main source of refugees in the years to come does not of course mean there will not be others. The wave of Polish refugees and "strandees" that followed on the Jaruzelski coup of December 1981 reminds us that the periodic eruptions of Eastern Europe in the last generation are not finished. And in these nervous years of missile deployments we are not, alas, assured that a cataclysmic war might not bring flights of scarcely imaginable horror. But reasonable expectations must focus on the third world, and to formulate the likely course of policy we must seek to understand what determines who will be treated as a refugee, who will feel responsibility for action, and what form of response can be expected. Reflection on current practice and what has happened in the past suggests three such determinants: senses of affiliation and antipathy of political, ethnic, cultural, and historical sorts; senses of national strengths and competencies; and broader concerns for equity, humanitarianism, and international responsibility. Realistic expectations for refugee policy and practice must conjure with all these determinants, and it seems prudent to approach what may be ideal through what is likely to occur.

An even-handed regard for all refugees may be a necessary international ideal. But ideal responses are always bent by special senses of affiliation and antipathy.

The litany of twentieth-century forced movements recited at the beginning shows the end of migrants' journeys to be commonly with their own kind. The great reshuffling of populations in Central and Eastern Europe, the exchanges of Greeks and Turks, the separation of Muslims, Hindus, and Sikhs in the Indian subcontinent were moves toward the consolidation of nation-states. So also were the retreats of Europeans from their colonial empires. The acceptance of refugees in places they can claim as their "homelands" is not always ungrudging or generous — Jane Kramer has told us of Provençal villagers who looked curiously to see if the returning *pieds-noirs* had black feet and never made neighborly visits with those who found a kind of refuge among them (Kramer, 1981, p. 171 ff). The hard test of hospitality is personal and local, and complaints of localities and their governments that they are bearing unfair burdens because of the incomers are endemic features of refugee affairs. But national and official responses have normally been warmly accepting to their own kind, though there are exceptions, most conspicuously the Palestinians.

Special ethnic, religious, or tribal ties within nations provide receptivity, too. Jewish emigrés from the Soviet Union have found ready acceptance and special provisions to assist their settlement in the United States; Cuban-Americans have put the name of another Cuban bay in U.S. history; and the Poles since 1981 have had eloquent advocates among Polish-Americans. In the third world, the remarkable acceptance of literally millions of Afghans in Pakistan, and Somalis from the Ogaden into Somalia, has rested on ethnic and cultural ties. The generally celebrated receptivity of African countries to refugees from neighboring countries had been commonly credited to hospitality within related groups of peoples who straddle borders. Such cases certainly exist and they have been important in the "spontaneous settlement" that has gone on without benefit of national or international assistance, but in fact few instances have been seriously reported and receptivity may be as much a consequence of limited control as deliberate hospitality (see Hansen, 1981; Rogge, 1981; and Betts, 1981).

Revolutions and civil wars often propel peoples into wide diasporas: the White Russians after the Russian Revolution, the Hungarians in 1956, Indochinese since 1975, and Iranians from 1979. Responses to these refugees have been based more on political and ideological sympathies or historical connections than on established ethnic and cultural links. Thus, for the United States, provisions were made under the Displaced Persons Act of 1948, the Refugee Relief Act of 1953, and the 1965 amendments to the Immigration and Nationality Act for admission of refugees from Nazi, Fascist, or Communist persecution. Most of the refugees who were admitted to the United States between the Hungarian exodus of 1956 and the passage of the Refugee Act of 1980 entered under a so-called parole procedure which has applied to refugees from Eastern Europe, Cuba, and Indochina who were seen as fleeing Communism. It is a common complaint that stranded and refugee Poles since 1981 have been received with much less enthusiastic generosity than the Hungarians of 1956, but generally sympathetic responses have marked the treatment of those fleeing Communist countries to the present.

Beyond current politics and ideology, a sense of historical connection and responsibility has played an evident role in responses to refugees. The American response to Indochinese refugees, both in the immediate circumstances of the 1975 collapse in South Vietnam and in later responses to Vietnamese, Cambodians, Laotians, and Hmongs, has been stimulated by such feelings. The same holds for the generous response of France to Indochinese refugees.

The responses to the Palestinian refugees are in some apparent contrast to the patterns of hospitality that have prevailed in many other cases. In the years after the flight of 500,000 Palestinians from the Arab-Israeli war of 1948–1949, only Jordan among the neighboring Arab countries responded with substantial acceptance of them as citizens. As David Forsythe, a long-time student of the subject, has recently written, the political symbolism of these refugees has dwarfed other reactions, with the result that we now have a quasi-permanent population, mostly born as internationally recognized refugees and assisted as such since 1949 by the UNRWA (Forsythe, 1983, p. 99). The United States, the principal source of support for this agency, had contributed nearly $1 billion to it by 1982; in some recent years, the oil-rich Arab countries have also been important sources of support, their $51.5 million of contributions to the international refugee organizations in 1981 going mostly to UNRWA (*World Refugee Survey*, 1982, p. 48). The Palestinian situation has unique features in its protractedness and the massive international support for Palestinian self-determination as a nation. But the resistance to treating Palestinians as refugees to be settled in the countries of first asylum, or resettled elsewhere, is certainly not unique.

Where mass exoduses have occurred, it has been common and typically necessary to regard asylum as temporary, whether or not the receiving country felt ties of affinity. Thus President Siad Barre of Somalia has repeatedly declared that the Somalis from Ethiopia must ultimately return there; the same is said of Afghans now in Pakistan. In many other African situations and particularly in the cases of "freedom fighters" against a lingering colonial presence, an expectation of return has accompanied hospitality. Repatriation of refugees is indeed one of the standing possibilities of permanent or durable resolution of refugee problems sought by the UNHCR, and it is not confined to third world situations. Poles seeking refuge in Western countries since December 1981 have encountered various legal devices providing temporary status as alternatives to permanent settlement. In the United States, the Immigration and Naturalization Service (INS) set a succession of "extended departure dates" for Poles who were unwilling to return to Poland under existing circumstances there, and they have been permitted to work if in need (*Refugee Reports*, July 1, 1983, p. 3). France and the Federal Republic of Germany followed similar practices, which have been represented to UNHCR as alternatives to setting generous quotas for permanent refugee settlement. In addition to features it has in common with worldwide treatment of refugees, the Palestinian diaspora in the Arab countries has been treated much like other Arab migrants. These countries show a jealous reserve in granting citizenship that is common among third world countries. Citizenship has been granted only in rare cases, even for long-established residents, and numerous restrictions exist on access to education, the holding of property, or the establishment of businesses.

Such unwillingness to give foreigners citizenship or economic and educational opportunities is, of course, in some measure normal and universal. But in the countries of the third world it may be that there are distinctive and especially pronounced resistances that derive from the freshness of independence and the legitimacy that principles of self-determination give to quite narrow and particularistic senti-ments. The independence of new nations has been an aggressively egalitarian rejection of the ascendancy of outsiders. The relative ease with which colonial regimes exercised peaceful control of large sub-ject populations is difficult to understand without some acceptance of their legitimate occupation of positions of authority and advantage, and hence in some sense of their "superiority." The rejection of this accepted hierarchy could hardly be a simple and straightforward political act. Independence has been a potent symbol of social revo-lution, asserting the proper claims of previously subject peoples to fundamentally equal rights and competencies. Such social revolu-tions could hardly be neatly confined to their effects on outsiders of other races and cultures. They have had complex and diffuse effects that are broadly captured in Clifford Geertz's conception of an "in-tegrative revolution." One such effort appears in the familiar dis-junction between such very broad solidarities as Pan-Arab national-ism or Pan-Africanism, and the solidarities around which nation-states and the parts of them have formed. The fiercely nativist sen-timents which made the recent expulsion of foreign migrants popular among Nigerians, or have afflicted internal migrants in India, seem to be normal features of this integrative revolution. As Zolberg ar-gues, they are major generators of flight and expulsion, and they also raise barriers to the acceptance of refugees, even where there are favoring ethnic, cultural, or political solidarities. A sense of the need and legitimacy of protecting what one has and so recently has gained is reinforced by awareness of the meager resources and eco-nomic opportunities that characterize great parts of the third world. But as the oil-rich countries show, poverty is not the sole basis of coolness toward accepting refugees, and visions of an international strategy for coping with third world refugees must conjure with the strength of national egotisms there.

If this analysis is sound, the prospects of long-term settlement of refugees in places of first asylum in the third world do not look very encouraging. Resistances may harden, not only to accepting mass exoduses but also to receiving the kind of professional, intellectual, and political refugees that we began by calling to mind. Fighters against colonial regimes have been welcomed in neighboring coun-tries, as several recent African examples show. Political sympathies have also made refuge possible for deposed leaders like Sihanouk in Peking, or Kwame Nkrumah in Sekou Touré's Guinea. This is also evidence of a growing disposition to respond to the chronic precariousness of third world political careers by offering refuge, as in the Latin American tradition, to deposed figures with whom the hosts share no clear political sympathies — possible cases in point are the Emperor Bokassa's stay in the Ivory Coast or Sadat's willingness to receive the Shah. Intellectuals and scholars fleeing South Africa have been welcomed in independent African countries and in some cases given good positions. But the jealous protection of a limited array of opportunities and the frequent thinness of intellectual life in third world countries have often made lasting refuge uncomfortable or disillusioning.

The possibilities of resettlement have lain principally in Western Europe, North America, and Australia, and have depended much on special political, ideological, and historical connections such as we have seen in the Indochinese exodus. The presumption seems strong that these connections will only rarely be powerful enough in mass exoduses to overcome the host populations' sense that their ties to third world peoples are tenuous or lacking. For political leaders and intellectuals the prospects of refuge in Europe and America would seem to be considerably better; indeed, such diverse figures as Somoza, Gowon, the Kabaka of Buganda, Ben Bella, and many others have found homes abroad. The costs to the countries of refuge can sometimes be very high, as the United States found when it admitted the Shah for medical treatment. Often political and historical affiliations make for sympathetic reception, but whether or not such sympathies are present, the conceptions of being free and tolerant nations, able to harbor diversity, undoubtedly favor receptivity. Making place for political and intellectual refugees who cannot be tolerated in their home countries conforms to the ideals of "free societies." It has symbolic importance over against the Communist bloc and as an example to the third world, and Western nations have shown themselves ready to face controversy over loyalty to these ideas.

How ready a country is to respond to the needs of refugees — to offer them temporary asylum or permanent settlement — obviously depends on its feelings about security and absorptive capacity. In the nineteenth century Great Britain took in Italian, Polish, French, German, Hungarian, and Russian political refugees, before and after the great upheavals of 1848. In addition to Karl Marx, it took in Louis-Philippe, Metternich, Louis-Blanc, Mazzini, Victor Hugo, Kossuth, Garibaldi, and Bakunin — the whole spectrum of contemporary continental politics. British self-confidence of the time seems to have been the crucial factor in this hospitality to refugees, many of whom had no place else to turn. Continentals who were thought to be threats to their governments at home were no threat in the eyes of the British parliament and public opinion. British governments were often embarrassed by the political and conspiratorial activities of refugees but, between 1828 and 1905 (except for one brief interval), there was nothing to prevent aliens from entering Britain as they pleased and no provisions existed for expelling them.

Mark Bonham Carter points out in a review of a book on this history (*Times Literary Supplement*, Feb. 22, 1980, p. 200) that Britain did not face any large-scale influx of refugees from a foreign country during this period; he thought that restrictions would have been imposed on the Irish refugees fleeing the famine had they come from a foreign country, and indeed it was the coming of Jews from Eastern Europe in substantial numbers which brought about the Aliens Act of 1905.

The great hospitality of the United States to refugees and indeed immigrants of nearly all kinds during much of its history has been similarly grounded in national self-confidence. When that confidence was shaken in the 1930s by the Great Depression, a darker mood prevailed; what happened to the spurned refugees has become a matter of lasting regret.

At the present time a mood of contraction looms again, despite generous principles in existing legislation, with the latest years showing declines in the authorized numbers of refugee admissions and failures of the numbers of admissions actually to reach authorizations. The reasons for this growing parsimony have evidently to do with concerns that are now widespread among nations and not peculiar to the United States.

Anxieties over capacity to provide a haven for refugees come from several sources: a fear that their political activities may be disruptive internally or disturb foreign relations; a sense that the country is already overcrowded and that newcomers will be competitors for employment and other opportunities; a sense that the refugees will not be assimilable or that the social composition of the population will be adversely affected by the incoming refugees. The mass exodus from Indochina since 1978 has shown these resistances in various forms. The Thai government reacted in June 1979 to the influx of Cambodians following the December 1978 Vietnamese invasion of Cambodia with a violation of the principle of refugees that was widely condemned inside and outside Thailand. Its reaction was caused by anxieties over the spread of the war within Cambodia and fears of closer engagement with the Vietnamese (*Refugee Reports*, July 13, 1983).

The unwillingness or utter refusal of other Southeast Asian nations to accept Indochinese refugees has been rationalized on grounds of the limited resources and economic opportunities these nations have for their own citizens, although concerns about the ethnic composition of the refugee flows, particularly for the Sino-Vietnamese, manifestly played a role. The responses of Japan and most European countries to appeals that they accept quotas for resettlement were meager and bespoke doubts about the assimilability of these refugees. In the Western countries at the present time, acceptance of these refugees hinges more on broader concerns of control and restriction of immigration than on concerns over foreign relations or hazards from the continuing political activities of the refugees (Jaeger, 1981, p. 55). Fears and calculations like the ones that drove Trotsky after 1928 from Turkey to France to Norway and to his death in Mexico in 1940 continue to preoccupy governments. Public order is disturbed by assassinations, terrorist bombings, kidnappings, and violent demonstrations. The French government has had to face troubles with Iran over Bani-Sadr, the British to extricate a drugged Nigerian ex-minister from a shipping crate, and currently, France and Switzerland had to jockey for a time on who should allow the presence of the Syrian president's exiled brother. In all matters of immigration, present-day governments seem much less at ease than Britain was at the height of its self-confidence. The United States maintains the much-criticized exclusions of the 1952 McCarran-Walter Act for intellectuals and politicians with alleged Communist affiliations, but on the whole fears of subversion or disturbances to foreign relations by refugees seem less troubling than more general anxieties about the volume of immigration.

The nature of these concerns and such justification as they may have are considered in other essays in this volume, and I will not dwell on them here. But they have had direct effects on the disposition to receive refugees, as we have seen in efforts in the U.S. Congress to keep refugee admissions within overall annual totals for immigration under the Simpson-Mazzoli bill, rather than leaving refugee admissions to be determined by humanitarian need or other reasons. There is, in the political struggle over such provisions, a direct confrontation between different determinants of refugee policy, but it has not yet given cause for discouragement to the advocates of broad humanitarian concerns.

One must nevertheless expect that the present caution about capacity to absorb immigrants in Western and other countries will persist and be a strong influence on refugee policy. Wealthy countries facing expectations that they help with world refugee flows are thus likely to seek other ways of helping — through support to international refugee organizations, assistance to refugees in countries of first asylum, or otherwise. We have observed such responses in the Indochinese case and they occur in a broad variety of proposals and efforts in refugee relief and development programs.

Poor countries, on the other hand, with their sense of limited powers, offer limited receptivity to refugees and expect that they will be assisted by the richer countries. The delicate problems of mutual expectations that arise in such situations have been well illustrated by the Indochinese experience where the readiness of Southeast Asian countries to provide asylum has been critically dependent on prospects of resettlement in the United States or other countries, and on other forms of assistance. Refugee flows characteristically involve such international relations, sometimes in starkly political bargaining, and sometimes in a broad frame of commonly accepted principles and responsibilities.

Affiliations, antipathies, and cautious measuring of response to national capacities certainly play major roles in the making of refugee policy and practice, but they are not all the story. Various organizations and individuals exert pressures to find generally acceptable and defensible ways of responding to refugees. Countries are typically proud of their traditions of hospitality to refugees and want to maintain these traditions if they can do it within carefully controlled bounds — hence the great current interest in legal definitions of refugees and the procedures for applying these definitions.

Legal definitions of refugees are provided by the legislation of individual countries and by the 1951 UN Convention Relating to the Status of Refugees and a 1967 Protocol following thereon. Under the UN definition a refugee is a person who, "owing to well-founded fear of being persecuted for reasons of race, religion, nationality, membership in a particular social group, or political opinion, is outside the country of his nationality and is unable or, owing to such fear, is unwilling to avail himself of the protection of that country." Prior to 1980 the United States in its domestic legislation had only narrower legal definitions of refugees, requiring that they come from Communist countries and the Middle East. But in the Refugee Act of 1980 the United States adopted the UN definition with significant extension, at the president's discretion, to persons within their own countries who are persecuted or have "a well-founded fear of persecution." Admission of refugees requires that they be of "special humanitarian concern" to the United States. Other countries have shown a similar progression to generalized definition with variations of the UN definition. As refugee flows within and from the third world have become the principal focus of concern, the limitations of the UN definition have been evident. It does not embrace the victims of natural disasters, or of generalized conditions of oppression, insecurity, and economic deprivation. A 1969 Convention of the Organization of African Unity recognized the importance of such reasons for flight and liberalized the definition accordingly. Other countries did not follow this liberalization, but in fact many migrants from and within the third world could make some claim to be regarded as refugees in this wider sense. They arouse humanitarian concerns and issues of equitable treatment and thus pose problems to countries seeking to maintain respectable standards of behavior. Thus, for example, legislation has recently been proposed in the United States for a "stay of deportation" for certain Salvadorans who have reached the United States but have not been granted refugee status.

The treatment of refugees widely appears as a sensitive test of the political character of a national state; it has symbolic links to the rule of law and civil rights that tap sentiments reaching far beyond the specific subject. All the Western countries and a great many third world countries now have an important constituency watching over the observance of civil rights and due process of law. This group typically has strong concerns with nondiscriminatory treatment of both citizens and resident aliens, and scrutinizes the treatment of refugees of different ethnic, religious, and political characters. The legal provisions and administrative procedures that are applied to applicants for refugee status are subject to sharp debate and zealous contention, as currently in the United States over the relevant provisions of the Simpson-Mazzoli bill, the detention provisions introduced by the Reagan administration, and the litigation over treatment of Haitian, Cuban, Afghan, and other groups.

There can be little doubt that a crisis now exists over the handling of asylum applications in the United States and in Europe. W. Scott

Burke, head of the asylum division in the State Department, asserted in 1983 that his office received 30,000 to 40,000 asylum applications a year, and had a backlog of more than 170,000 cases (*New York Times*, July 7, 1983; for detailed discussion of the legal issues, see Scanlan, 1981). Ten years earlier there were only a couple of hundred per year. The critical change came with the passage of the Refugee Act of 1980 which, by adopting the definition of refugees in the 1951 Convention and the 1967 Protocol, opened claims to asylum from countries other than the Communist countries and the Middle East. The subsequent increase in applications was massive, with Cuba, Iran, El Salvador, and Nicaragua the source of two-thirds of them. That other nations share these problems was evident in a 1983 conference sponsored by the German Marshall Fund. There the director for Refugee and Humanitarian Affairs in the Ministry of the Interior of the Federal Republic of Germany reported that the number of asylum applications had risen from 5,000 in 1976 to 108,000 in 1980 (with 58,000 of these from Turkey alone), and it was estimated that as much as 1 billion DM per year had been spent in adjudicating asylum claims. Subsequent measures to "streamline legal procedures" reduced the numbers of applications to 38,000 in 1982 and 20,000 in 1983, but they rose again to 35,000 in 1984 (and were expected to rise still higher in 1985 with a particular influx of Sri Lankans). Representatives of other countries at the conference reported less spectacular numbers but sharp rises in applications (up 260 percent since 1979 in the United Kingdom), backlogs of cases, and complex procedures with numerous appeals from first determinations. There was much talk at this conference of "bogus" refugees, meaning for the most part people who were fleeing bleak economic situations in their own countries but claiming that they were persecuted there. No country has been willing to treat those fleeing economic deprivation as refugees and all are concerned to control the various forms of illegal entry which the search for better livelihoods and opportunities has been producing. Advocates of generous policies toward refugees typically attack not the rejection of economic refugees as such, but the real or alleged insensitivity to claims of some of them that they are vulnerable to persecution. The difficulty of getting reliable evidence on the likelihood of such persecution for sizable refugee groups before their arrival or after deportation seems manifest. Thus when Senator Kennedy asked the U.S. Coordinator for Refugee Affairs and INS officials in 1983 about the alleged persecution of Salvadorans who had returned to their country after being expelled from the United States, he was asking about some 26,000 such people; any serious effort to trace these people after their return to El Salvador would obviously be an extraordinary undertaking, hardly possible without cooperation of the government of that country, which would be itself suspect (*Refugee Reports*, Sept. 7, 1984, pp. 1–3).

This intrinsic difficulty of determining the vulnerability to persecution of large numbers of present or potential applicants for asylum is only one among many difficult points in the administration of refugee policy. There are many others in the balancing of administrative feasibility with assurance of fair and careful procedure. Clearly no ideal and perfectly defensible set of laws and procedures can be achieved that will serve to the satisfaction of all. It is difficult to balance the public interest and private interests, and to assure adequate representation of the groups and issues involved. The complex and costly procedures now provided for the handling of refugees have the merit of giving such representation and are one important means of securing equitable treatment of groups of refugees within the bounds of national generosity. But such procedures require supplementation by organizations that deal with refugees of all kinds.

It is a common complaint that the world's attention goes to the dramatic and spectacular while equal suffering and need go neglected or unnoticed. Thus the Indochinese boat-people in 1979 brought a massive international response that provoked a bitter commentary from a specialist on African refugees:

> The refugees from Czechoslovakia in 1968, from Chile after 1973, and from Vietnam in 1979 have been blazoned across the headlines of the world's press; many have been accepted into the industrialized countries as individual cases which require close personal assistance. But Guineans in Senegal and Ivory Coast, Equatorial Guineans in Gabon and Cameroon, Angolans in Zaire, Zairians in Angola and Ugandans in South Sudan have not moved the conscience of the rich world in the same way. Dying in rural Africa is less dramatic than drowning in the South China Sea.   (Chambers, 1979, p. 384)

The ideal of fair and even-handed attention to all refugees is an ideal of humanitarians and of some officials and it has detectable consequences. One of the leading American concerned institutions, the International Refugee Committee, some time ago launched an appeal on behalf of Kurds, not because it is a committee of Kurds, but plainly because many Kurds were in a woefully deprived and neglected state after an agreement between the Shah and Saddam Hussein. The U.S. Committee on Refugees makes its annual effort to record and enumerate refugees wherever they are, and the Refugee Act of 1980 provides for a process of setting numbers of admissions from a worldwide assessment of needs.

There is unquestionably a body of universalistic humanitarian sentiment that, once aroused, can bring a response to the needs of refugees, whoever and wherever they may be. But this sentiment must actually be aroused among people and organizations capable of response. It is evident that a kind of economy of attention characterizes human behavior very generally. The occasions for sympathetic concern with the problems and needs of others are enormous — perhaps effectively infinite — and some principle of habitual exclusion is a normal requirement of everyday living. When someone like Solzhenitsyn condemns our callous indifference to far-off injustice, we may for a time throw off the protective inattention that enables us to go about our daily lives. But such arousals must be episodic, like the coursing of adrenalin when the organism senses crisis, and must have some sense of immediacy to our identity as citizens of a country or members of some other group. Hence the common tendency toward limited and selective responses we have described, and the talk of "compassion fatigue," when claims for sympathetic attention seem too numerous and recurrent.

The world has come only slowly to accept the need to view refugees as a general and chronic problem. The editors of a recent publication of the American Academy of Political and Social Science devoted to "The Global Refugee Problem: U.S. and World Responses" recall that in a 1939 issue on refugees the editor argued that "the attitude that the present is only a temporary crisis must give way to recognition of the fact ... that the refugee problem is a permanent one" (*Annals*, 1983, p. 9). When refugee "crises" have been recognized, organizations and programs develop to meet the demands of the moment and then fall away or collapse when the crisis has passed, or is declared to have passed. Losses in experience, expertise, and organizational strength have been evident and much deplored, but there are good reasons to want crisis programs to terminate promptly. The schemes for solving the Palestinian refugee problem in four or five years and dissolving UNRWA now make very melancholy reading, but it is understandable that its sponsors would not have wanted UNRWA to last as long as it has.

Despite these resistances an array of organizations and international and domestic legislation has grown to provide a basis for general and persisting concern with refugee problems. A body of international humanitarian law dating from the last century is watched over with good Genevan rectitude by the International Committee of the Red Cross. The Universal Declaration of Human Rights is indeed a universal document, with obligations for all, if not toward all. The 1951 Refugee Convention and the 1967 Protocol have superseded more limited definitions of refugees; they had by 1981 only some 90 adherents among the states of the world. The Office of the United Nations High Commissioner when it was established in 1951 followed a series of organizations of briefer life and narrower mandates, and the Intergovernmental Committee on European Migration has become simply the Intergovernmental Committee on Migration, and in other contexts there has been growth toward continuity and universality. The U.S. Refugee Act of 1980 was intended to provide "a permanent and systematic procedure for refugee admissions," and Victor Palmieri, the U.S. Refugee Coordinator under the Carter Administration, lauded this act as "a rare model of the legislative art" that promises "some measure of order and rational planning on what had traditionally been a chaotic process" (Kritz, 1983, p. xix).

The advance of general and humanitarian concern for refugees depends on the erection of specialized organizations. The existence of these organizations assures the continuity of concern, both official and private. What they can do depends on laws and procedures and on the support they get from governments and citizens. But they are in a position to uphold with constancy an equitable and humanitarian regard for refugees that others can do only sporadically. They provide organizational resources for coping with the problems of protection, relief, transportation, and settlement without which nations may plead incapacity to cope, and they have a natural disposition to become a lobby for refugees, as the voluntary organizations for settling refugees in the United States have been.

Most of the determinants of response to refugees that we have been surveying have their roots in special attachments and interests of nations or parts of them, and it would be foolish to think that partisan considerations will not continue to play major roles in refugees' fates. But the strength of worldwide concerns for humanitarian and equitable treatment of refugees and the sharing of international responsibility for them are not now feeble. How adequate this mix of motivation and strength is to cope with present and foreseeable refugee flows, particularly in the third world, is the question to be answered in the final section of this chapter.

Refugees are in some sense a manifestation of pathologies in the functioning of societies. What makes them take to the international airlines or flee more tediously and dangerously across land and water has to do with features of the modern world that are deep and lasting. People in the third world seek refuge from the persisting difficulties of that world in its poverty and awareness of it, the precariousness of national integration and political stability. The great disparity in the rates of population growth between North and South promises to exacerbate these conditions in the decades ahead and to feed the migrations in which refugee flows are embedded. Real or feigned desperation will presumably continue to make migrants of many sorts seek refugee status and arouse the defenses of countries that they seek to enter, but no dearth of indisputable refugees seems likely. The frustrations of third world countries promise harsh controls and oppressive or precarious governments. Freedom of thought and expression hardly flourishes in these circumstances, and many educated individuals who can find opportunities to do so will continue to risk the pains of exile. Whether the dominant political authority resides in the military, as it now does in so many countries, or totalitarian ideological control spreads to other countries, independent thought promises to make uneasy heads.

A continuing stream of political and intellectual refugees mixed in larger flows of migrants, and varying greatly in their attractiveness to countries that are their destination, will almost certainly persist. Like Dante, some of the intellectuals will have been deeply engaged in politics, and will continue to speak out in exile. Some, like Lenin or Khomeini, will be awaiting a triumphant return. Some will have past associations, Communist and otherwise, that make their welcome grudging or uncertain. Others, like Russian and East European refugees of the present and past generations, will be concerned with the maintenance of cultures that are threatened or destroyed by totalitarian controls. In the midst of so much diversity of purpose, merit, and affiliation, a rich variety of responses is likely, but with cases to trouble the bureaucracies and arouse public passions. Undoubtedly sentiments will shift and times of generous sympathy will alternate with times of niggardly restraint. But a continuing receptivity to political and intellectual refugees among the Western countries seems assured by their self-image as free societies and their principled opposition to the Communist societies. The price for this hospitality may sometimes be troubling, and the easy self-confidence of nineteenth-century Britain will doubtless remain unmatched. But the posture of the first world toward the second and third worlds will remain a principled and ideological one in which political and intellectual freedoms remain important, and refugees of conscience a test of these principles. Dispositions in the rich countries toward mass exoduses thus seem likely to be shaped by a continuing receptivity to smaller flows of individuals.

As conviction has slowly grown that mass exoduses are not merely sporadic occurrences, but common enough to be regarded as endemic, analysts have called for reducing the likelihood of refugee flows by attacking the conditions that cause them. Refugee policy and assistance have commonly been bureaucratically separated from national and international concerns with development and human rights, but they now tend to converge from both sides. The disposition in the past decade to pay careful attention to equity and the basic needs of the poor has brought development policy closer to eleemosynary concerns; and the international attention to the observance of human rights, however uncertain and limiting in its results, has certainly expanded in many countries. Frequent pleas are heard for "early warning" systems that would identify potential refugee problems and direct development and human rights efforts to their mitigation or prevention. Not much has yet come from these pleas, given the difficulty and political sensitivity of the analysis. The statute of the Office of the High Commissioner for Refugees requires that its work be "of an entirely nonpolitical character," and it clearly cannot undertake such early warning analysis alone.

A recent report by Sadruddin Aga Khan to the UN Commissioner on Human Rights has recommended that the UN system be broadly mobilized to provide such timely warnings (United Nations, 1981, p. 61 and annexes). Various private organizations that watch over human rights or the management of disasters have been attracted to the subject, but have lacked the resources for major efforts. Some of the scholarly efforts noted above may in the years ahead provide a more solid basis for anticipating and preventing refugee flows. But given the uncertainties of prediction, it seems more likely that any effective prevention of refugees through development and human rights efforts will be an incidental consequence of programs undertaken for other reasons.

The fate of refugees depends on the response they find at two stages — first in their need for immediate asylum and later in the provision of a long-term abode, or a "durable solution," as the UNHCR has described it. The Indochinese crisis has shown how unsatisfactory present assurances of asylum are. The UN Convention provides against the forcible return of refugees. It does not include obligations to provide asylum; an effort in 1977 to secure a convention on territorial asylum through a UN Conference broke down. There appears at present little or no prospect of a universal consensus on the subject. The OAU Convention mentioned above does include an obligation to provide asylum, but it is no more followed in this than in other respects. The capacities of the Western countries to improve prospects for the granting of asylum in the third world would appear to depend on their own behavior and on the assistance they may provide in long-term solutions. Scrupulous and orderly handling of asylum applications to their own countries involves much cost and vexations, and there are temptations to reduce these problems by strong measures in interdictions, protracted detentions, or summary deportations. But troubling procedures and vulnerabilities to doubtful cases at home are prices paid to encourage better treatment of asylum seekers elsewhere. The experience in Southeast Asia also shows that the granting of even temporary asylum may require help with funds, organizational resources, and opportunities for resettlement.

There are three classic ways of providing for refugees beyond their immediate needs for asylum and relief: repatriation; settlement in the country of first asylum; and resettlement elsewhere. When at all possible, repatriation has naturally been favored, and has been earnestly pursued in recent years, even for Cambodians and Chadians. The resolution of independence struggles and civil strife has brought some successful examples, but the assessment of the frequency with which repatriation may be a satisfactory solution in the future is generally pessimistic. Difficult political problems, the trend toward demands for uniformity in nation-states, and population pressures commonly stand in the way, and the need for recourse to other long-term solutions has been manifest. The possibility of permanent settlement in countries of first asylum has been naturally appealing to the Western countries, and Vice-President Mondale proposed at a 1979 conference a $200,000,000 international fund for durable solutions of this sort to be administered by the UNHCR. But the United States failed to provide its share of this fund and the initiative has languished (Scheinman, 1983). Recognition that poor countries must be assisted if they are to assume the burdens of settling any substantial groups of refugees is nonetheless generally accepted. And any consideration of cases leads quickly into general developmental questions, since refugees can hardly be better treated than the needy populations among which they are to be settled. Present efforts to link refugee assistance and development programs include Sadruddin Aga Khan's proposals; other studies have sought to find ways in which the programs and organization of development and refugee agencies might be usefully brought together. The effort is a difficult one — as indeed the long history of development schemes for the Palestinians reminds us — and seems likely to be vigorously pursued only in situations of special political interest.

Resettlement of third world refugees in the way that several hundred thousand Indochinese refugees have been resettled in Western countries seems clearly to be an exceptional solution. It is not impossible to imagine that such cases should recur, say from major conflagrations in Mexico or South Africa, or a catastrophe befalling Israel. But in the more normal course of events, the distant resettlement of refugees seems likely to follow the carefully screened and individualized procedures described above. Since the passage of the Refugee Act of 1980 the American experience suggests that the familiar determinants of response to refugees will continue to bring very uneven treatment to different groups, but within a formal responsibility to attend to claims from anywhere.

This summary view is certainly not reassuring. It leaves the likelihood that there will be badly served masses of refugees over much of the world in the years to come. But a general obligation to receive and assist some refugees has been sustained, and scrupulous and orderly national means for screening refugees' claims are supported by domestic pressures in many countries and specialized organizations for dealing with them are well established. Various efforts to strengthen these aids and resources for refugees are notable. The notorious inadequacy of research and analysis on the origins of refugee flows, experience in dealing with them, and the effects of settlement and resettlement have been finding remedies in scholarly efforts and in such ventures as the Refugee Policy Center in Washington and another under the International Council of Voluntary Agencies in Geneva. Efforts also continue, both within countries and internationally, to secure equitable and humanitarian treatment of refugees, over against the endemic strengths of special and selfish national interests. Sadruddin's report has called for the establishment of a UN Special Representative for Humanitarian Affairs, and he has taken leadership in convening an independent commission on international humanitarian issues in response to a resolution of the UN General Assembly (Sadruddin, 1983).

Skepticism about the likely effectiveness of such efforts comes easily, and one may doubt a substantial growth of humanitarian sentiment through deliberate education and exhortation. But prospects of strength in such sentiments are not lacking. Much of the nongovernmental responsibility for refugees has been assumed in the Western world by religious groups, and religiously based, charitable principles have been a source of the universalistic humanitarianism that has appeared in the West. Very narrow loyalties to kin and community have marked many cultures, leaving a vast indifference to the fates of others, but expectation of non-Western receptivities to general humanitarian principles need not rest solely on cultural and religious counterparts to Western traditions elsewhere. The worldwide growth of nationalism and the spread of egalitarian principles involve a receptivity to universalistic doctrine. Indeed, the sense of weakness and disadvantage which marks the third world has reinforced an attachment to universal claims. Universalistic principles may be only weakly honored, but deference to them provides a basis for benign treatment of refugees, whoever they may be.

Reconciling a special concern for leaders and intellectuals with an even-handed concern for all refugees is not always easy. Resentment bursts out occasionally in complaints that the famous and respected get too much attention while the poor and anonymous are neglected. It may be that these perturbations are now more troubling than they were in the past, when numbers were smaller, long moves more difficult, and mass exoduses less likely to be frequent. But we should remember that anonymous Whites fled Florence and wandered with Dante, and lesser folk, now forgotten, kept company with later famous exiles. How they were received depended on sympathies and calculations not fundamentally different from those we have surveyed in the present time, and will persist in the future. Universalistic principles may lead to better minimal assurances for future refugees, but their fortunes are no more likely to be free from disparities, accepted or deplored, than those of other humans.

NINE

The Emerging West Atlantic System: Migration, Culture, and Underdevelopment in the United States and the Circum-Caribbean Region

Orlando Patterson

AT THE individual level, most people move voluntarily for much the same reasons: they learn of opportunities to improve their standard of living elsewhere and, in the absence of restraints, they move. At a larger level, however, such movements always involve social groups and political entities. An understanding of migration therefore needs to look at the interface of micro- and macro-sociological processes, and in the process it must consider cultural and moral issues. Most societies accept the right of individuals to emigrate, but few accept the symmetric right of entry. The apparent contradiction is rooted in the conflicting interplay of group and individual interests (Zolberg, 1978).

Neo-Marxians, especially world-system and dualistic theorists, have gone further than most in their explanations of the wider socioeconomic contexts of migration. Capitalism, they argue, as a worldwide system promotes an international division of labor which maximizes the profits of center countries, drains the human and material resources of peripheral areas, and exploits the workers of the periphery, both those who stay at home and those who migrate to the center. In so doing it also reduces the bargaining power and lowers the wages of workers in the center. The emphasis on the systemic nature of migratory processes and on their being part of a wider exchange of socioeconomic forces is an important contribution of such theories, and there is some truth to the view that labor markets are increasingly international (Portes, 1978a; Piore, 1979). These theories oversimplify, however, especially in their tendency to look at center-periphery relations in terms of a single global capitalist system.

There is not one but several systems of international migration, for capitalism itself has several centers and these have radically different relationships to their respective peripheries. Political, cultural, and moral particularities play havoc with purely material global theories, as shown by the very different experiences of Japan and the United States with their respective and partly overlapping peripheries. To develop a satisfactory understanding of migration as a systemic process we must go beyond materialist, one-world assumptions and explore the interaction of social, economic, geographic, political, and ideologic forces. Here I propose to sketch one framework for such an approach by examining in broad terms what may be called the emerging West Atlantic system. By this I mean the interaction of the United States with its Central American and Caribbean neighbors.

In considering migration as a system it is best to adopt the most comprehensive definition of the process. A migration system, then, is any movement of persons between states, the social, economic, and cultural effects of such movements, and the patterned interactions among such effects. Duration of stay is often cited as an important criterion for distinguishing genuine migration from other forms of movement, but I think it is an error to exclude short-stay visitors in some cases. In many societies today, especially in the third world, such visitors are often powerful change agents. Tourism provides a case in point. At any given time, tourists constitute over a third of the population of many Caribbean societies. They are a significant and permanent force in these societies, though individual tourists may stay on average only a couple of weeks. We must also distinguish between high-impact and low-impact migrants. A team of development experts from the World Bank or the International Monetary Fund (IMF) sent on a structural adjustment mission to some financially beleaguered third world society can have a far more radical impact on its fortunes than, say, a group of several thousand laborers brought in on a permanent basis to harvest its sugar cane.

The West Atlantic migration system is quite different from other contemporary systems, such as the flows of third world workers to and from industrial Europe or the oil-rich Arab states. It is also different from the systems of the historic European empires where the peripheral regions interacted little with each other, and the imperial center (London or Paris), although functionally distant, mediated the multidimensional flows of voluntary and involuntary migrants, of capital, ideas, and cultural patterns. In the West Atlantic, by contrast to the old metropolitan systems, the peripheral areas are within easy reach or even adjacent to the powerful center. The peripheral regions are highly dependent economically on the center; they are not, however, colonies but politically autonomous states, at least legally or constitutionally. Although legal restrictions regulate the flow of persons, communications are well developed and relatively inexpensive, and there is a high level of information about opportunities available throughout the system. Voluntary movement is not confined to elites, as in the old metropolitan systems, and what is more, significant movements occur among the peripheral areas. Finally, the directional flow of people, culture, capital, and ideas is multiplex. There is no simple flow of cheap labor to capital, or vice versa. Everything that is capable of flowing moves in all directions.

What are the origins of this system? How does it work? What are its consequences for the economies, cultural patterns, and notions of ethnic and racial identity in the region?

The Constitutive Socioeconomic and Cultural Systems

Four kinds of sociocultural systems have converged in the emerging West Atlantic system.

1. The pluralistic capitalist center, the United States
2. The Central Latin American societies
3. The insular and South Caribbean Latin societies
4. The Afro-Caribbean societies

The Center

What is striking about the United States in this West Atlantic context is its vastness. It is the dominant industrial and military state, not only in the hemisphere, but in the world. It is infinitely wealthier and more powerful than its southern neighbors, yet this economic and political distance between center and periphery is accompanied by geographic proximity. The peripheral regions are not undifferentiated, however, and the United States is the center for not one, but several peripheries to which it relates in different ways.

The American economic system is currently undergoing important changes, all relevant to the problem of immigration. The first change affects the system insofar as it is a capitalist economy; the second affects the system as an industrial system. For a summary we draw on the literature on economic dualism, especially the work of Michael Piore (1979; Berger and Piore, 1980). Capitalism in its pure form involves a continuous process of differentiation and simplification of tasks. Mass production methods do not require skilled workers and an unskilled labor force is vulnerable in relation to the owners of capital. This work force is shifted to a secondary labor market in which wages are low and there is little or no job security. On the other hand, operations which require high levels of skill, especially given a variable demand for products, reward workers with high pay and job security. Labor unions and other institutions intervene in this process of labor-market dualism, allowing many workers "to escape the role that the logic of the system assigns to them" (p. 38) and to become a "quasi-capitalistic" element. The secondary labor market becomes a means by which capitalists evade the skilled workers' evasion of the logic of the system. Migrant labor, along with marginal native workers — minorities, women, teenagers — reinforce the capitalist hand in this struggle.

As an industrial society America is also subject to "the flux and uncertainty that inheres in economic activity" (p. 43), something it shares with all such systems, including socialist and mixed economies. Because capitalists control the production process there is a strong tendency to force labor to bear the major cost of uncertainty and change. Large firms, with stable demand through political and monopoly power, can afford and will pay high wages and job security for skilled workers to ensure continuity of operations. On the other hand, small, competitive firms employ low-paid, usually nonunionized workers with little job security. The resulting dualism is greatly facilitated by the incorporation of foreign laborers.

A third kind of change is also taking place — the evolutionary shift from a goods-producing industrial society to a high-technology, service-oriented, postindustrial one (Bell, 1973; Bluestone and Harrison, 1982; Singelmann, 1978). However, the several kinds of service industries have grown at different rates. Producer services (engineering, computer technology, banking, insurance, legal services, real estate) and social services (health care, education, government) together grew from 11.5 percent of the labor force in 1920 to over 30 percent in 1970. On the other hand, personal services, such as domestic labor, hotel waiters, repair, entertainment, and all the dirty jobs that remain essential for an industrial society, grew only from

8.2 to 10 percent over the period (Singelmann, pp. 145–146). The evolutionary transformation of the economy bears upon the problem of migration in several critical ways. We shall see in a later section that in the same way that attempts are made to evade the flux and uncertainty of the normal capitalist and industrial system, similar attempts are made to evade the evolutionary transformation to a postindustrial society: immigrants play a pivotal role in such evasions.

Immigrants are also important in another respect. Society will continue to need personal services, for many dirty jobs can simply not be automated away. What is more, a postindustrial society is positively associated with the liberation of female labor — native women not only enter the labor force in greater numbers but at higher levels of the occupational hierarchy, thus creating a growing need for persons to do the work traditionally done by women as full-time homemakers. With growing affluence, too, there is also a growing demand for services like providing fast food. These vitally needed jobs, however, are nearly all traditionally low-status occupations. In the face of growing affluence, the native lower class of postindustrial America is increasingly disinclined to perform them.

American culture consists of a mainstream with several pluralistic variants. The mainstream is the peculiarly American version of West European civilization. The remarkable thing about it is its continent-wide uniformity. Social norms, civic values, popular arts, and attitudes reveal a distinctive American character. At the mass level it is an open culture and, like the version of English which it uses, it is a relatively easy culture to learn. In addition to the mainstream, various ethnic subcultures continue to exist in the wake of the immigrant communities that began to develop in America from the nineteenth century onward.

One of the most distinctive features of American society and culture is its pattern of race relations. It is a racist society, though one which has struggled, especially during the last quarter-century, to overcome this failing. Legal segregation is now a thing of the past, although economic support for segregation is still strong. During this period the black population has gone through a radical change (Williams, 1977; Wilson, 1978). About 40 percent of the black population is now middle and lower-middle class, with life-styles not much different from those of their white counterparts, in sharp contrast with the situation in 1940 when only 5 percent held such positions. At the same time a large black underclass has grown, to become the main victim of the declining industrial economy. There is no room for its members anywhere and very little hope that they can be retrained to be made relevant to the postindustrial economy. This group is now more segregated than blacks have been at any time in American history.

Economic and class factors are critical in explaining this extraordinary bifurcation in the black group, as William Wilson has shown. But race remains crucially important, and race and social class "increasingly interact to produce critical effects that cannot be explained by simply combining the main effects of the two factors" (Pettigrew, 1981). Old-style, legally sanctioned, dominative discrimination has been replaced by newer, "secondary forms of racial discrimination that are more indirect, more subtle, more procedural, more ostensibly non-racial, and more centered on demographic and housing patterns."

In cultural terms American racism is based on an unusual conception of racial differences. Race is perceived in binary or dichotomized terms. People are either white or black, with no intermediary groups. This binary conception is accepted both by blacks and by whites, which is not to say that somatic differences are not significant. The important point is that races are formally conceived of and legally defined in these dichotomized terms. As we shall argue, it is precisely this unusual conception of race which has been most open to influences by the new wave of immigrants.

The Central Latin American Societies

Mexico and the other Central American societies constitute a distinct sociocultural grouping. Highly developed and densely populated pre-Columbian civilizations existed here and, in spite of their early devastation, the native populations were not eliminated but instead largely absorbed the Hispanic conquerors. Spanish colonial society was also distinctive. Based on mining and hacienda farming, the colonial economy was essentially an autonomous enclave within the broader context of a large, highly localized, peasant economy, and a smaller, isolated highland Indian communal system (Chevalier, 1963; Rivas, 1973).

Between the wars of independence and the end of the nineteenth century the area went through a prolonged period of crisis, verging on chaos, in which North American domination and capitalist penetration of the most ruthless sort prevailed. Since the late 1930s and

1940s all of these societies have gone through varying degrees of modernization, but none of them has succeeded in achieving anything approaching autonomous growth. Modernization has meant growing class inequities, declining rural sectors, overdeveloped urban centers, and a chronic incapacity to meet basic social needs (Fagen and Pellicer, 1983; Newfarmer, 1984).

The traditional cultural patterns of this area are complex. The elites all share a highly creolized version of Spanish culture, but the masses vary considerably from one part to the next. The populations of the area are primarily *mestizo*. Race has a quite different meaning in this area than it does in America; indeed it is doubtful whether the term is meaningful at all. Some anthropologists have suggested that a concept of "social race" would be appropriate. An Indian is primarily one who behaves culturally like an Indian. Interestingly there is no single term for non-Indians; no racial identity may be constructed upon the basis of racial exclusiveness.

One should be careful not to idealize this situation. Throughout the area there seems to be real contempt for Indianness. Massacres of Indian communities are still not uncommon (*Cultural Survival Quarterly*, 1983; on the concept of social race, Wagley, 1965). Such contempt may not be racist, but one wonders how different is the experience of such culturally based prejudice from the racial prejudice of North America.

The Insular and South Caribbean Latin Group

This group of societies includes Cuba, Puerto Rico, the Dominican Republic, and the South American states of Colombia and Venezuela. All share with Central America a common Spanish colonial past and cultural heritage, but beyond this radical differences set them apart. The Indian populations of this region were either totally eliminated or excluded entirely from the process of colonization and capitalist development. Export-oriented economies eventually developed in all of these societies. The plantation, rather than the hacienda, was the norm in most of them during the colonial period. African slavery was an important mode of labor exploitation, and blacks constitute a significant proportion of these populations. By the end of the nineteenth century nearly all of these societies had become enmeshed in a special relationship with the United States. In addition to its economic domination of the region the United States has directly involved itself in the political life of these countries.

Cultural and racial patterns were also quite distinctive. Unlike Central America, racial and somatic factors are highly salient in these societies. In contrast with North America, however, race is not a binary concept but is used denotatively. Somatic differences are considered socially significant by all members of the society. Color is both an index of, and a partial determinant of, status. The system is flexible, allowing the upwardly mobile some leeway in redefining their color identification, and permitting between generations a lightening process (in physical terms) through intermarriage.

The demographic majority of these populations is either lightly mixed or white. Unlike in the United States, working-class whites and blacks mix freely, with relatively little racial animosity. Nonetheless, and throughout, these societies exhibit a strong sensitivity to differences in shade and practice at all levels a constant trade-off between color and class, especially in marital relations. And the elites tend to be exclusively white.

The Afro-Caribbean Group

This group includes all the non-Latin islands of the Caribbean in addition to the mainland states of Guyana, Surinam, and Belize. The complete creation of West European imperialism, these were for centuries the classic colonial societies. Pure plantation systems were developed in this region, all of them originally based on harsh slave regimes involving the mass migration of millions of Africans, so that by the early part of the eighteenth century the societies were all overwhelmingly black. Since emancipation, a dual socioeconomic system emerged consisting of a plantation sector tied to a metropolis and the world economy, alongside a peasant society based on farming of the marginal lands.

A peculiar cultural and racial system evolved in Afro-Caribbean societies. Like the insular Latin group these societies manifested a color-class pecking order, but here blacks, because they constitute the majority, have been able to take over the political control of the area. These societies are all culturally dualistic: an Afro-Caribbean culture, with its roots in the peasantry, which developed out of the fragments of African cultures that survived slavery; and a Euro-Caribbean culture, which is a creolized version of the culture of the former colonial elite. While the society remains culturally bifurcated, some integration has taken place through shared institutions such as schools, European law, and political parties. Within recent years there has been increasing legitimization of the African component in the culture, especially its vibrant urban shanty-town variant, the variant that has given the world reggae music, calypso, and Rastafarianism.

Converging Economic Trends on the Periphery

The socioeconomic diversity of the circum-Caribbean area is being eroded by certain shared economic problems and processes and by its position within the immediate geopolitical and cultural sphere of the United States. The basic economic data make this apparent. Apart from Haiti, at one extreme, and the oil-rich states of Trinidad, Venezuela, and Mexico at the other, the circum-Caribbean states all fall in the lower-middle-income range of developing countries. The economies of all, however, are very precarious. Compared to lower-middle economies elsewhere, their growth rates are below average while their inflation is well above average; and their exceptionally high urbanization rates testify to social and economic costs greater than the norm for societies at their level of development. It is extraordinary, for example, that 53 percent of the population of the Dominican Republic, 68 percent of Mexico's, and 84 percent of Venezuela's should be in urban areas (World Bank, 1984).

Employment in these countries' agricultural sectors is declining faster than in comparable countries elsewhere and, more importantly, this decline in agriculture is in no way matched by growth in industry generally and even less so by growth in the manufacturing sector. An unusually high proportion (over 50 percent) of their gross domestic product (GDP) is in services, reflecting the urban bias of development in the area. Most of the available jobs are not in producer services but in public and personal service activities.

The fragile nature of these economies is reflected in their increasingly unfavorable balance of payments, slim reserves, and large external public debt. Nearly all of them depend on external trade for their survival. World Bank figures (1984) show that in this region as a rule the more prosperous the country in terms of per capita GNP, the more dependent it is on foreign capital and markets, and the greater the tendency for it to produce what it does not consume and consume what it does not produce. When the economies are viable there is, of course, nothing wrong with this. The trouble is that they export only a few products in an uncertain market for most of the foreign exchange earnings on which they survive. The wealthier the country, the more vulnerable the economy, measured in terms of dependence on a limited number of products and markets. The major cause and focus of this precarious dependency is the United States core economy, as we shall see when we look at the dynamics of the interaction between core and periphery.

Migration Flows in the Region

Legal flows. Migration has been a major factor in the development and underdevelopment of all the societies in this region. Up to the middle of the nineteenth century, contact between the four groups was mediated largely through the metropolitan system of the European empires and there was little direct contact across metropolitan boundaries. Even within the boundaries of the imperial systems, contacts were surprisingly attenuated. All this was to change after about the beginning of the nineteenth century. Spain departed from its traditional policy by encouraging immigration, not only from Spain and Latin America but from elsewhere in the Americas, to its last remaining colonies of Puerto Rico and Cuba, in an effort to develop large-scale sugar plantations.

By the middle of the last century the United States began to flex its imperial muscles in the area, culminating in the Spanish-American War and the occupation of the Spanish islands. Long before these wars, however, the United States was to become a haven, especially in New York, for Cuban and other radical exiles. Thus from the very beginning we find a complex exchange of people and ideas in the area. Capital and ideological flows from the Southern states encouraged slavery and annexation sentiments in Cuba, while Northern money and abolitionist and revolutionary sentiments encouraged abolitionist and independence movements against Spain.

In the British Caribbean equally important migratory changes were taking place. In response to the ex-slaves' abandoning the plantations, the planter class recruited vast numbers of East Indian indentured laborers from the Indian subcontinent. Toward the end of the nineteenth century the black working class retaliated by staging a mass exodus to Panama, where they constituted the main labor force in the excavation of the Canal, and to other Central American societies, including Cuba.

The twentieth-century patterns of movement of populations have occurred in four major waves. The first took place between the beginning of the twentieth century and the 1920s. Large numbers of West Indians moved to the United States during this time, some re-migrating from Central America. There was also a small but steady flow of Puerto Ricans, most of whom went to the West Coast of America. The flow of West Indians to the United States was brought to an abrupt end with the passage of racist immigration laws in the 1920s. Within the Caribbean, racist sentiments accounted for the encouragement of immigrants to Cuba from other parts of Latin America and Spain. It was the objective of the Cuban elite at this time to reduce the proportion of nonwhites in the population of the island.

The second wave of migrations took place between 1940 and 1960. Its main features were the following: a substantial increase in the number of Puerto Rican and Mexican migrants to the United States; the first mass migration of the Cuban elite following the Cuban revolution; the movement of over one million migrants to Venezuela, a substantial proportion of whom came from Colombia; and a fairly sizable inter-island movement in the eastern Caribbean, mainly from the poorer British islands, to Trinidad, the oil-refining Dutch islands, the American Virgin Islands, and the Bahamas.

The third wave of migrations occurred between 1960 and 1973. The dislocation and eventual failure of Operation Bootstrap in Puerto Rico resulted in a mass exodus involving over one-third of the entire population. In 1962 the migratory wave of West Indians to Britain was brought to a halt by the British government. At about the same time the United States changed its immigration laws to favor states in the hemisphere. West Indians immediately took advantage of this new opening and a new wave of migrants from the British islands to the mainland began. During this period too the number of Haitians illegally entering the Bahamas multiplied rapidly, bringing the total up to over 40,000 by the mid-1970s.

The main feature of the fourth wave, which can be placed between 1973 and the present, has been the massive increase in the number of illegal migrants to the United States from Mexico and the poorer Caribbean islands. The second vast exodus of Cuban migrants also occurred during this period. An interesting feature of this latest wave, however, has been the movement of professional and other elite-status people from all over the Caribbean basin to the United States, with a special concentration developing in Miami.

The dominance which the West Atlantic region has assumed in

Table 9.1.   United States immigrants from the circum-Caribbean area by country of birth, 1951–1980 (in thousands)

Region and country	1951–1960	1961–1970	1971–1980	Percent 1951–1960	Percent 1961–1970
Mexico	319.3	443.3	637.2	63.3	39.2
Colombia	17.6	70.3	77.6	3.5	6.2
Central America	44.6	97.7	132.4	8.8	8.6
El Salvador	4.8	15.0	34.4	1.0	1.3
Guatemala	4.1	15.4	25.6	0.8	1.4
Panama	9.7	18.4	22.7	1.9	1.6
Other	26.0	48.9	49.7	5.2	4.3
West Indies	122.8	519.5	759.8	24.4	45.9
Barbados	1.6	9.4	20.9	0.3	0.8
Cuba	78.3	256.8	276.8	15.5	22.7
Dominican Rep.	9.8	94.1	148.0	1.9	8.3
Haiti	4.0	37.5	58.7	0.8	3.3
Jamaica	8.7	71.0	142.0	1.7	6.3
Trinidad & Tobago	1.6	24.6	61.8	0.3	2.2
Other	18.8	26.1	51.6	3.7	2.3
Total	504.3	1,130.8	1,607.0	100.0	100.0

Source: U.S. Bureau of the Census, *Statistical Abstract of the United States*, 1984, table 126.

United States immigration can be seen in Tables 9.1 and 9.2: in the 1970s it accounted for over 80 percent of all legal immigrants from this hemisphere and over one-third of immigrants from all parts. As Kritz (1981) has observed, this is extraordinary when we consider that, excluding Canada, the rest of the Americas have about the same population as the Caribbean basin but contribute under 5 percent of all legal immigrants.

But there is another side to this migratory movement: the flow of persons from the United States to the rest of the region. These migrants included the colonial administrators and military personnel who directly ruled Puerto Rico, Haiti, the Dominican Republic, and Nicaragua. During the United States occupation of these areas, soldiers also occupied camps in Jamaica and Trinidad, up until the end of the 1950s. Accompanying them were the agents of U.S. multinational corporations, beginning with the United Fruit Company. Since the late 1940s, such migrants have moved throughout the area, now

Table 9.2.   United States immigrants from the Americas, from the circum-Caribbean, and total, 1951–1980 (in thousands)

Immigrants	1951–1960	1961–1970	1971–1980
Total United States	2,515.5	3,321.7	4,493.3
Total from Americas	841.3	1,579.4	1,929.4
Americas minus circum-Caribbean	337.0	448.6	322.4
Total circum-Caribbean	504.3	1,130.8	1,607.0
As percent of total from Americas	59.9	71.6	83.3
As percent of total United States	20.0	34.0	35.8

Source: U.S. Bureau of the Census, *Statistical Abstract of the United States*, 1984, table 126.

with the invitation of the modernizing elite. A new kind of migrant emerged after the early fifties — the corps of development experts from the various lending agencies, such as the World Bank and AID, all of which have permanent missions in nearly all the states of the region.

Finally, an important aspect of migration is the mass movement of tourists to Mexico and the Caribbean islands. These impermanent visitors not only contribute substantially to the economies of the region, but, as noted earlier, in many of the smaller islands constitute up to a third of the resident population at any given time. They bring with them attitudes, expectations, and styles of living which have significantly altered the world view of the native populations. In addition to short-term visitors many foreign-born permanent residents live in the peripheral areas. Their share of the population is particularly high in the Caribbean island states, especially in the Afro-Caribbean countries that have no oil; by contrast, the proportion of foreign-born residents is low in the Latin Central American nations. It is worth noting as well that the countries with higher per capita GDP tend to have proportionally larger foreign-born populations. While many of the foreign-born in these societies come from the poorer islands, in cases such as Bermuda and the Bahamas a substantial proportion of the foreign-born are from the United States and other advanced societies.

The illegal flow to the United States. In addition to the legal migrants there is a very large but indeterminate number of illegal migrants — indeterminate because by their very nature such data are not likely to be accurate. Estimates of the number of illegal aliens living in the

United States have ranged from 3 to 12 million, and currently are conventionally placed in the lower third of this range. It is commonly believed that about half of these are of Mexican origin, and that nearly all of the non-Mexicans come from the Caribbean area — the Dominican Republic, Haiti, Jamaica, Guatemala, and Colombia, in that order. While the vast majority of Mexicans enter the United States illegally, most migrants from the Caribbean societies enter legally through Miami and New York as visitors or students, then simply fail to go back. A major exception in this pattern has been the waves of Haitian boat-people, which began arriving in southern Florida in the early seventies.

Despite the lack of hard information, there is no question that the number of illegal migrants in the United States at any given time is large, as is the number of those moving across the national frontiers in either direction without taking up long-term residence. Moreover, the public perception of these movements, whether or not it is accurate, has come to play a significant role in national and international policy.

Economic Flows and Patterns of Interdependence

Legal economic flows. An asymmetric pattern of interdependence exists between the United States and the peripheral circum-Caribbean states. These are increasingly dependent on the United States for their economic survival, and their peculiar pattern of distorted growth is related directly to the nature and magnitude of economic flows in the area.

The flows go both ways. The center's dependence on the periphery, although not as critical as the periphery's on the center, is all too easily underestimated (Muñoz, 1981). Part of this dependence is due to the United States' need for certain vital resources from the region, especially oil and bauxite. But other forms of this dependence become clear when we begin to view the United States in regional rather than continental terms, for it is in the eastern seaboard and the southern border states that the economic flows from the Caribbean show their importance.

The dependence of the region's countries on trade with the United States can be seen in a few statistics. In 1983 46 percent of all exports from the circum-Caribbean region were to the United States; the share for individual countries ranged from nil for Cuba to about 60 percent for Barbados, Mexico, Trinidad, and Tobago, and between 70 and 80 percent for the Bahamas, the Dominican Republic, and Haiti. Similarly, the share of the region's imports from the United States amounted to 42 percent and ranged from less than 1 percent for Cuba to 60 percent for Mexico (IMF, 1984).

If we look at the region's share of United States worldwide trade, what impresses us is not how small but how large it is given the region's relative poverty: in 1983 it accounted for 10 percent of U.S. exports and 12 percent of imports (IMF, 1984). Similarly, in 1980 12 percent of all U.S. investments went to the region, which returned 14 percent of all foreign income. Even more striking, however, is the fact that these figures amounted to 38 percent of all U.S. investment and 52 percent of all U.S. income from all of Latin America (Bureau of Economic Analysis, 1982).

Illegal economic flows. Paralleling the illegal flow of migrants from peripheral areas to the United States is the illegal flow of wealth. This flow assumes two principal forms: shipments of illegal drugs and the largely illegal transfer of flight capital into southern Florida and the southwestern portion of the United States.

Although, as in the case of illegal immigration, the flows of illegal drugs can at best be only roughly estimated, some figures for 1978 provide a sense of their magnitude. The retail value of imported illicit drugs was estimated at over $40 billion. Mexico accounted for the bulk of the heroin, while Colombia was the principal trafficking source for cocaine, which was imported mostly through southern Florida. However, marijuana remains the top income generator among the illicit drugs, and it is estimated that over 90 percent of that came from Mexico and the Caribbean (National Narcotics Intelligence Consensus Committee, 1982). This flow of illegal drugs has had major effects on the economy of southern Florida, and its importance to several of the nations of the region, especially Colombia, Jamaica, Mexico, and the Bahamas may be sensed by comparing the above figures to the region's total legal exports of $14 billion to the United States in 1977 (IMF, 1984).

The intake of flight capital has also had major effects on the economies of southern Florida and many of the region's nations. It is estimated that over $4 billion in Latin exile money has passed into the banks of Miami (*The Economist*, October 16, 1982). In a cover story on the area, *Time* magazine reports that, "inspired by the Nicaraguans who fled their country after the downfall of President Anastasio Somoza in 1979, wealthy families from El Salvador, Guatemala,

Venezuela and Argentina are nervously preparing a South Florida refuge in case their own governments totter" (Nov. 23, 1981). One could add to this list the elites of Jamaica, Barbados, and Trinidad and Tobago. In most cases the flow of capital to the United States is illegal, given the exchange control regulations in many of these societies. A variety of ways, some of them quite ingenious, exist to get around these legal obstacles.

Asymmetric Interdependencies: Gains and Losses in the Center and the Periphery

What have been the effects of all these flows on the societies of the region? In any assessment of costs and benefits we must distinguish between individual, collective, and system effects. The three rarely coincide.

Moreover, formal governmental policy statements about these flows must be distinguished from what is really going on, even where no official deceit is intended. Institutions and individuals often find themselves in self-contradictory positions regarding these movements — this is as true of nationalist leaders who unwittingly undermine their cherished national cultures with misbegotten economic policies, as it is of U.S. leaders who call for tougher immigration policies while protecting elements of the capitalist sector which benefit from the cheap labor of illegal migrants. Alejandro Portes has put the matter neatly:

> Illegal or not, the fundamental point, however, is that international labor immigration responds to structural determinants in both sending and receiving countries. Such determinants exist independent of the apparatus of legal regulation, the national pride and culture of the exporting society, and the intentions of political leaders.
>
> International labor migration also establishes a symbiotic bond between countries in different positions in the capitalist economy. It simultaneously alleviates labor scarcity and high labor costs in core areas and conditions of labor oversupply, capital scarcity, and difficulty in controlling the labor force in peripheral ones.   (1978b, p. 477)

The traditional assessment of migratory flows, based mainly on classical international trade theory, is that such flows amount to a positive sum exchange. On the individual level, the migrants gain in increased income and opportunities, while producers in the host country gain by lower wages, resulting in gains to consumers through lower prices of the goods produced by the migrants. The sending countries, it is further claimed, gain through relief of their unemployment problems and increased foreign exchange earnings of hard currency through remittances; and on the individual level, the bargaining power, and hence wage level, of those left behind are increased by the out-migration of labor.

This is not so much an inaccurate as an incomplete and simplistic interpretation of the real world. As Philip Martin and Alan Richards have pointed out, the traditional approach fails to take account of at least three important factors (p. 477). First, while migration may benefit migrants, employers, and consumers, it may reduce the overall bargaining power of all workers in the host society. Second, the traditional view neglects the "limited substitutability among workers of different skill levels" in the sending, peripheral countries and, as such, "may generate manpower shortages in precisely those areas of the economy that are essential for economic growth." Third, this approach fails to distinguish between flows of people and flows of goods and capital. The human costs of migration for both sending and receiving countries are not insignificant.

The data on migration flows in the West Atlantic region suggest that, on the whole, the United States center is a net gainer; however, the effect on the sending countries is mixed. Some individuals and sectors gain more than others in each country; and the net macroeffects vary from one country to the next, but are in general negative.

Effects on the center. In the United States center the inflow of migrants dovetails with the prevailing structural evolution of the economy. Migration facilitates dualism. The great majority of the migrants go to work for low wages either in the service sector or in those areas of the agricultural- and goods-producing sectors which would otherwise collapse under competition from foreign countries. They thus give capitalists in the declining goods-producing sector an alternative to moving their firms out of the United States to the third world. Part of the reason for the shift of industry from the frostbelt to the sunbelt within the United States was the search for cheap migrant labor, especially from Mexico (Bluestone and Harrison, 1982, especially ch. 6).

The opposite argument is that the inflow of migrants restrains the increased capitalization needed to revitalize the traditional goods-producing industries; or, just as problematic, that it conflicts with the transformation of the United States into a postindustrial system.

This is greatly to be doubted. There is no evidence that the process of capitalization or reindustrialization of the goods-producing sector bears any relationship to the supply of immigrant labor, legal or illegal. As to the evolution of the postindustrial society, migrants enter all sectors of the economy, including services, although they take on the dirtiest jobs, which native workers rightly feel are dead-ends not worth the effort.

While the great mass of immigrants earn low wages, a growing share of migrants to the United States consists of professionals or entrepreneurs. This significant recent development has led to what Portes (1981) calls the "enclave" immigrant economic sector made up of firms created by immigrant entrepreneurs, partly to meet the needs of the migrant community, but also — and it is in this respect that the pattern differs from previous immigrant firms — those of the host community. The Cubans in Miami are the most obvious case in point; but the same is true of many other groups.

The consequences of this migration for labor markets have been the subject of much dispute. Here I shall focus on the case of Mexican migrants, drawing heavily on Cornelius (1978), because these are the most numerous of the migrants and because the issues are generic for other migrants from the circum-Caribbean region.

It is often contended that the migrants, by increasing the supply of labor, affect wages and job opportunities adversely for the poorest of America, especially blacks, Chicanos, and Puerto Ricans. Cornelius shows that half of illegal Mexican migrants work in agriculture, and the great majority of the others take jobs as janitors, garbage collectors, dishwashers, unskilled construction workers, gardeners, and the like — jobs requiring little or no skill, with low security and few prospects, which are unattractive to native workers.

It is also suggested that illegal aliens undermine the structure of the labor market further because, being illegal and hence vulnerable, they allow employers to provide miserable working conditions in addition to low wages. According to this view, if there were no illegal migrants employers would be forced to make these jobs more desirable to native workers. While plausible in theory, the data do not support this argument. Cornelius shows that the lowest unemployment rates in the United States are primarily in the areas with the highest concentration of illegal migrants.

Nor does it appear that migrants undercut organized labor by working below the minimum wage. Admittedly few Mexican workers are unionized, but this is largely because of the deliberate hostility of the unions to these workers. Moreover, a recent study in Chicago by Marcus Alexis and his associates (1983) found that it is black workers rather than Latin migrants who tend to work below the minimum wage. On the whole, Cornelius argues persuasively, Mexican migrants, like the guestworkers in Western Europe, contribute significantly to the nation's economic growth. Moreover, the American poor also benefit from the lower costs and prices which the use of migrant labor makes possible.

On quite another dimension, advocates of zero population growth have expressed concerns about high Hispanic fertility rates — concerns which are at best alarmist, at worst racist. Mexican immigrants do have high fertility rates, but they rapidly adopt the fertility patterns of the native population, especially as they urbanize. What is certain, however, is that the ethnic mix of the U.S. population will change significantly as a result of the ongoing migration. The oft-repeated proposition that the Mexican-ancestry group will constitute the single largest non-European ethnic group by the turn of the century is basically correct. This will have important sociological implications, but as we shall argue later, the overall effects are likely to be positive.

Finally, there is the controversial issue of the effect of the migratory flow on social services and taxes. Cornelius underestimates this impact by emphasizing that illegal migrants, while paying for such tax-based programs as employment compensation, welfare assistance, and public education, make little use of them. While this may be so, the picture alters radically when we consider the longer term. Martin and Richards (1980) observe that host countries initially benefit from the fact that imported workers do not require social infrastructure, but that permanent immigrants do require social investments if they and their children are to be brought up to host-country norms.

Perhaps the most significant socioeconomic effect on the United States of the mingled flow of migrants, capital, and cultural patterns has been the growth of the southern Florida area. Miami has come to the fore as the financial, political, and cultural center of the emerging West Atlantic system. There is a real sense in which it is no longer an exclusive American city but the heart of an international metropolitan region. Legal and illegal migrants and capital find a haven there. Five years ago only five banks in the Miami metropolitan regions were chartered to engage in international finance; now over forty-four banks are so chartered. Of these, at least thirty-six are foreign banks. These banks account for 25 percent of southern Florida's regional product and 20 percent of all jobs. An indicator of the region's financial vitality is the $6 billion cash surplus run by the regional office of the Federal Reserve; this is more than the combined reserves of the nation's other Federal Reserve Banks, and much of it comes from the inflow of illegal drug funds and from the nest eggs accumulated by the elites of the region. Florida has also become the corporate headquarters for Latin America for at least 110 multinationals, and many Latin American companies have moved their headquarters there.

Miami serves as the political hub of the larger region. It is well known as the center for conservative political exiles and terrorists from the region. "International intrigue," according to the *New York Times*, is "turning Miami into the Casablanca of the New World." Miami has become "a magnet for a mixed bag of Caribbean and Latin American strongmen, revolutionaries, exiles, arms merchants, Colombian cocaine cowboys, spies and buccaneers of every calling" for four principal reasons: "Geography, language, ambiance and money" (Dec. 29, 1984).

The city now plays an increasingly active role in the national politics of the circum-Caribbean region. Two examples provide striking illustrations. Belisario Betancur, the successful presidential candidate for Colombia, campaigned in Miami, and financial and other support by Colombians resident in that city were important factors in his victory. Similarly, the current Jamaican prime minister, Edward Seaga, planned part of his campaign strategy in Miami and received support from upper-class Jamaicans who had fled the incumbent democratic socialist government. From his Florida base he was able to gain support from a number of conservative American groups and to influence the American press and corporate leaders.

Southern Florida is likewise the academic and intellectual center of the region. Numerous newspapers, journals, and trade reports in Spanish and English cater to the information needs of this constituency. The *Miami Herald*, especially the Sunday issue, is the newspaper of choice for the elites of nearly all the states of the circum-Caribbean. The universities of southern Florida are not only the preferred institutions for their children but havens for academics and journalists from the peripheral states.

The counterpart to the Americanization of the periphery has been the Latinization and Caribbeanization of substantial parts of the United States. Miami is, of course, by now as much a Latin as an Anglo city, a development strongly resented by the Anglo community (Portes, 1984). But migrants from the region have had a significant impact on American culture far beyond southern Florida. In New York and other northeastern cities Puerto Ricans and other West Indians have influenced cultural life not only through their carnivals and their music but in race relations and attitude to race (Flores et al., 1981; Cortes et al., 1976).

It is on matters of racial attitude and relations that the joint impact of the West Atlantic migrants will likely be strongest. Already there are clear signs that the traditional binary racial classification of the United States is breaking down. This stems in part from the different conceptions of race which the immigrants themselves hold, but even more from their very presence. For the first time in its history America has a large segment of its population which cannot be classified as either black or white, which does not wish to be classified as either, but which cannot be hidden away on reservations, as were the native Americans. It is difficult to say just where American racial values will go as a result of this impact. What is certain, however, is that the situation cannot stay as it is (Sudarkasa, 1983; Safa, 1983).

Migrants from the region have played, and will increasingly play, an important role in the national political life of the United States. Historically, black West Indians have contributed to the American civil rights struggle out of proportion to their numbers. Marcus Garvey, the back-to-Africa leader, was a Jamaican who first migrated to Panama and moved among other Central American countries before coming to the United States. Since his time other West Indians have been prominent in American radical politics, and were overrepresented in the Communist and Socialist parties before the war. More recent leaders such as Malcolm X, Stokely Carmichael, and Shirley Chisholm have come from the West Indies (Forsythe, 1976).

If black West Indians have been disproportionately influential in radical politics, their counterparts from Cuba and Latin America have had a disproportionate impact on conservative American politics. The Cubans, however, are an isolated case, and not even all Cubans, since the latest wave of migrants seem more inclined to identify with other migrants from the region (Dixon, 1983; Bach, 1980). There is every indication that the great majority of the Latin migrants will not only become actively involved with the political life of America but will increasingly identify their interests with those of the black and other disadvantaged groups in the United States. Such a coalition of interests will be of tremendous importance not only for America but also for the peripheral states of the region from which the migrants came (London, 1980; Valentine, 1985; Portes, Parker, and Nash, 1980).

Effects on the periphery: dualism and underdevelopment. Earlier we saw how change and contradictions in the center led to the development of a dualistic socioeconomic system. Much the same process of dualism has taken place in the peripheral states. Perhaps, as Berger and Piore (1980) have suggested, dualism is a necessary feature of all industrializing societies, attributable to flux and uncertainty on the one hand, and to differentiation on the other. But this is too general a statement of the problem. In specifying the processes of underdevelopment in the periphery we will draw not only on dependency theory but also on some recent work in social ecology (Hannan and Freeman, 1977).

The dualistic underdevelopment of the region has emerged over the centuries since its discovery and settlement. At different times the various social units in the region have used different strategies based on two criteria of adaptation to find a niche in the West Atlantic environment. The first criterion is whether the social unit adapts by employing a specialist or a generalist strategy. A specialized economy concentrates on producing one or two goods, aims for efficiency, and seeks to exploit some comparative advantage. Specialism is, however, a high-risk mode of adaptation and works best in stable environments. By staking so much on so few productive enterprises the society runs the risk of total collapse if conditions change. The classic example in the West Atlantic peripheral states are the predominantly plantation economies operating in the protected imperial systems of the region.

The generalist strategy emphasizes diversification. Its advantage is that it is a low-risk mode of adaptation to an environment which may change. There are many eggs in the production basket. The flip side of generalism, however, is the danger of chronic inefficiency. The economy may end up in the jack-of-all-trades dilemma. Economies of scale are often sacrificed, an acute problem for economies with small internal markets. Organizational redundancy is also a major problem. An ideal-type pure-plantation economy producing only sugar needs only one marketing board; an economy producing coffee, sugar, and yams needs a board for each crop, and the yields from each may not be great enough to justify all its institutional costs.

The viability of generalism as a strategy is a function of the amount of resources controlled by the social unit. The more limited the land

and other resources, the lower the efficiency of such systems. Haiti represents the inefficient end of the generalist strategy among West Atlantic societies (Leyburn, 1941; Charles, 1967; Moore, 1972). It is predominantly a peasant society with a small plantation and even smaller industrial sector. The slash-and-burn hoe culture of the peasants, a survival from West Africa, works best under conditions of low population density. With its population growing and its land resources finite, indeed dwindling, the generalist strategy has become a disaster for Haiti. Malnutrition is chronic, famine imminent. Not all generalist strategies have been as disastrous as Haiti's in the West Atlantic; but it is significant that nearly all have been failures.

The second criterion used in classifying strategies is whether the dominant mode of production (by which I mean simply what generates most of the national product) is agricultural or industrial (more accurately, nonagricultural). These two criteria form the basis for four basic strategies or modes of adaptation to the West Atlantic environment. The four socioeconomic strategies have generated four kinds of dualisms. What follows is a schematic account of each.

1. *Agricultural Generalism (AG)*. The best examples are Haiti, Dominica, Grenada, and Honduras, where the informal or secondary sector overwhelms the tiny formal sector. They are nonetheless dualistic because the small formal sector sustains the all-important urban elites which dominate the mass of peasants in the informal sector (Garrity, 1981).

2. *Agricultural Specialism (AS)*. Examples are Cuba, Nicaragua, Colombia, Guatemala, and St. Kitts, which are classic plantation economies. The formal sector is overwhelmingly rural, with the rural proletarian being the distinctive and typical formal worker. The formal urban sector is based on industries related to or ultimately supported by the plantation sector. Taken together, workers in the formal sector make up between a third and a half of the total work force. The remaining workers are in the informal peasant sectors or the informal, unproductive urban service jobs, or are simply unemployed (Beckford, 1972).

3. *Industrial Generalism (IG)*. These societies have made efforts to diversify through import substitution and export-oriented industrial strategies. The formal sector dominates in terms of both employment and contribution to GNP. It is mainly urban industrial, but includes a formal farm sector. The informal sector is increasingly urban, consisting mainly of shanty-town dwellers, most of whom are unemployed or self-employed. It also includes workers in the rapidly

declining peasant or small-farming sector. The U.S. center is, of course, the most successful example of this mode of adaptation. While this strategy has worked well for the central society, it has been conspicuous for its failure in the peripheral systems. Puerto Rico, Jamaica, Mexico, Costa Rica, and Barbados are the best examples of this strategy (Beckford, 1975; Jefferson, 1970; Demas, 1965; Lewis, 1963; Carr, 1984; Payne and Sutton, 1984; Sanchez Tarnielloa, 1973). The temporary successes (during the fifties and sixties) and ultimate failure of this mode of adaptation in the peripheral states is closely related to its success in the center for reasons already discussed. I will return to certain other problems of center-periphery relations in the use of this strategy.

4. *Industrial Specialism (IS)*. This mode places an overwhelming reliance on one or two nonfarm products for export. In this respect the IS strategy bears a superficial resemblance to AS, and some Caribbean economists have argued that it is merely a version of AS. I disagree sharply with this "plantationist" theory. The systems are internally very different. First, in IS the formal sector is overwhelming larger proportionally than even that of the U.S. center. Second, when it works, this strategy is highly efficient and societies employing it tend to have high per capita income and low unemployment levels. Like all specialist modes of adaptation, however, it is a high-risk strategy, much more so than the AS classic plantation strategy. When AS strategies fail either for production or market reasons, the whole system does not collapse, only the formal sector. The informal peasant sector remains intact and workers often seek refuge in it. It is the consumption levels of the elite which are most at risk. But when the IS strategy fails, the entire social order is at risk. A good example is the mini-state of Aruba, where an Exxon oil refinery has been generating over half of all government revenue. Exxon's recent decision to close down its refinery means that, at one corporate stroke, the entire economy faces collapse (de Cordoba, 1984). Other examples in this group are the oil states of Venezuela and Trinidad and the tourist-based states of the Bahamas, Bermuda, Antigua, and St. Croix (Bond, 1977; Robinson, 1971; Sutton, 1984; Andic and Andic, 1971). All of these rank among the top third of the peripheral states in terms of per capita income. However, they are all high-risk societies. The volatility of oil-based economies is by now well known, and so is the weakness of those which are tourist-based. Indeed, the experience of St. Croix during the early 1970s is instructive. When a maniac ran loose and killed a couple of vacationing golfers, the

immediate reaction was a temporary drying up of the tourist trade. Overnight the economy collapsed. It took months of expensive public relations to restore it.

Figure 9.1 shows the pattern of asymmetric interdependency in the West Atlantic system as capital flows back and forth between the center and the peripheral states. Countries which have adopted the center's strategy of Industrial Generalism have not been able to replicate its success, and in spite of their high per capita income find themselves in the most precarious and the most dependent situation. As the figure shows, their dependence on the center for investment loans and other capital is matched by counterflows amounting to a net loss of capital and severe structural problems. The second reason, not illustrated, for these countries' lack of success is the fact that the center is a global power for which the West Atlantic periphery is merely one of several peripheral societies (Cheng and Bonacich, 1984). For reasons we cannot enter into here, the IG strategy has been far more successful in other peripheral systems, most notably the East Asian societies of Korea, Taiwan, and Singapore. Resources have accordingly been shifted from the West Atlantic periphery to the East Asian; one configuration's gain has been the other's loss. The West Atlantic region and the center, by virtue of their proximity, nonetheless share a special relationship that includes national security and has resulted in the growing dualism of both parties.

It is in this context that we come, finally, to the problem of migration. The demand for labor at the center and the supply from the periphery are both products of a single process of structural dualism extending over the West Atlantic region. Capital flows from the center to the periphery to evade the contradictions of capitalism, industrialism, and postindustrial change. In the periphery, multinational capital dualizes the economy by creating a formal modern sector and an informal one; but here the disruptive effects of dualism are much greater than in the center. Capital takes flight from the periphery to the center as a safeguard against the uncertainties of dependent dualism. Peripheral unemployment is greatly increased. Migration is often promoted as a safety valve in the expected transition to modernity, benefiting the peripheral states by relieving their labor surpluses, providing hard currency through remittances, and eventually putting to use the entrepreneurial skills of returning migrants.

Empirical studies have cast serious doubt on all these expectations. Migration, economists have shown, has almost no effect on the rates

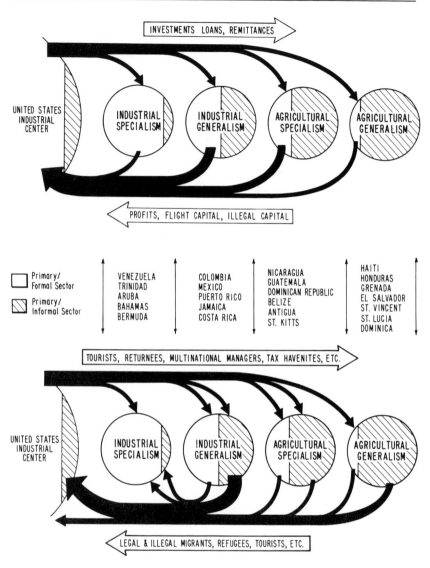

Figure 9.1.   Capital and migration flows in the West Atlantic system.

of unemployment in the peripheral states. With the questionable exceptions of northern Mexico, and those small islands where the entire economy depends on the remittances of the majority of the male labor force working abroad (Montserrat, Providencia, Carriacou, a few of the Grenadines, Saba, Anguilla and Andros islands), the evidence suggests that "despite the large sums remitted and their importance for individual well-being and social mobility, there is no positive contribution to rural economic rejuvenation" (Rubenstein, 1983, p. 295; Stinner, de Albuquerque and Bryce-Laporte, 1982; Cornelius, 1978). The migrants' funds usually support imported consumer durables, not locally produced goods. Returning migrants rarely become creative entrepreneurs. Indeed, they often return with attitudes more appropriate to the life-styles and business practices of the center; in the case of Puerto Rico, they have brought back the worst social problems of the U.S. ghetto way of life (Johnson, 1982). Rather than promoting entrepreneurship, one of the most significant negative effects of migration is that it drains the periphery of its most motivated and skilled labor (Bhagwati, 1979; Hope, 1976; Portes, 1976; UN, 1971).

Further, the very ease of migration in the West Atlantic makes progressive political change impossible; even moderate reforms, essential for the viability of these systems, are likely to be met with massive capital flight, followed by elite and even blue-collar flight. In all these respects, migration from the periphery becomes self-reinforcing, promoting the very structural dualism that generates it. The degree to which the process of dualistic interdependence influences migration, however, varies with the prevailing adaptive strategy. Emigration is highest from those societies that employ industrial generalism and are politically closest to the center. These two characteristics are linked in that an IG strategy depends on heavy foreign investment, which in turn requires the right political climate, another name for strong pro-Americanism. By contrast, the states employing industrial specialism have the lowest migration rates. This is because they have the highest per capita incomes and the lowest rates of unemployment. Indeed, they tend to be migrant-receiving states.

One more aspect of migration in the peripheral societies must be noted. Not only are they regions of emigration but also of immigration in the form of returning migrants, tourists, tax-haven seekers, and change agents. These have reinforced the artificial modernization of values, intensifying the process of rising expectations, which can often be met only by migrating to the center.

The effect of American values has not, however, been all negative. Racial values in the periphery have been favorably influenced by both tourists and returning migrants. Ideas of racial pride and political independence from the center have had liberating consequences (Sutton and Makielski, 1975; Green, 1975; Oxaal, 1971; Coombs, 1974). And tourists have revolutionized the primitive racist and sexist as well as racial-sexual norms of the traditional peripheral cultures. Thus the willingness of North American female tourists to sleep with working-class black Barbadians undermined almost overnight the vicious pattern of racial exclusiveness and notions of racial purity that prevailed before the tourist era. On the whole, however, the effect of immigration on traditional values has not been to alter but to eliminate and replace them with those of North America (Peace, 1982, especially chs. 2 and 4; Bryden, 1973; Matthews, 1977; Manning, 1982).

Under the conditions obtaining in the West Atlantic region, illegal migration is inevitable. Even when migration to the United States is legally blocked, the potential rewards for a worker from the periphery are so high that to attempt illegal entry is now the most highly rational decision. "In this sense," Piore has written, "the migrant is initially a true economic man, probably the closest thing in real life to the *homo economicus* of economic theory" (1979, p. 54).

From the point of view of the United States, the cost-benefit equation reinforces the rationality of illegal entry. The only benefit which American citizens would derive from keeping migrants out would be the monopolization of resources within the United States, which is of dubious value, for the costs of exclusion are incomparably greater. These include, first, the enormous expense of patrolling the thousands of miles of border with Mexico and of shoreline. Even were this possible, the expense would far outweigh the economic benefits of resource monopolization. But there are greater costs. Migrants are a selective group of highly motivated people who contribute substantially to the national product of the United States; keeping them out entails significant opportunity costs. And at a regional level there are the sociopolitical costs of keeping individuals trapped in peripheral states which can no longer support them. The United States as a collective actor has not been able to solve the problems of these states. Hence, the United States increases the risk of political instability and Communist penetration in its security perimeter by refusing to allow the disenchanted to enter its borders. The economic costs of clandestine CIA operators and of supporting repressive, parasitic regimes are extremely high. Even higher, however, are the political and prestige costs to the leader of "the free world."

Our conclusion about the impossibility of sealing U.S. borders to migration is reminiscent of two of the most common principles of environmental economics, that of proprietorial nonexcludability and mutually beneficial usage. Some environmental resources cannot be privately owned because it is too impractical and costly to keep other people from using them, and it is pointless to own something which one cannot prevent others from enjoying. Environmental goods also have the characteristic of mutually beneficial usage in "that there are likely to be enormous economies in the joint consumption or use of the resource as contrasted with individual use" (Dorfman and Dorfman, 1972, p. xv).

Both the physical and the socioeconomic structures of the West Atlantic region have increasingly become like nonexcludable environmental resources. This includes the center's industrial system and its opportunities. When a worker from the periphery contemplates illegal entry into the United States, he has merely adopted an attitude of nonexcludability comparable to the one that U.S. policy makers and multinational executives have held from the early part of the nineteenth century toward the countries of the periphery. In undercutting the national sovereignty of the peripheral states and in its refusal or incapacity to assist the region with a level of aid that would restore their economic viability, the United States has set in motion forces that now undercut the most important element of its own sovereignty, the defense of its own borders.

Migration and the Ethics of Domination

Although our discussion has been in sociological terms, important moral precepts are involved. One is the principle that domination always incurs a moral obligation on the part of the dominator. In simple terms: "If you come uninvited to my turf and exploit my resources, I at least have the right to go to your turf and do the same." In more sophisticated terms, subjection establishes a communal bond, however unequal. From ancient Roman times imperial powers have implicitly accepted this principle. The Romans took this principle to its extreme limits in that the greater the subjection the closer was the implied bond. Only this can explain the extraordinary fact that the simplest way of becoming a Roman citizen was to be manumitted from enslavement by a Roman citizen. The modern European imperial states continued to act on this principle in that all subjects of their empires were citizens and had the right of entry to any part of the empire, including the metropolis.

In its domination of the West Atlantic region the United States has incurred a similar obligation in the moral world view of the dominated peoples; one that it has only halfheartedly recognized. Ironically, it uses the fiction of national sovereignty and the fact that it has not formally colonized most of the states of the region as excuses for not facing up to this obligation. No one in the periphery takes this seriously. The United States has not only dominated the region economically and by direct and indirect political means, but the almost daily statements of its leaders clearly indicate that it considers the region vital to its national security. From a geopolitical perspective the region is within its military boundaries. The attitudes of its leaders to Cuba and to Central America only make sense in these terms. The Caribbean is the American lake as certainly as the Mediterranean was considered "our sea" by the Romans. The recent invasion of Grenada and current covert action in Central America confirm all this.

It is in the light of this moral obligation that we must interpret the attitude of persons who illegally enter the United States. Basically, these people do not consider their action to be wrong or illegal in any way. We detect no sense of shame on the faces of those who are apprehended by the border police. Instead, the attitude seems to be, "I'll be back." Most poor Mexicans, according to a *New York Times* report, regarded the ill-fated Simpson-Mazzoli bill on immigration as something of a "cruel joke" as well as an added burden.

> It is cruel, they say, to them — another obstacle to be overcome, like the Mexican police who try to shake them down when they arrive in this gritty border city [Tijuana] from the south, or the "baja pollos" who rob them as they are trying to cross or the border patrols who catch them and turn them back. "Baja pollos" means to take money from chickens. It is also a joke, they say, on anyone who thinks it will stop them from crossing the border to find work to feed themselves and their families. "They're trying to mess around with us," said a 33-year-old carpenter — "But there will still be work and as long as there's work there will still be 'mojados.'" Mojados is slang for illegal aliens. (Meislin, 1984, p. 10)

The attitude of the Mexican government toward U.S. immigration policies and its treatment of "illegal aliens" is also only comprehensible in these terms.

The behavior of American capitalists who benefit from the labor of migrants, legal and illegal, reinforces nonexcludability. To be sure, economic considerations are uppermost in their thinking, but it may well be that an acceptance of the migrants' basic right to enter the United States also plays a part in their extraordinary willingness to subvert the immigration laws of their own country. Moral precepts and obligations are most clearly understood and diligently pursued when they are congruent with economic interests. This is a strongly ingrained Anglo-American tradition, as the abolition of the slave trade and slavery so nicely illustrate.

It may well be, too, that a more primitive moral precept is at work in the movement of people into the United States. This is the simple conviction that it is not right that one's neighbor should monopolize vast resources while one struggles to survive with very little. Mexico (from which vast land and mineral resources were seized in the last century) and most of the Caribbean islands are hopelessly over-crowded and resource-poor societies. It may be that in simple economic terms most of these societies are not viable economic entities. In the light of this brutal disparity between the United States and its neighbors, it will take nothing short of repressive and possibly totalitarian means on the part of the U.S. authorities to keep out migrants from the periphery. There is some evidence that American immigration authorities are already fully alive to this fact.

What all this amounts to is that it makes less and less sense to speak of nation-states in the West Atlantic. The communities of the region already spread across political boundaries. Puerto Rican society encompasses the 60 percent of Puerto Ricans who live in Puerto Rico, "the inner community," and the 40 percent who live on the mainland, "the outer community." The same holds for Jamaican society, a quarter of whose members live in the United States, as it does for Mexicans.

This also means that the idea of ethnicity is of little relevance. Migrants from the region cannot be expected to replicate the ethnic experience of earlier migrants from Europe. The latter severed most social bonds with their parent societies. They sought to become Irish-Americans, Italian-Americans, Polish-Americans, and the like, in all cases respecting the fact that they were members of a different sovereign state. It is different with the migrants from the West Atlantic region. They do not recognize the need to become new citizens, not out of disrespect for American citizenship but because the idea of citizenship has lost its meaning. Nor have they changed their communities. They have simply moved from the periphery to the center of their own communities. What Elsa M. Chanery (1976) wrote of Chapinero, the Colombian section of Queens, could just as easily describe other Caribbean "outer" communities on the mainland: "Chapinero is more like a remote province of Colombia than an ethnic barrio of New York City."

The West Atlantic as an Emerging Postnational Environment

In this essay I have followed the lead of some recent scholars in arguing that migration flows between rich and poor countries can be properly understood only in terms of the wider system of socioeconomic interactions between them. I have parted company with world-system analysts, however, in emphasizing the distinctively regional nature of the West Atlantic system of migration. This system shares many features with other systems of flows to the U.S. and other capitalist centers, but is unique in the peculiar configuration of geographic contiguity and long political involvement between the center and the periphery.

Originally a region of diverse cultures and economies operating within the framework of several imperial systems, the West Atlantic region has emerged over the centuries as a single environment in which the dualistic United States center is asymmetrically linked to dualistic peripheral units. Unlike other peripheral systems of states — those of the Pacific, for example — the West Atlantic periphery has become more and more uniform, under the direct and immediate influence of the all-powerful center, in cultural, political, and economic terms. Further, unlike other peripheral states in their relation to their centers, the West Atlantic system has a physical nexus in the metropolis at the tip of Florida.

I have argued that four paths have led to the evolutionary sink that is peripheral dualism. These different paths, despite their common outcome, are nonetheless important in accenting four different migratory patterns and volumes of flows. The more dualistic the society, and the greater the modernization of the economy, the higher the volume of flows out of the society to the center.

The migratory flows have, in turn, certain important consequences for both the center and the periphery, beyond the more obvious economic effects. In cultural terms, a significant regional segment of the center has been thoroughly Latinized. But even more important in its long-term implications is the radical change in the center's traditional conception of race which will come about as a result of the immigrant group. I predict, and already see clear indications of, a major shift from the Anglo-Saxon binary conception of race to one that is descriptive. The mere demographic presence of the Latin and Afro-Caribbean migrants would have brought about this change. A binary conception of race is possible only when all major population groups can be unambiguously classified as belonging to the "white" or "black" race. With the growing presence of working-class Latins who refuse to be classified as either, the binary conception of race is bound to collapse. In addition to this powerful demographic fact, there is also the descriptive conception of race which the immigrants bring with them, reinforcing the changes that their mere presence initiated.

The newcomers will also most certainly bypass the classic cycle of ethnic assimilation, mobility, and third-generation nostalgic "cut-flower" consciousness. This is yet another major difference from the center's relation to its Pacific immigrants. Many factors account for the difference — the volume of the West Atlantic migration, its timing with respect to the evolution of American capitalism, and the structural role of the immigrants, but perhaps most important of all are geographic proximity and co-historical intimacy with the center. A major sociopolitical implication of the systemic flows in the West Atlantic is the emergence of transnational communities and the decline of the nation-state — both in the center and the periphery — as a boundary maintaining entity.

In the peripheral states three powerful currents are undermining the integrity of national boundaries. The first is the long and continuing history of direct political and economic intervention by the United States, invited and uninvited, in overt and covert ways. The second is the complex of political and economic forces which are in direct conflict with traditional notions of sovereignty. Some of these forces restrict the options on all sides. As Fagen and Pellicer (1983) have pointed out, "it is becoming increasingly difficult for any one country to develop unless its neighbors enjoy peace and prosperity" (p. 5). But others exert positive pressures toward transnational development. It is increasingly apparent that for most states internal markets are too small, and the goods they produce are too much in competition with each other. The obvious alternative is some form of regional cooperation. Past and current attempts at such integration are hardly encouraging because they fly in the face of local bourgeois nationalism. But any meaningful socioeconomic change has to be within the context of such transnational integration. Pedro Vuskovic (1983) observes that future development must consider alternative schemes of either isolated national development or a common integrated development.

The third current undermining the nation-state is that of migration. The societies of many of the peripheral states no longer coincide with political boundaries. Economic dualism has generated sociodemographic dualism. These same migratory flows also undermine the national integrity of the center. Having spent the last century and a half violating militarily, economically, politically, and culturally the national boundaries of the region, the center now finds itself incapable of defending the violation of its own national borders. The costs of doing so are administratively, politically, and, most important, economically too high. Trade, and the international division of labor, follows the flag. But they also set in motion winds that tear it down. Irrevocably, the West Atlantic emerges as a postnational environment.

Bibliography
Contributors
Index

Bibliography

Abadan-Unat, N. 1976. Turkish migration to Europe, 1960–1975: A balance sheet of achievements and failures. In *Turkish Workers in Europe 1960–1975: A Socioeconomic Reappraisal*, ed. N. Abadan-Unat. Leiden: E. J. Brill.

Abbott, E. 1926. *Historical Aspects of the Immigration Problem*. Chicago: University of Chicago Press.

Alexis, M., N. DiTomaso, and C. Kyle. 1983. Impact of Hispanics on Black workers in Chicago. Paper given at the International Conference on Immigration and the Changing Black Population in the United States, May 18–21, University of Michigan, Ann Arbor.

Anderson, B. A., and B. D. Silver. 1983. Estimating russification of ethnic identity among non-Russians in the USSR. *Demography*, 20:461–489.

Anderson, P. 1974. *Lineages of the Absolutist State*. London: New Left Books.

Andic, F. M., and S. Andic. 1971. The economy of the Netherlands Antilles. In *Politics and Economics of the Caribbean*, ed. T. G. Matthews and F. M. Andic. Puerto Rico: Institute of Caribbean Studies.

Anstey, R. 1975. *The Atlantic Slave Trade and British Abolition 1760–1810*. London: Macmillan.

Armstrong, W. 1962. Godkin and Chinese labor: A paradox in nineteenth-century liberalism. *The American Journal of Economics and Sociology*, 21:91–102.

Asiegbu, J. 1969. *Slavery and the Politics of Liberation*. London: Longmans, Green.

Bach, R. L. 1980. The new Cuban immigrants: Their background and prospects. *Monthly Labor Review* (Oct.): 39–46.

Barth, G. 1964. *Bitter Strength: A History of the Chinese in the United States, 1850–1870*. Cambridge, Mass.: Harvard University Press.

Bass, J. R. 1976. The South-east Asian Chinese: Accommodation without acceptance. In *Case Studies on Human Rights and Fundamental Freedoms: A World Survey*, vol. 3, ed. V. A. Veenhoven. The Hague: Martinus Nijhoff.

Bastid-Bruguière, M. 1980. Currents of social change. In *The Cambridge History of China*, II, Part 2, ed. D. Twitchett and J. Fairbank. London: Cambridge University Press.

BBL (*Bundesblatt*). 1951. *Botschaft (II) vom 9. August zum Entwurf zu einem Bundesgesetz über Erwerb und Verlust des Schweizerbürgerrechts.*

Beckett, J. 1973. *The Making of Modern Ireland 1603–1923*. New York: Knopf.

Beckford, G. L. 1972. *Persistent Poverty: Underdevelopment in Plantation Economies of the Third World*. New York: Oxford University Press.

―――― 1975. *Caribbean Economy: Dependence and Backwardness*. Kingston, Jamaica: I.S.E.R.

Beer, W. R. 1976. Language and ethnicity in France. *Plural Societies*, 7:85–94.

Bell, D. 1973. *The Coming of Post-Industrial Society*. New York: Basic Books.

Berger, S., and M. J. Piore. 1980. *Dualism and Discontinuity in Industrial Societies*. Cambridge: Cambridge University Press.

Best, L. 1968. Outline of a model of pure plantation economy. *Social and Economic Studies* (Sept.), 17:283.

Betts, T. F. 1981. Rural refugees in Africa. *International Migration Review*, 15(1-2):213–218.

Bhagwati, J. N. 1982. Shifting comparative advantage, protectionist demand, and policy response. In *Import Competition and Response*, ed. J. N. Bhagwati. Chicago: University of Chicago Press.

―――― , ed. 1976. *The Brain Drain and Taxation, Theory and Empirical Analysis*. Amsterdam: North-Holland.

Bhagwati, J. N., K-W Schatz, and K. Wong. 1983. The West German system of immigration. *Columbia University, International Economics Research Center Paper*, 24. New York.

Bluestone, B., and B. Harrison. 1982. *The Deindustrialization of America*. New York: Basic Books.

Bohning, W. R. 1975. Some thoughts on emigration from the Mediterranean basin. *International Labor Review*, 3:251–277.

―――― 1979. International migration and the international economic order. *Journal of International Affairs*, 2:182–200.

―――― 1981. Elements of a theory of international economic migration to industrial nation states. In *Global Trends in Migration*, ed. M. M. Kritz, C. B. Keely, and S. M. Tomasi. New York: Center for Migration Studies.

Bolland, O. N. 1981. Systems of domination after slavery: The control of land and labor in the British West Indies after 1838. *Comparative Studies in Society and History*, 23:600–615.

Bonacich, E. 1976. Advanced capitalism and black/white relations in the United States: A split labor market interpretation. *American Sociological Review*, 41:34–51.

Bond, R. D., ed. 1977. *Contemporary Venezuela and Its Role in International Affairs*. New York: New York University Press.

Boyd, M. 1970–1971. Oriental immigration: The experience of the Chinese, Japanese, and Filipino populations in the United States. *International Migration Review*, 5:48–61.

Brana-Shute, R., and G. Brana-Shute. The magnitude and impact of remittances in the Eastern Caribbean: A research note. In *Return Migration and Remittances: Developing a Caribbean Perspective*, ed. W. F. Stinner, K. de Albuquerque, and R. S. Bryce-Laporte. Washington, D.C.: Smithsonian Institution.

Braun, R. 1970. *Sozio-kulturelle Probleme der Eingliederung italienischer Arbeitskräfte*. Zürich: Eugen Rentsch.

Bryden, J. 1973. *Tourism and Development: Case Study of the Commonwealth Caribbean*. Cambridge: Cambridge University Press.

Bundesamt für Industrie, Gewerbe und Arbeit, ed. 1964. *Das Problem der ausländischen Arbeitskräfte*. Bern: Bericht der Studienkommission für das Problem der ausländischen Arbeitskräfte.

Burawoy, M. 1976. The functions and reproduction of migrant labor. *American Journal of Sociology*, 81:1081–1095.

CAJ/E (Christliche Arbeiter-Jugend "Emigrante"). 1980. *Wer sind sie? Schweizer und/oder Spanier. Die zweite Generation spanischer Immigranten in der Schweiz*. Zürich.

Campfens, H. 1980. *The integration of ethno-cultural minorities: A pluralist approach. The Netherlands and Canada: A comparative analysis of policy and programme*. The Hague: Government Publishing Office.

Carr, R. 1984. *Puerto Rico: A Colonial Experiment*. New York: New York University Press.

Castles, S., and G. Kosack. 1973. *Immigrant Workers and Class Structure in Western Europe*. London: Oxford University Press.

Chambers, R. 1979. Rural refugees in Africa: What the eye does not see. In *Disasters*. London: Journal of the International Disaster Institute, 3(4).

Chaney, E. M. 1976. Colombian migration to the United States (Part 2). *The Dynamics of Migration: International Migration*. Interdisciplinary Communications Program, Occasional Monograph Series, 2(5). Washington, D.C.: Smithsonian Institution.

Charles, G. P. 1967. *L'économie haitienne et sa voie de développement*. Paris: Larose.

Cheng, L., and E. Bonacich, eds. 1984. *Labor Migration under Capitalism*. Berkeley: University of California Press.

Chevalier, F. 1963. *Land and Society in Colonial Mexico*. Berkeley: University of California Press.

Clapham, J. 1931. Irish immigration into Great Britain in the nineteenth century. *Bulletin of the International Committee of Historical Sciences*, 5:596–604.

Colloque. 1983. Diversité culturelle, société industrielle, état national. Communication finale (Créteil, May 9–11).

Commissariat général du plan. 1982. *L'impératif culturel*. Rapport du groupe de travail "long terme" et culture. Paris: La documentation française.

Coolidge, M. 1909. *Chinese Immigration*. New York: Henry Holt.

Coombs, O., ed. 1974. *Is Massa Day Dead? Black Moods in the Caribbean*. New York: Anchor Books.

Cornelius, W. A. 1976. Outmigration from rural Mexican communities. In *The Dynamics of Migration: International Migration*. Interdisciplinary Communications Program, Occasional Monograph Series, 2(5). Washington, D.C.: Smithsonian Institution.

——— 1978. *Mexican Migration to the United States: Causes, Consequences, and U.S. Responses*. Cambridge: Migration and Development Study Group of the Massachusetts Institute of Technology.

Cortes, F., A. Falcon, and J. Flores. 1976. The cultural expression of Puerto Ricans in New York: A theoretical perspective and critical review. *Latin American Perspectives*, 3:117–152.

Craig, G. 1978. *Germany 1866–1945*. New York: Oxford University Press.

Crum Ewing, W. 1975. Discrimination in Great Britain. In *Case Studies on Human Rights and Fundamental Freedoms: A World Survey*, vol. 1, ed. V. A. Veenhoven. The Hague: Martinus Nijhoff.

Cumpston, I. M. 1953. *Indians Overseas in British Territories 1834–1854*. London: Oxford University Press.

Curtin, P. 1969. *The Atlantic Slave Trade: A Census*. Madison: University of Wisconsin Press.

Curtis, L. P., Jr. 1971. *Apes and Angels: The Irishman in Victorian Caricature*. Washington, D.C.: Smithsonian Institution.

Davids, J., ed. 1979. *American Diplomatic and Public Papers: The United States and China*. Ser. II, vols. 12 and 13. Wilmington: Scholarly Resources.

Davies, N. 1981. *A History of Poland, God's Playground*, vol. 2. New York: Columbia University Press.

Davis, D. B. 1966. *The Problem of Slavery in Western Culture*. Ithaca: Cornell University Press.

——— 1975. *The Problem of Slavery in the Age of Revolution 1770–1823*. Ithaca: Cornell University Press.

Dawson, H. 1908. *The Evolution of Modern Germany*. New York: Scribner's.

Death and disorder in Guatemala. 1983. *Cultural Survival Quarterly* (Spring), 7(1).

de Cordoba, J. 1984. Aruba faces rough times without refinery. *Boston Globe* (Dec. 16).

Deer, N. 1949, 1950. *The Story of Sugar*, 2 vols. London: Macmillan.

Degler, C. N. 1981. *Neither Black Nor White*. New York: Macmillan.

Demas, W. 1965. *The Economics of Development in Small Countries*. Montreal: McGill University Press.

Dibble, V. 1968. Social science and political commitments in the young Max Weber. *European Journal of Sociology*, 5:92–110.

Dixon, H. 1983. An overview of the Black Cubans among the Mariel entrants. Paper given at the International Conference on Immigration and the Changing Black Population in the United States, May 18–21, University of Michigan, Ann Arbor.

Dohse, K. 1981. *Ausländische Arbeiter und bürgerlicher Staat. Genese und Funktion von staatlicher Ausländer politik und Ausländerrecht Vom Kaiserreich bis zur Bundesrepublik Deutschland*. Köningstein: Verlag Anton Hain.

Domar, E. 1970. The causes of slavery or serfdom: A hypothesis. *Journal of Economic History*, 30:18–32.

Donges, J. B. 1983. Re-appraisal of foreign trade strategies for industrial development. In *Reflections on a Troubled World Economy*, ed. F. Machlup et al. London: Macmillan.

Donges, J. B., and D. Spinanger. 1983. Interventions in labour markets: An overview. *Kiel Working Papers*, 175 (May).

Dorfman, R., and N. Dorfman. 1972. *Economics of the Environment*. New York: W. W. Norton.

Duncan, B. 1972. *Atlantic Islands: Madeira, the Azores, and the Cape Verdes in Seventeenth Century Commerce and Navigation*. Chicago: University of Chicago Press.

Ecevit, Z., and K. C. Zachariah. 1980. International labor migration. *Finance and Development*, 17(3).

Erickson, C. 1976. *Emigration from Europe, 1815–1914: Selected Documents*. London: Adam and Charles Black.

Esser, H. 1980. *Aspekte der Wanderungssoziologie: Assimilation und Integration von Wanderern, ethnischen Gruppen und Minderheiten. Eine handlungstheoretische Analyse*. Darmstadt: Luchterhand.

——— 1982. Sozialräumliche Bedingungen der sprachlichen Assimilation von Arbeitsmigranten. *Zeitschrift für Soziologie*, 11:279–306.

Fagen, R. R., and O. Pellicer, eds. 1983. *The Future of Central America*. Stanford: Stanford University Press.

Flores, J., J. Attinasi, and P. Pedraza, Jr. 1981. La carreta made a U-turn: Puerto Rican language and culture in the United States. *Daedalus*, 110:193–217.

Forsythe, D. 1976. West Indian radicalism in America: An assessment of ideologies. In *Ethnicity in the Americas*, ed. F. Henry. Chicago: Aldine.

Forsythe, D. P. 1983. The Palestine question: Dealing with a long-term refugee situation. *Annals of the American Academy of Political and Social Sciences*, 467.

Frank, I. 1980. *Foreign Enterprise in Developing Countries*. Baltimore, Md.: The Johns Hopkins University Press.

Freeman, G. 1979. *Immigrant Labor and Racial Conflict in Industrial Societies: The French and British Experience, 1945–1975*. Princeton: Princeton University Press.

Frisch, M. 1967. *Oeffentlichkeit als Partner*. Frankfurt: Suhrkamp Verlag.

Furnivall, J. S. 1948. *Colonial Policy and Practice*. London: Cambridge University Press.

Galenson, D. 1981. *White Servitude in Colonial America: An Economic Analysis*. Cambridge: Cambridge University Press.

Garcia, J. A. 1981. Political integration of Mexican immigrants: Explorations into the naturalization process. *International Migration Review*, 15:608–625.

Garrity, M. 1981. The assembly industries in Haiti: Causes and effects. *Journal of Caribbean Studies*, 2(1):25–37.

Garza, R. O. de la. 1976. Mexican Americans in the United States: The evolution of a relationship. In *Case Studies on Human Rights and Fundamental Freedoms: A World Survey*, vol. 5, ed. V. A. Veenhoven. The Hague: Martinus Nijhoff.

Gerstenmeier, J., and F. Hamburger. 1974. Bildungswünsche ausländischer Arbeiterkinder. Ergebnisse einer Befragung von Eltern und Kindern. *Soziale Welt*, 25:278–293.

Gilani, I., M. F. Khan, and M. Iqbal. 1982. *Labor Migration from Pakistan to the Middle East and Its Impact on the Domestic Economy*. Final Report, Research Project on Export of Manpower from Pakistan to the Middle East. Washington, D.C.

Gille, H. 1982. International population assistance. In *International Encyclopedia of Population*. New York: The Free Press, 1982.

Giordan, H. 1982. *Démocratie culturelle et droit à la différence. Rapport présenté à Jack Lang, Ministre de la Culture*. Paris: La documentation française.

Glazer, N. and D. Moynihan. 1970. *Beyond the Melting Pot*. Cambridge, Mass.: MIT Press.

———, eds. 1975. *Ethnicity: Theory and Experience*. Cambridge, Mass.: Harvard University Press.

Gordon, D. M., R. Edwards, and M. Reich. 1982. *Segmented Work, Divided Workers: The Historical Transformation of Labor in the United States*. New York: Cambridge University Press.

Green, V. 1975. Racial versus ethnic factors in Afro-American and Afro-Caribbean migration. In *Migration and Development*, ed. H. I. Safa and B. M. Du Toit. The Hague: Mouton.

Green, W. 1976. *British Slave Emancipation. The Sugar Colonies and the Great Experiment, 1830–1865*. Oxford: Clarendon Press.

Griffin, K. 1976. On the emigration of the peasantry. *World Development*, 4:353–361.

Grubel, H. G., and A. D. Scott. 1966. The international flow of human capital. *The American Economic Review, Papers and Proceedings*, 56:268–274.

Gulati, L. 1983. Impacts of male migration to the Middle East on the family: Some evidence from Kerala. Paper given at the Conference on Asian Labor Migration to the Middle East, Honolulu, East-West Population Institute.

Gurny, R. 1978. *Die zweite Generation. Die spezifischen familiären und schulischen Probleme der zweiten Ausländergeneration*. Zürich: Soziologisches Institut der Universität Zürich.

Gurny, R., et al. 1983. *Karrieren und Sackgassen. Wege ins Berufsleben junger Schweizer und Italiener in der Stadt Zürich*. Zürich: Soziologisches Institut der Universität Zürich.

Hannan, M. J., and J. Freeman. 1977. The population ecology of organizations. *American Journal of Sociology*, 82:829–864.

Hansen, A. 1981. Refugee dynamics: Angolans in Zambia 1966–1972. *International Migration Review*, 15:175–194.

Heath, D., and R. Adams, eds. 1965. *Contemporary Cultures and Societies of Latin America*. New York: Random House.

Hechter, M. 1975. *Internal Colonialism*. Berkeley: University of California Press.

Hiemenz, U., and K-W Schatz. 1979. *Trade in Place of Migration*. Geneva: International Labour Office.

Hitchins, F. 1931. *The Colonial Land and Emigration Commission*. Philadelphia: University of Pennsylvania Press.

Hobsbawm, E. 1962. *The Age of Revolution, 1789–1848*. New York: Mentor.

Hoffmann-Nowotny, H-J. 1970. *Migration — Ein Beitrag zu einer soziologischen Erklärung*. Stuttgart: Enke Verlag.

———— 1973. *Soziologie des Fremdarbeiterproblems. Eine theoretische und empirische Analyse am Beispiel der Schweiz*. Stuttgart: Enke Verlag.

———— 1974. Rassische, ethnische und soziale Minderheiten als Zukunftsproblem internationaler Integrationsbestrebungen. In *Minderheiten*, ed. R. Kurzrock. Berlin: Colloquium Verlag.

———— 1978. European migration after World War II. In *Human Migration: Patterns and Policies*, ed. W. H. McNeill and R. S. Adams. Bloomington: Indiana University Press.

———— 1981. A sociological approach toward a general theory of migration. In *Global Trends in Migration: Theory and Research on International Population Movements*, ed. M. M. Kritz, C. B. Keely, and S. M. Tomasi. New York: Center for Migration Studies.

Hoffmann-Nowotny, H-J., and K. O. Hondrich (Hrsg.). 1982. *Ausländer in der Bundesrepublik Deutschland und in der Schweiz. Segregation und Integration: Eine vergleichende Untersuchung*. Frankfurt: Campus Verlag.

Holborn, L. Refugees: World problems. *International Encyclopedia of the Social Sciences*, 13:361–373.

Hsu, I. 1980. Late Ch'ing foreign relations, 1866–1905. In *The Cambridge History of China*, II, Part 2, ed. D. Twitchett and J. Fairbank. London: Cambridge University Press.

International Monetary Fund (IMF). 1984. Direction of trade statistics. *Yearbook*. Washington, D.C.

Jaeger, G. 1981. Refugee asylum — policy and legislative developments. *International Migration Review*, 15.

Janich, H. 1971. The Chinese and the courts, 1850–1902. J.D. diss. University of Chicago.

Jefferson, O. 1970. *The Post-War Economic Development of Jamaica*. Kingston, Jamaica: I.S.E.R.

Johnson, R. A. 1982. The New Yorican comes home to Puerto Rico: Description and consequences. In *Return Migration and Remittances: Developing a Caribbean Perspective*, ed. W. F. Stinner, K. de Albuquerque, and R. S. Bryce-Laporte. Washington, D.C.: Smithsonian Institution.

Johnston, H. J. M. 1972. *British Emigration Policy 1815–1830, Shovelling Out Paupers*. Oxford: Clarendon Press.

Kerr, B. 1942–43. Irish seasonal migration to Great Britain, 1800–1838. *Irish Historical Studies*, 3:365–380.

Kindleberger, C. P. 1967. *Europe's Postwar Growth: The Role of Labor Supply*. Cambridge, Mass.: Harvard University Press.

Kinzer, S. 1983. Nicaragua: The beleaguered revolution. *New York Times Magazine* (Aug. 28).

Klein, H. 1967. *Slavery in the Americas: A Comparative Study of Virginia and Cuba.* Chicago: University of Chicago Press.

Kloosterboer, W. 1960. *Involuntary Labour Since the Abolition of Slavery.* Leiden: E. J. Brill.

Kohler, M. 1936. *Immigration and Aliens in the United States: Studies of American Immigration Laws and the Legal Status of Aliens in the United States.* New York: Bloch.

Körner, H., and M. Werth, eds. 1981. *Rückwanderung und Reintegration von ausländischen Arbeitnehmern in Europa.* Saarbrücken: Breitenbach Publishers.

Korte, H. (coordinator). 1982. *Cultural Identity and Structural Marginalization of Migrant Workers.* Strasbourg: European Science Foundation.

Koschitzky, A. von. 1983. *Die schulische Integration der spanischen Fremdarbeitkerkinder.* Zürich: Soziologisches Institut der Universität Zürich.

Kramer, J. 1981. *Unsettling Europe.* New York: Random House.

Krausz, E. 1976. Ethnic pluralism and structural dissonance. *Plural Societies,* 7:71–83.

Kremer, M., and H. Spangenberg. 1980. *Assimilation ausländischer Arbeitnehmer in der Bundesrepublik Deutschland.* Königstein: Hanstein.

Kritz, M. M. 1981. International migration patterns in the Caribbean: An overview. In *Global Trends in Migration,* ed. M. M. Kritz, C. B. Keely, and S. M. Tomasi. New York: Center for Migration Studies.

Kritz, M. M., C. B. Keely, and S. M. Tomasi, eds. 1981. *Global Trends in Migration.* New York: Center for Migration Studies.

Kubat, D., U. Mehrlander, and E. Gehmacher, eds. 1979. *The Politics of Migration Policies: The First World in the 1970s.* New York: Center for Migration Studies.

Lebon, A. 1983. Maintien des liens culturels et insertion des migrants: quelles relations? *Revue française des affaires sociales,* 37:89–114.

Levine, B. B. 1982. The Puerto Rican circuit and the success of return migrants. In *Return Migration and Remittances: Developing a Caribbean Perspective,* ed. W. F. Stinner, K. de Albuquerque, and R. S. Bryce-Laporte. Washington, D.C.: Smithsonian Institution.

Lewis, G. 1963. *Puerto Rico: Freedom and Power in the Caribbean.* New York: Monthly Review Press.

Ley, K. 1981. Migrant women: Is migration a blessing or a handicap? Situation of migrant women in Switzerland. *International Migration,* 19:83–93.

Leyburn, J. G. 1941. *The Haitian People.* New Haven: Yale University Press.

Lipsky, S. 1983. Invite the Palestinians to America. *Wall Street Journal* (Aug. 31).

London, C. G. 1980. On Afro-American and Afro-Caribbean cooperation. *Journal of Ethnic Studies,* 8(3):142–147.

Ma'oz, M. 1976. Homogeneity and pluralism in the Middle East: The case of Lebanon. In *Case Studies on Human Rights and Fundamental Freedoms: A*

World Survey, vol. 3, ed. V. A. Veenhoven. The Hague: Martinus Nijhoff.

Makielski, S. J., Jr. 1976. America's minorities. In *Case Studies on Human Rights and Fundamental Freedoms: A World Survey*, vol. 3, ed. V. A. Veenhoven. The Hague: Martinus Nijhoff.

Manning, F. E. 1982. The Caribbean experience. In *The Tourist Trap: Who's Getting Caught?* special issue of *Cultural Survival Quarterly* 6(3), Summer.

Marangé, J., and A. Lebon. 1982. *L'insertion des jeunes d'origine étrangère dans la société française. Rapport, considérations générales et propositions.* Paris: La documentation française.

Martin, P., and A. Richards. 1980. International migration: Boon or bane? *Monthly Labor Review* (Oct.): 4–9.

Matthews, H. G. 1977. Radical and Third World tourism: A Caribbean "focus." *Annals of Tourism Research*, 5:20–29.

Mayo-Smith, R. 1890. *Emigration and Immigration: A Study in Social Science.* New York: Charles Scribner & Sons. (New York: Johnson Reprint Corporation, 1968.)

McIntosh, C. A. 1981. Some social consequences of labor migration to the Middle East for sending countries in Asia. Paper given at the Conference of Asian Labor Migration to the Middle East, Honolulu, East-West Population Institute.

McNeill, W. H. 1976. *Plagues and Peoples.* New York: Anchor Books.

McNeill, W. H., and R. Adams, eds. 1978. *Human Migration.* Bloomington: Indiana University Press.

Meislin, R. J. 1984. Immigration law is joke to Mexican. *New York Times* (June 24).

Menard, R. 1977. From servants to slaves: The transition of the Chesapeake labor system. *Southern Studies*, 16:355–390.

Miller, S. 1969. *The Unwelcome Immigrant: The American Image of the Chinese, 1785–1882.* Berkeley: University of California Press.

Mines, R. 1981. *Developing a Community Tradition of Migration: A Field Study in Rural Zacatecas, Mexico and California Settlement Areas.* Monograph no. 3, U.S.-Mexican Studies. San Diego: University of California.

Mitchell, B. 1976. *European Historical Statistics, 1750–1970.* New York: Columbia University Press.

Moch, L. P., and L. A. Tilly. 1979. Immigrant women in the city: Comparative perspectives. University of Michigan, Center for Research on Social Organization, Working Paper No. 205.

Moore, O. E. 1972. *Haiti: Its Stagnant Society and Shackled Economy.* New York: Exposition Press.

Morison, S. 1974. *The European Discovery of America: The Southern Voyages.* New York: Oxford University Press.

Mörner, M. 1976. Spanish migration to the New World prior to 1810: A report on the state of research. In *First Images of America: The Impact of the New World on the Old*, ed. F. Chiappelli. Berkeley: University of California Press.

Muñoz, H. 1981. The strategic dependency of the center and the economic importance of the Latin American periphery. In *From Dependency to Development*, ed. H. Muñoz. Boulder: Westview Press.

National Narcotics Intelligence Consensus Committee. 1982. *The Supply of Drugs to the U.S. Illicit Market from Foreign and Domestic Sources in 1978*. Washington, D.C.: Government Printing Office.

Nauck, B. 1983. *Arbeitsmigration und Familienstruktur. Eine soziologische Analyse der Migrationsfolgen fur türkische Familien in der Bundesrepublik Deutschland*. Bonn: Habilitationsschrift, Universität Bonn.

Nelli, H. 1964. The Italian padrone system in the United States. *Labor History*, 5:153–167.

Neubach, H. 1967. *Die Ausweisungen von Polen und Juden aus Preussen 1885–1886*. Wiesbaden: Otto Harrassowitz.

Newfarmer, R., ed. 1984. *From Gunboats to Diplomacy*. Baltimore: The Johns Hopkins University Press.

Newton, A. 1937. *The European Nations in the West Indies, 1493–1688*. London: Adam and Charles Black.

Nichtweiss, J. 1959. *Die ausländischen Saisonarbeiter der Landwirtschaft des östlichen und mittleren Gebiete des deutschen Reiches 1890–1914*. Berlin (Ost): Rütten & Doening.

Nolli, M. 1982. *Italienische Mädchen in der Freizeit. Eine empirische Studie zum Freizeitverhalten italienischer Mädchen am Beispiel der Stadt Zürich*. Zürich: Soziologisches Institut der Universität Zürich.

North, D., and R. Thomas. 1973. *The Rise of the Western World: A New Economic History*. London: Cambridge University Press.

Oberai, A. S., and H. K. Manohan Singh. 1980. Migration, remittances and rural development: Findings of a case study in the Indian Punjab. *International Labor Review*, 5:119.

OECD. Various years. *Continuous Reporting System on Migration*. Paris: SOPEMI.

Oxaal, I. 1971. *Race and Revolutionary Consciousness*. Cambridge, Mass.: Schenkman Publishing Co.

Paine, S. 1974. *Exporting Workers: The Turkish Case*. Cambridge: Cambridge University Press.

Papademetriou, D. 1979. Greece. In *International Labor Migration in Europe*, ed. R. E. Krane. New York: Praeger Publishers.

Parry, J. H. 1966. *The Establishment of European Hegemony: 1415–1715*. 3rd ed. New York: Harper and Row.

Patterson, O. 1972. Toward a future that has no past: Reflections on the fate of Blacks in the Americas. *The Public Interest* (Spring 1972) 27:25–62.

———— 1982. *Slavery and Social Death: A Comparative Study*. Cambridge, Mass.: Harvard University Press.

Payne, A., and P. Sutton, eds. 1984. *Dependency Under Challenge: The Political Economy of the Commonwealth Caribbean*. Manchester: Manchester University Press.

Peace, L. P. 1982. *The Social Psychology of Tourist Behavior*. New York: Pergamon Press.

Pettigrew, T. W. 1981. Race and class in the 1980's: An interactive view. *Daedalus*, 110: 233–255.

Piore, M. J. 1979. *Birds of Passage: Migrant Labor and Industrial Societies*. New York: Cambridge University Press.

Portes, A. 1978a. Migration and underdevelopment. *Politics and Society*, 8:1–48.

―――― 1978b. Introduction: Toward a structural analysis of illegal (undocumented) immigration. *International Migration Review*, 12(4):469–484.

―――― 1979. Illegal immigration and the international system: Lessons from recent legal Mexican immigrants to the United States. *Social Problems*, 26(4).

―――― 1981. Modes of structural incorporation and present theories of labor immigration. In *Global Trends in Migration*, ed. M. M. Kritz, C. B. Keely, and S. M. Tomasi. New York: Center for Migration Studies.

―――― 1984. The rise of ethnicity: Determinants of ethnic perceptions among Cuban exiles in Miami. *American Sociological Review*, 49:383–397.

Portes, A., R. N. Parker, and J. A. Cobas. 1980. Assimilation of consciousness: Perceptions of U.S. society among recent Latin American immigrants to the United States. *Social Forces*, 59(1): 200–224.

Portes, A., and J. Walton. 1981. *Labor, Class, and the International System*. New York: Academic Press.

Possony, S. T. 1976. Apartheid in India. *Plural Societies*, 7:3–11.

Poussou, J.-P. 1970. Les mouvements migratoires en France et à partir de la France de la fin du XVème siècle au début du XIXème siècle. Approches pour une synthèse. *Annales de démographie historique*: 11–78.

Ranis, G. 1979. Appropriate technology: Obstacles and opportunities. In *Technology and Economic Development: A Realistic Perspective*, ed. S. M. Rosenblatt. Boulder: Westview Press.

Rees, T. 1979. The United Kingdom. In *The Politics of Immigration Policies*, ed. D. Kubat, U. Mehrlander, and E. Gehmacher. New York: Center for Migration Studies.

Refugee Reports. Various dates. Washington, D.C.: The American Council for Nationalities Service.

Reichert, J. S. 1981. The migration syndrome: Seasonal U.S. wage labor and rural development in Central Mexico. *Human Organization*, 40(1).

Rist, R. C. 1978. *Guestworkers in Germany: The Prospects for Pluralism*. New York: Praeger. (German translation, 1980. Stuttgart: Ernst Klett.)

Rivera-Batiz, F. L. 1983. Trade theory, distribution of income, and immigration. *The American Economic Review, Papers and Proceedings*, 73:183–187.

Robinson, A. N. R. 1971. *The Mechanics of Independence: Patterns of Political and Economic Transformation in Trinidad and Tobago*. Cambridge, Mass.: MIT Press.

Rogge, J. R. 1981. Africa's resettlement strategies. *International Migration Review*, 15:195–212.

Rose, A. M., and C. B. Rose, eds. 1972. *Minority Problems*, 2nd ed. New York: Harper & Row.

Rubenstein, H. 1983. Remittances and rural underdevelopment in the English-speaking Caribbean. *Human Organization*, 42(4):295–304.

Safa, H. I. 1983. Caribbean migration, cultural identity and the process of assimilation. Paper given at the International Conference on Immigration and the Changing Black Population in the United States, May 18–21, University of Michigan, Ann Arbor.

Safa, H. I., and B. M. Du Toit, eds. 1975. *Migration and Development*. The Hague: Mouton.

Sánchez Tarnielloa, A. 1973. *La Economía de Puerto Rico*. Puerto Rico: Ediciones Bayoan.

Sapir, A. 1983. Foreign competition, immigration and structural adjustment. *Journal of International Economics*, 14:381–394.

Sassen-Koob, S. 1978. The international circulation of resources and development. The case of migrant labour. *Development and Change*, 9(4):509–545.

Saxton, A. 1971. *The Indispensable Enemy. Labor and the Anti-Chinese Movement*. Stanford: Stanford University Press.

Scanlan, J. A. 1981. Regulating refugee fear: Legal alternatives and objectives under the Refugee Act of 1980. *The Notre Dame Lawyer*, 56:618–643.

Schatz, K-W. 1974. *Wachstum und Strukturwandel der westdeutschen Wirtschaft im internationalen Verbund — Analysen und Prognosen*. Tübingen: J. C. B. Mohr.

Scheinman, R. 1983. Refugees: Goodbye to the good old days. *Annals of the American Academy of Political and Social Sciences*, 467.

Schmidt, A. 1981. Refugees and immigrants: In conflict with the American poor. *Migration Today*, 9:17–21.

Schofler, L. 1975. *The Formation of a Modern Labor Force. Upper Silesia, 1865–1914*. Berkeley: University of California Press.

Singelmann, J. 1978. *From Agriculture to Services: The Transformation of Industrial Employment*. Beverly Hills: Sage Publications.

Singhanetra-Renard, A. 1983. Going abroad: Thai labor movement to the Middle East from the village standpoint. Paper given at the Conference on Asian Labor Migration to the Middle East, Honolulu, East-West Population Institute.

Skoog, B. 1981. *Cultural Identity of Immigrants and Foreign Workers in Five European Towns*. Strasbourg: Council of Europe.

Smith, A. E. 1971. *Colonists in Bondage: White Servitude and Convict Labor in America, 1607–1776*. New York: W. W. Norton.

Stahl, C. W. 1982. Labor emigration and economic development. *International Migration Review*, 16:869–899.

Stark, O. 1979. On the role of urban-to-rural remittances in rural development. *Journal of Development Studies*, 5:119.

——— 1982. Research on rural-to-urban migration in LDCs: The confusion frontier and why we should pause to rethink afresh. *World Development*, 10:63–70.

Stinner, W. F., K. de Albuquerque, and R. S. Bryce-Laport. 1982. *Return*

Migration and Remittances: Developing a Caribbean Perspective. Special issue: *International Migration Review*, 16. Washington, D.C.: Smithsonian Institution.

Stuart, J., and Kearney, M. 1981. Causes and effects of agricultural labor migration from the Mixteca of Oaxaca to California. Working paper no. 28, U.S.-Mexican Studies. San Diego: University of California.

Sudarkasa, N. 1983. Race, ethnicity and identity: Some conceptual issues in defining the Black population in the United States. Paper given at the International Conference on Immigration and the Changing Black Population in the United States, May 18–21, University of Michigan, Ann Arbor.

Suhrke, A. 1983. Global refugee movements and strategies of response. In *U.S. Immigration and Refugee Policy: Global and Domestic Issues*, ed. M. Kritz. Lexington, Mass.: Lexington Books.

Sutton, C. R., and S. J. Makielski. 1975. Migration and West Indian racial and ethnic consciousness. In *Migration and Development*, ed. H. Safa and B. M. Du Toit. The Hague: Mouton.

Sutton, P. 1984. Trinidad and Tobago: Oil capitalism and the "presidential power" of Eric Williams. In *Dependency Under Challenge: The Political Economy of the Commonwealth Caribbean*, ed. A. Payne and P. Sutton. Manchester: Manchester University Press.

Swanson, J. 1979. *Emigration and Economic Development: The Case of the Yemen Arab Republic*. Boulder: Westview Press.

Thomas, B. 1973. *Migration and Economic Growth*. Cambridge: Cambridge University Press.

Thomas, L. 1979. *The Medusa and the Snail*. New York: The Viking Press.

Thompson, E. P. 1963. *The Making of the English Working Class*. New York: Vintage Books.

Thorud, E. 1982. *Labor and Immigration Policy: The U.S. Case in Theoretical Perspective*. M.A. diss., University of Chicago.

Tilly, C. 1978. Migration in modern European history. In *Human Migration*, ed. W. H. McNeill and R. Adams. Bloomington: Indiana University Press.

Tinker, H. 1974. *A New System of Slavery: The Export of Indian Labour Overseas, 1830–1920*. London: Oxford University Press.

Torres Rivas, E. 1973. *Interpretación del Desarrollo Social Centroamericano*. Costa Rica: EDUCA.

Tumlir, J. 1982. International economic order: Can the trend be reversed? *The World Economy*, 5:29–41.

United Nations. 1981. *Study on Human Rights and Mass Exodus*. New York: E/CN.4/1503.

——— 1982. *International Migration Policies and Programmes: A World Survey*. New York: ST/ESA/SER.A/80.

United States, 48th Congress, 1st Session, House of Representatives. *Report No. 144* (Feb. 23, 1884).

United States Department of Commerce, Bureau of Economic Analysis. 1982. *Survey of Current Business.* (August).

Untersuchung der Determinanten der beruflichen Ausbildungsbeteiligung von ausländischen Jugendlichen in Berlin (West). 1980. Berlin: Vorgelegt von der Prognos AG im Auftrag des Regierenden Bürgermeisters von Berlin.

Valentine, A. C. 1985. Voluntary ethnicity and social change. *Journal of Ethnic Studies*, 3(1):1–27.

Veenhoven, V. A., ed. 1975. *Case Studies on Human Rights and Fundamental Freedoms: A World Survey*, vol. 1. The Hague: Martinus Nijhoff.

—— 1976a. *Case Studies*, vol. 3.

—— 1976b. *Case Studies*, vol. 5.

Verlinden, C. 1970. *The Beginnings of Modern Colonialism.* Ithaca: Cornell University Press.

Vuskovic, Pedro. 1983. Los Problemas Económicos de la Transición. *El Trimestre Económico* (Jan.–March), 197:473–518.

Wagley, C. 1965. On the concept of social race in the Americas. In *Contemporary Cultures and Societies of Latin America*, ed. R. Heath and D. Adams. New York: Random House.

Walker, M. 1964. *Germany and the Emigration, 1816–1885.* Cambridge, Mass.: Harvard University Press.

Waltner, P. 1982. *Auswanderung marokkanischer Arbeitskräfte nach Deutschland und ihre Rückkehr.* Tübingen: Forschungsbericht.

Warwick, D. P. 1982. *Bitter Pills.* New York: Cambridge University Press.

Williams, E. 1980. *Capitalism and Slavery.* New York: Perigee.

Williams, R. M., Jr. 1977. *Mutual Accommodation: Ethnic Conflict and Cooperation.* Minneapolis: University of Minnesota Press.

Wilpert, C. 1980. *Die Zukunft der zweiten Generation. Erwartungen und Verhaltensmöglichkeiten ausländischer Kinder.* Königstein: Anton Hain.

Wilson, W. J. 1976. The changing context of American race relations: Urban Blacks and structural shifts in the economy. In *Case Studies on Human Rights and Fundamental Freedoms: A World Survey*, vol. 5, ed. V. A. Veenhoven. The Hague: Martinus Nijhoff.

—— 1978. *The Declining Significance of Race.* Chicago: University of Chicago Press.

Wirtschaft und Statistik. 1965. 2:93–94.

Woodside, A. 1979. Nationalism and poverty in the breakdown of Sino-Vietnamese relations. *Pacific Affairs*, 52:381–409.

World Bank. 1984. *World Development Report 1984.* New York: Oxford University Press.

World Refugee Survey. 1961–1984. Now published by the U.S. Committee for Refugees, under the auspices of the American Council for Nationalities Service.

Yinger, M. J. 1975. Discrimination against American Blacks. In *Case Studies on Human Rights and Fundamental Freedoms: A World Survey*, vol. 1, ed. V. A. Veenhoven. The Hague: Martinus Nijhoff.

Yletyinin, R. 1982. *Sprachliche und kulturelle Minderheiten in den USA, Schweden und der Bundesrepublik Deutschland. Ein Minderheiten und bildungs-politischer Vergleich*. Frankfurt: Haag & Herchen.

Young, A. 1951. *Bismarck's Policy Toward the Poles, 1870–1890*. Ph.D. diss. University of Chicago.

Zolberg, A. 1974. The making of Flemings and Walloons, 1830–1914. *Journal of Interdisciplinary History*, 5:179–235.

——— 1978. International migration policies in a changing world system. In *Human Migration*, ed. W. H. McNeill and R. Adams. Bloomington: Indiana University Press.

——— 1978. The main gate and the back door. Paper given at the Workshop on Current Immigration Issues, Council of Foreign Relations, Washington, D.C.

——— 1983. The formation of new states as a refugee-generating process. *Annals of the American Academy of Political and Social Sciences*, 467:24–38.

——— *Alien Flows: The Politics of International Migrations in Western Development*. Forthcoming.

Contributors

William Alonso is Richard Saltonstall Professor of Population Policy at Harvard University.

The late Hedley Bull was the Montague Burton Professor of International Relations and Fellow of Balliol College, Oxford University.

Juergen B. Donges is Vice-President of the Kiel Institute of World Economics and Professor of Political Economy (hon.) at the University of Kiel.

Hans-Joachim Hoffmann-Nowotny is Professor of Sociology at the University of Zurich.

William H. McNeill is Robert A. Milliken Distinguished Service Professor, University of Chicago.

Orlando Patterson is Professor of Sociology at Harvard University.

Francis X. Sutton is a retired Ford Foundation officer and in 1985–86 served as Acting President of the Social Science Research Council.

Myron Weiner is Ford International Professor of Political Science at MIT.

Aristide R. Zolberg is University-in-Exile Professor and Chairman of the Department of Political Science at the New School for Social Research.

Index